PIONEERS IN MACHINIMA

The Grassroots of Virtual Production

by

Tracy G. Harwood

and

Ben Grussi

Series in Critical Media Studies

VERNON PRESS

Copyright © 2021 Vernon Press, an imprint of Vernon Art and Science Inc, on behalf of the author.

All rights reserved. No part of this publication may be reproduced, stored in a retrieval system, or transmitted in any form or by any means, electronic, mechanical, photocopying, recording, or otherwise, without the prior permission of the copyright holder and Vernon Art and Science Inc.

www.vernonpress.com

In the Americas:
Vernon Press
1000 N West Street, Suite 1200,
Wilmington, Delaware 19801
United States

In the rest of the world:
Vernon Press
C/Sancti Espiritu 17,
Malaga, 29006
Spain

Series in Critical Media Studies

Library of Congress Control Number: 2021930170

ISBN: 978-1-64889-206-6

Also available: 978-1-62273-273-9 [Hardback]

Product and company names mentioned in this work are the trademarks of their respective owners. While every care has been taken in preparing this work, neither the authors nor Vernon Art and Science Inc. may be held responsible for any loss or damage caused or alleged to be caused directly or indirectly by the information contained in it.

Every effort has been made to trace all copyright holders, but if any have been inadvertently overlooked the publisher will be pleased to include any necessary credits in any subsequent reprint or edition.

Cover image: Machinima Europe 2007.

Cover design by Vernon Press.

Table of Contents

Key Terms

.dem	Type of file, demonstration file
AAA (Triple A)	Top tier games developer, best funded for game development and marketing
AMAS	Academy of Machinima Arts & Sciences
AR	Augmented reality
BBSs	Electronic bulletin boards
EULA	End user license agreement
Indie (Independent)	Independent game developer or film studio
LAN	Local area network
LED	Light emitting diode (screens)
Machinima	3D real-time animated filmmaking (machine-animation-cinema)
Machinimator	Machinima creator
MMO	Massively multi-user online [game/environment]
Mods/modding	Modification, process of modifying
NCP	Network channel partner/ship
P2P	Peer to peer (sharing)
SFX	Special effects
VFX	Video effects (a variation of special effects, SFX)
VJ	Video jockey
VR	Virtual reality

List of Figures and Tables

Figures

Tables

Prologue: An interview with Kim Libreri, Chief Technology Officer at Epic Games

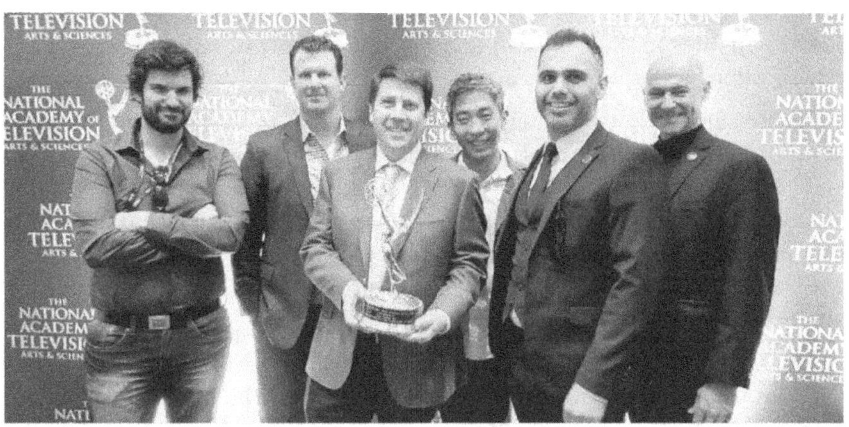

Kim Libreri (centre) holding the first *Technology and Engineering Emmy* for *Unreal Engine* in the category '3D Engine Software for the Production of Animation' at the 2019 70th *Annual Science & Technology Emmy Awards* hosted by the *National Academy of Television Arts & Sciences.*

(L-R: Epic Games' David Hurtubise, Craig Laliberte, Kim Libreri, Ryan Mayeda, Ben Lumsden and David Morin). Image used with permission, source: Epic Games ©.

Biography: Kim Libreri has worked in film visual effects (VFX) for over two decades, starting out as a programmer before ultimately becoming Chief Technology Officer at *Epic Games* in 2014. Prior to this, he was *Lucasfilm* Chief Strategy Officer and *ILM* VFX Supervisor, supervising *LucasArts' Star Wars 1313* prototype and founding *Lucasfilm*'s *Real Time Group*. He has 25+ films credited to him, including *Event Horizon* (1997), *The Matrix* trilogy (2000, 2003/3), *Poseidon* (2006), *Speed Racer* (2008), *Super 8* (2011) and *Star Wars: Ep VII – The Force Awakens* (2015).

TH: Thanks for talking to us about machinima and virtual production. Our book is primarily focussing on the impacts of machinima on creators from mainly grassroots backgrounds, but also drawing in thoughts from game and film industry perspectives, so it is great to have the chance to talk to you about machinima things.

KL: I've always been really interested in previsualization using real-time computer graphics for making films. A lot of what I did pre-dates what people consider to be machinima; well, nowadays machinima is everywhere. At *Epic* our big focus now is cinematic creation through simulation. We have so many people using *Unreal Engine* for designing movies, previs, and final pixels. Take *The Mandalorian* for example; what you've got is basically in-camera machinima. A lot of people still think of game engines as things you can render prettier pictures in than you can in *Maya* or *Studio Max*. But rendering is not the only thing a game engine can do.

A game engine is a simulated world. Let's say you are doing a car chase. You set up the cars as drivable cars and you drive them like you would in live action, and you record all that data, and then you put cameras on it—you've basically built a simulation of the real world that can actually tell a story. That cross-over between film and games is still something not everyone gets. From the very early days, machinimists have been using real-time graphics, typically in game engines, to tell stories.

Colin Green ran Pixel Liberation Front, a very early previsualization company and his experience of using, I think it was *Softimage* at the time, would go back to probably 1997. Previs is the professional-grade version of what machinima is, because at the time, if you think about that era—digital cameras, pre-*Halo*, basically *Lara Croft* first iteration—the tools just weren't there then to do it in-game engine technology, but you could use professional tools to do some level of real-time visualization.

On the first *Matrix* movie, we did all the *Bullet Time* shots with previs and a few of the more complicated setups, but we weren't telling the story in its entirety. It was just pieces. It was like, how are we going to do these *Bullet Time* shots, what do they even look like, how do you translate Hong Kong Kung Fu action into something that can be shown in an interesting way with a camera that is free from the constraints of the physical world? But that's just a piece of using the tools, not an overall story itself. Most of my involvement, until the mid-2000s, was on that side of things. That's really the birth of computer graphics to tell stories, and some of it does pre-date a bunch of machinima stuff, because there are rigged characters in *Softimage* and *Maya*. If you want to look at the making of the *Matrix* and you look at our previs, there's an exact one-to-one correlation between what we previsualized and what we ended up making.

I think the first time we used real-time computer graphics for any movie visualization was in *Event Horizon*. You recall the big spinning ball they had? The production designer that fabricated the movie set out of bits of wood that had been tacked together and painted couldn't work out how to make it look cool when it spun. I was working in *Cinesite Studios* in London at the time, and out at *Pinewood Studios* we had a *Silicon Graphics Onyx* machine, a multi-million-British pound computer that could do very flashy things with graphics. It's funny because a few years later the *Nintendo 64* could do very similar things and basically ended up being a derivative of that hardware for a few hundred dollars rather than millions. My friend Dan Capone, who came from *Argonaut Games,* joined us at *Cinesite,* coded all the mass to generate the geometry of that thing. We would spin it until we thought it looked cool, and we got it designed. We used that as an early CAD-like thing because the construction people didn't know how to make it. That was our very first usage.

There were other crossovers into the games business in 2000. We did a demo for *SonyGSQ,* which was sixteen *PlayStation 2*s in a single box, which was meant to be machinima meets previs. We did a scene from *The Matrix,* although it wasn't in any of the original movies; the made-up scene was all real-time, and it was meant to be 'this is what machinima could be in the future'. Then another person, Habib Zargarpour, who now works for *Unity* but who was at *ILM*... his last movie at ILM was *The Perfect Storm,* and then he went to *EA,* where he worked on *Need for Speed.* He built a machinima system and all the cutscenes; all the marketing was done through a camera system and an action-replay system that Habib had the team build for *Need for Speed.* He was also responsible for the art direction of the game in that era. There's probably a pretty awesome machinima story in there.

TH: When did you first hear about machinima and what were your first thoughts about it?

KL: In terms of machinima the term, it would have been from John Gaeta. John was watching the stuff in the early 2000s—I think he knew the creators of the website. He was intrigued in using simulation for shot design, although for the level of sophistication that we needed to design something for *The Matrix* versus the level of sophistication in what you got in machinima tools then was night and day. It was partly his interest in that world that got us into doing that demo for *SonyGSQ.*

We started the work for that project immediately after finishing the first *Matrix* film. Ken Kutaragi [CEO of *Sony Computer Entertainment*], who was the father of the *PlayStation* and in charge of the *PlayStation* division at the time, was a huge fan of *The Matrix* movie. Within three months of the movie coming out, we got contacted by *Sony* asking whether we would make something *Matrix*-themed to show off this supercomputer they were making, the *GSQ,* which was these sixteen *PlayStation 2*s strapped together, before they even shipped. It was previewed at *SIGGRAPH* in July or August 2000.

TH: I guess then you won't recall any notable examples of machinima works you saw or any creators you are aware of?

KL: It was only a matter of time; it was obvious that eventually real-time graphics would be able to do amazing stuff. That's why we did that *GSQ* demo in 2000 because we wanted to show the world that real-time technology will be a filmmaking tool in the future. It was not a crack on what you were seeing at *Machinima.com* at the time, but it was obvious that eventually, with enough graphics power, you would be able to tell compelling stories.

TH: Were there any particular games engines you felt were better suited to producing machinima in the early days?

KL: When I did my degree at University of Manchester, I ended up specializing in real-time computer graphics so I was more into the real-time side of things than the software render side, but because when I went into movies there was just no way you could generate images of the quality we needed in movies. But I always kept my eye on it, and this is going to sound as though I'm making it up, but it's the honest truth: I was playing the first *Unreal* game. It basically starts off with a castle, I can't recall what the team at *Epic* called it at the time, but there was this fly-through where the camera flies around and through the castle, through the holes in the castle and, I'm like, 'my god, look at this, can you imagine this 20 years down the line? This is going to look like a totally real castle, and I feel like you could put it in a movie'. Then there's a moment in the game where all the lights go off and you are first introduced to the *Skaarj*, the bad guys in the game, and I felt like it didn't feel like a video game but more like I'm in an action shot in a movie. It started to connect that you would be able to use these tools.

A few years later, I went to *Digital Domain* to start up a game with *Unreal Engine,* working with Jerry O'Flaherty, who was art director on the first *Gears of War*. We were going to use *Unreal Engine* to make an animated movie… do you recall *Thundercats* from years ago? We said, why don't we remake it as a video game and a movie at the same time using *Unreal Engine 3*. That would have been around 2007. It's been something that I always knew was going to happen, to use games engines to make awesome linear narrative and you were going to be able to take advantage of that by making things playable. Because if you are building stuff in the same tool, you can have a playable component, you can have a linear story, and who knows what else will emerge if you have these two things mixed together.

TH: It is interesting that the machinima community always identified Tournament as one of the great games to create content, and the Matinee tool…

KL: Yes, the guy that wrote *Matinee* is James Golding, who works in our Guildford office, well he did when we worked in offices! Jerry O'Flaherty worked with James and talked him into making this toolset that is Matinee. I think Jerry was at *Midway* beforehand, or one of the Texas-based game studios, and he ended up applying to *Epic,* but he was really frustrated because he wanted to make movies and found himself stuck in games.

If you look at *Telltale Games* who made the *Sam & Max* games, and it has more recent history too, but that team goes back to the original *LucasArts Games* from the same era. I can't recall the name of the game the original engine that *LucasArts Games* was made on, but it's all machinima... Sam looks at Max, Sam opens door… they take the script that they write, and it automatically populates the scene. It takes the characters, the objects, like an animation, but all inside their system. It is basically the way that *Telltale* made all of their point-and-click adventure games, and it goes back to *LucasArts* and it's them building machinima systems to make games.

TH: How has the development of machinima techniques influenced you in your work over the years?

KL: It's almost the opposite way around. Seeing what's possible in video games over the years, I would look at machinima stuff—one of the great experiences was the crossover with the *Team Fortress* team at *Valve,* whilst they were building that tool. For me, I always wanted to make the visual quality better on this stuff, and so over the last seven years that I've been at *Epic,* a lot of what we've done is to replace *Matinee* because we wanted a tool that was much more filmmaker-friendly. With the new *Sequencer* tool you're now getting into the realms of making some pretty high-end, professional cinematic content. *Weta* put out a *Meerkat* movie recently that was made in *Sequencer.* It was this little animated short with a meerkat, and it was all done in the game engine. It is looking really great and you could make a full movie with it if you wanted to. So, it's more about how I add the knowledge that my team and I have had over the years into machinima tools, *Sequencer* being our machinima tool in *Unreal,* to produce motion-picture quality.

Machinima, and seeing what people are doing, has always reminded me and inspired me that one day you will be able to tell amazing stories that rival the traditional tools, but that are now accessible to everybody. It's driven a lot of our agenda with *Sequencer,* the lighting tools, the animation tools—look at what we can do with facial rigs now using tools like *MetaHuman Creator*—and all of it is available to everyone that downloads. It sounds like an advert now, but it's free for use with *Unreal Engine.* If you want to make a movie… I don't know if you've seen some of the stuff that people are making; there's a bunch of *Star Wars* content being made by fan teams… they're harvesting assets from games and getting them into *Unreal* and making full dramatic cinematic scenes with kick-ass motion—it's amazing!

My view for state-of-the-art machinima is that we take what the principles of this industry are and give everyone the tools that allow them to make even more beautifully crafted stuff.

TH: How does machinima align with what you discuss now in relation to virtual production?

KL: For us, it is all the same stuff. It is basically having a tool that can produce imagery that's compelling enough that an audience can watch it and believe it; producing imagery that looks so real that it looks like it was shot by a camera. You take that and incorporate it with the LED wall technology that's out there, and you've got the virtual production systems that we've got.

TH: Do you see that the film industry is forever being changed by the merger with the game industry?

KL: I do think that's going to happen. People are beginning to understand it and, classically in the creative realms, there is a visible wall between linear content creation and game content creation. The old guard are like, 'don't cross between these two things', but the reality is that consumers and kids and everybody that plays games and watches movies, they see them as entertainment.

Thanks to Jon Favreau and *The Mandalorian*, you can see that there is the possibility that you can make a game and TV show with the same assets. The ability to go back and explore environments and go off to alien worlds and play games that you've seen in TV shows, this is all possible. There are fewer barriers now. Almost everybody that has grown up in the last 30 years who plays games also watches movies and TV shows. I think there will be a whole new generation of creators who see it as one continuum, where they're making their own IP, a new world with a set of characters that can be experienced in all sorts of different ways. I think that not only is real-time going to revolutionize the filmmaking process, it's going to start to reimagine the way people think about building stories and worlds.

There are big differences between the two mediums, but I think there is a crossover place that's been unexplored as of yet that will actually yield new things. In much the same way that *2001* [*Space Odyssey*], *Star Wars*, and *Matrix* showed audiences something they had never seen before, I think this crossover between these two universes will give us new experiences.

TH: Machinima was all about making assets accessible so that those with limited skills or resources could still create compelling stories they wanted to tell... How does Unreal democratize the virtual production process?

KL: Not only is the tool available to anybody to download, but what we have done is made sure there is also a marketplace for the content—if you want a character, a vehicle or environment, there is loads of pre-made stuff on the marketplace. We added *Quixel* to the *Epic* family to help accelerate the ability to make natural phenomenon and environments in a really easy way. I think we've hit the critical mass and tipping point that it is so easy now that anyone who is willing to learn to use the software can pretty much tell a story. Sure, the tool isn't a watered-down, simple filmmaking tool. It's a sophisticated tool. But anyone who wants to tell a story deeply usually will invest the time in learning the tools or finding a group of friends to help.

If you look at the *Unreal Engine Virtual Production* group on *Facebook*, every week it welcomes another 5,000 people—it's over 38,000 members now—and the majority of those people are machinima makers. There's a lot of high-end professionals in there, but they are side by side with kids and hobbyists. I've never seen anything like it. It's got everybody at all levels, and they are all joyful about the exploration and this journey that they are all going on in terms of how virtual production changes the way they are making stories. It's awesome!

I don't know if you've seen Matt Workman's *Cinetracer*? It is built on *Unreal Engine*; it is sort of a mini virtual production system that's super accessible. It's like a video game. If you can play *Fortnite*, you can use *Cinetracer*. Almost every director of photography that is interested in technology has bought this app and is using it to design and pre-light sets and work out camera moves. It's super ubiquitous that they're using machinima tools now, and it's crazy that it sits side by side with kids using it that are working out what they're going to do in life and whether they're going to be a filmmaker.

TH: What do you see as the main barriers to virtual production now... and I'm using virtual production as synonymous with machinima, but maybe you're not?

KL: Yes, I think virtual production is the pro term for machinima. There is a very high-end use of it, but there is also just telling a story and that's still virtual production. Anything where the production involves using virtual interactive components is all virtual production.

Barriers... you need a computer, but then most gamers have a PC that's more than capable of doing this stuff. You have to invest a little bit of time in learning the tools, but there's a massive community of people, as I was saying earlier, and they all know *Unreal Engine* and are willing to help and are joyful that other people are learning from them.

The main challenge is how to tell a great story. Now that the tools aren't a barrier, it is about understanding human comprehension, understanding the light-depth field, writing, and placing things so that people can understand the story you are trying to tell. It's more now down to traditional film school education rather than pure tech skills... and you know you can also just watch loads of movies, not that film school isn't awesome, but if you watch enough movies you'll learn! Maybe you'll have a different take—sometimes someone informally trained has a different aesthetic than someone who has been professionally trained. We see that all the time in animators.

Animators in the movie business that did not go to animation school have a very different way of doing things—and this is probably going to upset the whole animation industry now, apologies if it does—but animating humans for action scenes, for example, is very hard to train an animator to do because they are about expressiveness and bigger-than-life performances. Actually, there are a lot of subtle nuances in human performance that someone who has learned by themselves. For example, one of my friends, Scott Benza, is one of the greatest animators on the planet for humans in action. When they needed to animate the features on *Hulk* at *ILM* for bookshots, they went to him because he just sees things in a different light. It's kind of cool that people can get access to these tools and teach themselves, and maybe they come up with a completely different language than others have before.

TH: What advice might you have for those new to storytelling using machinima and virtual production techniques?

KL: Create, watch, and share. You'll end up being in a vacuum if you don't share your work with anybody. Learn how to use the tool and remember that it's really important that when you are creating a story you're making it for an audience. So, find the audience and learn from their reactions. Create a lot. Watch a lot of movies. Play a lot of video games because the game aesthetic and link to the movie aesthetic is interesting. Share what you're making.

TH: Do you think the indie creator will take over the more professional sector going forwards?

KL: Anybody that is hugely talented and finds an audience for the stuff they make is inherently a professional; they will make money out of it somehow. I do think that the indie scene, especially the machinima scene, will be a great source of talent for storytelling creatives. I love the fact that there are so many people who love video games and video content that the worlds and characters that work from both types of consumption are going to be interesting. It's going to be a great place to source talent in the future. At some point, we may do some interesting stuff on this. We have the *Epic MegaGrants* program, so if you have a great concept for animated content that uses *Unreal Engine*, then we'll consider giving you a *MegaGrant*. I think you'll see some of these creatives become movie directors and TV directors of the future and game developers at the same time.

TH: Do you think COVID has accelerated the development of the sector?

KL: Yes, massively. People have had time on their hands, whereas traditional industries are very labor-intensive, so a lot of people have been working with *Unreal Engine* and experimenting with what can be done. We built this multi-user system that enables multiple people to collaborate together in a virtual production session, but it wasn't originally intended to run across the internet. It just happens that we are so blessed and our engineers are so awesome that because our networking works for video games, it also works across the internet. Obviously, multiplayer games have to work across the internet. You can see massive interest—just look at the growth curve on all of social media. It's crazy how many people are into it these days.

We've hit a visual quality level in real-time technology that almost all traditional visual effects artists are also interested in the possibilities. You're not going to be making the next *Avatar* in *Unreal Engine* in the next couple of years, but eventually you are going to be able to do that. The advantage of having everything interactive and in front of you on computers is being able to make changes. It's so huge that when people make that transition from traditional software packages to *Unreal Engine* they're not really going to want to go back unless they absolutely have to.

TH: Thank you so much for taking the time to talk to us today.

Interview by Tracy Harwood

30 November 2020

Chapter 1

Introduction

> It's funny, recently the term and practices around 'virtual production' are making waves across film, VFX and animation studios... one only needs to review the history of Machinima.com to see virtual production's roots are directly linked to it. That, to me, is how impactful the site was. It provided practices and language to a creative process before that process had fully formed. History should honor the site's foundation and how its grassroots filmmakers had nurtured this innovative approach that's causing fundamental shifts in how stories are now being told.
>
> Paul Marino, Lead Cinematic, *Aspyr Media* and Founder, *Academy of Machinima Arts & Sciences* (*AMAS*) (interview, 2020)

1.1 Introduction

This text explores the emergence of machinima through the lens of the original pioneers of the form. Much has now been written about machinima from theoretical and critical perspectives, from the roles of technological advancements to reviews of the machinima films that creators have produced since it was first recognized in 1996. We have not set out to provide a critical review the work of other authors on the subject or indeed a comprehensive review of the vast body of creative works that have been produced over the years, rather we have sought through this text to provide a different perspective which is complementary to others albeit one which they have not reported, or only fleetingly commented on.

We begin the text with a Prologue, an interview with Kim Libreri who is now the chief technology officer for *Epic Games* but whose previous roles and experiences have made him one of the world's leading figures in virtual production today. Whilst Libreri is perhaps best known for his work on the *Bullet Time* shots in *The Matrix*, his use of machinima tools and techniques over the years, and his passion for enabling emerging filmmakers to connect with increasingly professional tools for virtual production through his recent work at *Epic* on *Unreal Engine*, provide a unique insight into the convergence of film and game for real-time experiences. His words will resonate with many machinima filmmakers, and the stories he refers to give additional context to the battles faced by machinima creators and their emergent creative technologies practices. There are numerous touchpoints throughout the book that link back to Libreri's comments through the voices of others we have attempted to capture.

Through the chapters, our aim has been to tell the pioneering stories of creative practice which led to the now global recognition of the machinima phenomenon and its impact beyond into other creative forms, social contexts and creative industries. We do this by providing a detailed overview of the most influential key events from our perspective. We explore the producers and works that shaped how the community evolved from its earliest days to most recent times, reflecting the voices of members of the community by telling the stories through their memories and insights. Some of the key events we report will be familiar to some, but it is clear from our extensive research (which between us has been collected over 25 years since its earliest days) that the reach of machinima has far exceeded the roles of the original community of creators. Thus, we have attempted to bring the story of its evolution up to date: its boom and bust and re-emergence, reflecting the state of the art in 2020.

Specifically, our discussion leads us to conclude with four key themes emerging from our analysis of the earliest pioneers' works. These are the multifarious roles of community in shaping the trajectory of machinima's development; how the tentacles of commercialization impacted that trajectory; the influence of demand for converged media; and the potential of real-time creative practice.

We acknowledge that others may select different production lenses to review the world of machinima as it has evolved and, indeed, there are many perspectives that can be added to our text. This is our story and our selection but we are certainly open to discussion and welcome additions to this effort by others in the future.

1.2 Our roles in the Machinima story

As authors, we are connected with the machinima community in different ways.

Ben was part of the original core community whose earliest engagement with machinima began long before the term was coined. He describes himself as 'lucky to have been in the right place at the right time' for all the major developments in the story of machinima. In the early 1990s, he was knee-deep in the world of pre-internet and wandered the bulletin boards (BBS) following the Demoscene, enjoying pieces by *Future Crew*, *Renaissance* (*Second Reality/Panic*) and *Amnesia*. He intertwined this with PC gaming and, like most gamers back then, chewed through games and almost anything else he could get his hands on, amazed and hungry to see the next evolution of everything in the PC/gaming space, both technology and content. He explored *Wolfenstein3D* and *Doom* mods, then hooked on *7th Guest* and full-motion video storytelling, before finding *Quake*. Fascinated with *Quake* movie productions, starting with *Diary of a Camper* and everything that followed, Ben's pattern of curiosity and engagement continued until, purely by chance, he stumbled upon *Machinima.com* just a few days after it launched. As a committed fan, Ben offered a helping hand.

Figure 1.1: Ben Grussi with Ricky Grove, image captured at *Machinima Film Festival* 2008.

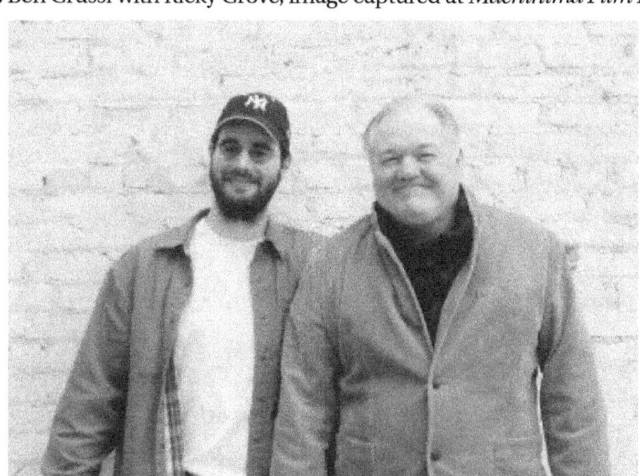

Author: Ben Grussi.

Little did he know this would be life-changing. Like many that became part of the machinima community, its force pushed Ben in an entirely unplanned and unexpected direction. He became a core part of the *Machinima.com* community, ultimately earning the distinction of once being described as its own *Wikipedia*! Ben was actively involved for twelve years in a variety of roles. He has also been news reporter, tech support and a community manager as well as a bit part actor from time to time. Most notably, he was the primary curator of machinima creative work from its earliest days. Even today, Ben describes himself as a bit of a ghost, happy to pop up here and there, surprise friends and colleagues, 'help out a bit' and equally happy to then disappear and observe from afar. He jokes that considering his role has involved every aspect of machinima right from its inception, the real surprise is that he never made any of his own films – but he did not need to, since he left the creative part to the community itself! This text draws on Ben's deep knowledge and insight of games, film, people, and events, from within the world of machinima as it emerged and evolved.

Figure 1.2: Author Tracy Harwood at *Machinima Europe Festival Awards* 2007.

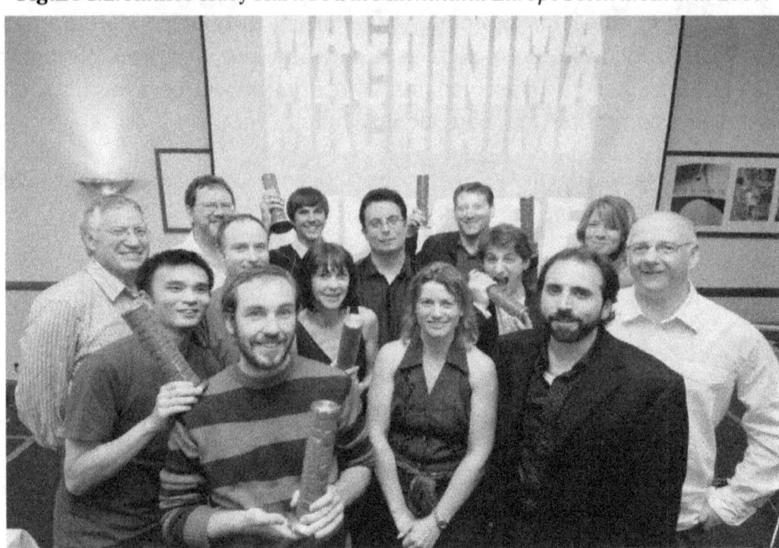

Author: Tracy Harwood. Back (l-r): David Asch (Deputy Vice Chancellor, *De Montfort University*), Andrew Hugill (Director, *IOCT*), Christian Kosta-Zahn (Best Commercial), Hugh Hancock (Keynote), Paul Jannicola & Kerria Seabrook (Best Series); middle (l-r): Alex Chan (Keynote), Xavier Lardy (*AMAS*), Ann Garner (Moviestorm), Ricard Gras (Best Technical Achievement), Toby Moores (Keynote); front (l-r): Friedrich Kirschner (*AMAS/Movie Sandbox*), Tracy Harwood, Paul Marino (*AMAS*).
Image used with permission, source: De Montfort University ©.

Tracy came to the machinima party much later as director of the *First European Machinima Festival* that took place in Leicester, UK in October 2007. The festival was the first major project to be developed by the newly formed *Institute of Creative Technologies* at *De Montfort University*, Leicester (IOCT). As a transdisciplinary institute, the *IOCT* was keen to support new practices that demonstrated the convergence of different disciplines drawing on science, arts, technologies and business. The festival reflected the institute's interests in time-based visual arts and multimedia technologies which collectively informed performance and production in both real and virtual environments. It was co-hosted with the *Academy of Machinima Arts and Sciences* (*AMAS*) including an annual awards ceremony (see Figure 1.2). The event was supported by transmedia academics, creative practitioners, games developers, media publishers (such as the *BBC*, *ITV*) and professional bodies (e.g., *TIGA*) with keynotes and panels by key innovators such as Paul Marino (*AMAS*), Hugh Hancock and Johnnie Ingram (*AMAS*/ *Strange Company*), Friedrich Kirschner and Klaus Neumann (*AMAS/Movie Sandbox*), Matt Kelland (*Moviestorm*), John C. Martin II (*Reallusion*), Ricard Gras (*La Interactiva*), Xavier Lardy (*AMAS*),

Burnie Burns and Jason Saldana (*Rooster Teeth*). Hancock and Ingram's 2007 book *Machinima for Dummies* was launched at the festival, as was *Moviestorm* (*Short Fuze*). The festival was also sponsored by *BEEPA* (maker of screen capture software, *FRAPs)* and attended by many community members who had hitherto struggled to attend the mainly US-based events that had taken place, drawing in an international audience. Subsequently, Tracy has researched community aspects of machinima and its impacts on digital culture, digital creativity and creative technologies practices, publishing in leading business and digital creativity academic journals, based on interviews with numerous community members over the intervening years. Her work on machinima has been funded by and contributed to the UK's *Arts and Humanities Research Council*'s major project on the future value of arts and culture, *Cultural Value Project* (Harwood, 2014; Crossick and Kaszynska, 2014).

Together, the authors have examined the history, backstories, recollections and impacts of machinima from its various annals which have been collated by ourselves (and many others) over the years.

1.3 Structure of the Text

Following this chapter, the text is divided into six core chapters and a conclusion chapter. The chapters are centred on pioneering contributions inspired by either a film, a producer or production studio. With each chapter, we highlight key games and tools used by the machinima community during the period represented in a series of vignettes. The final core chapter is focussed on the real-time concept as it was developed and evolved by a series of industrial contributors.

Chapter 2: In the Beginning: Diary of a Camper

A machinima text without *Diary of a Camper* is simply impossible! It is the story most often told by others in their review of all things machinima. In our chapter, however, we explore how it inspired others in the community directly and indirectly as the community began to take shape and coalesce around key creative practices, contributors and films.

Chapter 3: Machinima! [.com]

Founded by Hugh Hancock in 2000, *Machinima.com* was originally a part of his *Strange Company* production studio. It quickly grew and became a focus for the rapidly expanding machinima community, culminating in Hugh finding it a new home. Thereafter, the story of *Machinima.com* becomes blurred with a commercial pool of entrepreneurism under *Machinima Inc. Machinima Inc.* ultimately exploited the community and queered the term yet the community pioneers have survived. We review the trajectory of *Machinima.com* from beginning to its end in 2019, when it became subsumed by *Warner Bros.*, an *AT&T* company.

Chapter 4: Rooster Teeth Bites

As the most prolific and successful machinima production studio of all time, *Rooster Teeth*'s story is examined from the earliest days of its seminal *Red vs Blue Halo*-based series to most recent times as a let's play and podcast producer. As we were writing this text, its original founders had reached the end of their journey with the studio, albeit it continues as part of a major media conglomerate under *AT&T*'s ownership. We bring the story of *Rooster Teeth*'s longevity and successes up to date.

Chapter 5: The French Democracy in Action

This chapter examines the impact of a small film by a previously unknown filmmaker, Alex Chan. The film is raw in its storytelling power but impactful in its contribution to filmmaking, video journalism and politics as well as the machinima community. *The French Democracy* is often cited in media texts as an example of the democratizing capabilities of machinima, but few have examined how the full story of Chan's film was harnessed by others.

Chapter 6: Stolen Life Lives On

The chapter tells the story of the award-winning feature-length machinima film *Stolen Life*, produced by Peter Rasmussen and Jackie Turnure and released in 2007. The chapter particularly focusses on the contribution to the machinima community by Rasmussen. His repertoire of work was not large but its impact was significant, not least in the context of innovation in the Australian filmmaking scene. Rasmussen's life was sadly short but the struggles he faced as a pioneering filmmaker were recognized by his colleagues, culminating in an annual award at the *Sydney Film Festival* between 2009-2012. The chapter examines both the impact of the film and the award.

Chapter 7: Begin Again?

This chapter reflects the search for real-time 3D animated glory. We examine how machinima was viewed from different industry perspectives, focussing on pioneers from both the game and film sectors. Ultimately, the search is for new ways to tell stories, reflecting how audiences have evolved and developed their interests alongside technological advancements. In the end, nothing is new! We present a yardstick of *Epic Games' Unreal Engine* as a current force against which machinima is recognized as the foundational inspiration for future growth.

Chapter 8: Conclusion

Within this chapter, we summarize the key themes identified in each of the preceding chapters, setting out the contributions made and the future trajectory of machinima.

1.4 Contributors

The text draws on numerous contributors directly and others indirectly through their comments published in secondary sources. Specifically, we would like to thank the following contributors for their time and energy in answering our questions and providing us with meaningful details. Sadly, we were only able to use a fraction of the information collated from each in the process of writing this text:

Isabelle Arvers
Jason Boomer
Chris Burke
Ian Chisholm
Rob Connolly
Tina Crawford
Frank R. Dellario
Claude Errera
Joe Falcione
Joe Goss
Ricard Gras
Ricky Grove
James Hamer-Morton
Bryan Henderson
Chris Howlett
Xavier Lardy
Michele Ledwidge
Kim Libreri
Tawmis Logue
Leo Lucien-Bay
Laird MacLean
Paul Marino
Brian Mayberry
Gordon McDonald
Mary McDowell
Ingrid Moon
Peter Morse
Thuyen Nguyen
Michael Nikonov
Marc Petit
Caroline Piras
Phil Rice
John Romero
Tony Shiff
Ken Thain
Clive Thompson
Jackie Turnure
Damien Valentine
Reece Watkins
Christine Webster
Alexander Winn

We extend our thanks to contributors from earlier interviews for our respective research interests, whose commentary we have also reflected in this text:

Ebbe Altberg
Pooky Amsterdam
Russell Boyd
Heath 'ColdSun' Brown
Oscar Clark
Tony Dyson
Ernest Edmonds
Joseph DeLappe
Ian Friar
Chantal Harvey
Lynne Heller
Paul Jannicola
Tom Jantol
JayJay Jegathesan
Susan Johnson
Matt Kelland
Friedrich Kirschner
Scott Lamb
John C. Martin II
Ze Moo
Tutsy Navarathna
Chris Payne
Carol Rainbow
Crystel Schneider
Kerria Seabrook
Iain Simons
Mike Stubbs

Carl Goodman
Bibbe Hansen
Hugh Hancock
Patrick Lichty
Torley Linden
Jo Twist
Kelly Vero

We acknowledge the significant contributions of those who are no longer with us and without whose creative and documented legacy this book could not have been written:

Hugh Hancock, *Strange Company, Machinima.com* and *AMAS*

Peter Rasmussen, *Nanoflix Productions*

We owe a debt of gratitude to the *Internet Archive*'s *Wayback Machine* (created by Brewster Kahle and launched in 2001) without which much of the early community platforms we have trawled to verify various accounts of events throughout this text would not have been possible today.

Finally, we dedicate this book to the machinima community whose creative endeavours and pioneering works have founded a global interest in the convergence of game and film through real-time 3D production techniques, as reflected in Marino's quote at the beginning of this chapter. There are numerous others whose voices we have not had a chance to specifically include but whose contributions are nonetheless important to the story of the emergence of machinima.

Chapter 2

In the beginning: Diary of a Camper

ArchV: Is that who I think it is? ColdSun: Yeah... its John Romero.

Diary of a Camper (1996)

2.1 Introduction

Diary of a Camper (*DoC*) has long been recognized as the foundational machinima film by the community of creative practitioners. Over the years, numerous texts and articles have identified clear dimensions of machinima which make it unique from other similar forms, highlighting the creative process, method of production and the nature of the machinima product related to game of the day, *Quake*. In this chapter, we explore the backstory to the film alongside the story of the emergence of machinima through the influence and impacts of *DoC* and its production processes, discussing how its unique properties encompass both its methods of production and genre.

The early examples of machinima used a perfect capture method of recording from game play, with *Quake* and *Doom* being the founding games used as toolsets and assets for storytelling. These games offered limited support for machinima production as we now understand the term. As the machinima community began to develop and demand for creative toolsets began to grow, new tools emerged which facilitated gameplay for scenes as well as recording and editing. With these early tools and game modifications (mods), machinima quickly evolved, resulting in new creative forms from screen capture, asset compositing and 'bespoke' animation methods for filmmaking using game engines.

Alongside this, as games have themselves evolved from simple to complex formats, then so too have the creative juices of machinima creators flowed – machinima films quickly began to take shape as forms of fan fiction, parody, political commentary, experimental forms, fine art and music videos. Later, machinima would become a preferred pre-visualization tool. Somewhere in its evolutionary trajectory, other creative forms emerged such as historical drama and documentary, reportage and reconstruction, and education. But the journey into content creation as it became known, can be traced to one machinima film and a very small collection of other films it inspired. Following our review of the backstory and overview of *DoC*, we explore the impacts through the perspectives of the first key machinima producers.

2.2 Backstory

The word machinima is a combination of *machine* and *cinema*. The term was originally coined *machinema* (with an 'e') by Anthony Bailey and Hugh Hancock but, due to a happy accident involving the infamous Hugh Hancock, founder of the *Machinima.com* website years later, the term was misspelled and the word has ever since been part of popular geek culture. Some years ago, in conversation with Hugh Hancock, the authors discussed the impact of this misspelling: it was rationalized with the addition of animation as a middle part of the word. Other machinima creators also attribute the misspelling to the alignment of machinima with anime – Japanese for live – although anime animation is an entirely different genre of content (see, e.g., Ng, 2013). Machine-animation-cinema sums up what can be achieved with creative processes applied to games, where the games are animated assets for further development by artists.

But this was not always the case: at its earliest period it was referred to as the *demoscene*. During this period, games such as *Doom* and *Quake* were also noted to provide cinematic experiences and there were several theatrical performances at places such as the *Demoscene Convention* (Assembly) that showed off demos (demonstrations) of the capability of the game in a cinematic way. The demoscene did not, however, rely on games for their creative work. Creators used their own self-developed demo engines, and some of the best pieces of work became commercial demos for the then niche market of PC System Benchmarking (speed measuring) software which adopted a similar style but with a gamer focus (eg., *FutureMark/3DMark*). From a viewer's perspective, it was movie theatre with a cinematic score. This became a sophisticated game demo technique with further advancement of audio hardware and widescreen visual effects linked to developments in the complexity of computer hardware. Formally recognized (9 April 2020) as Intangible Cultural Heritage under UNESCO's 2003 Convention treaty for cultural heritage, demoscene is defined today thusly:

> The demoscene is a worldwide non-commercial network of creative minds involved in the making of so called 'demos'. Demos are computer generated music clips that show what kind of graphic and sound effects can really be done by using high-end computer hardware to its full potential.
>
> Demo-making is teamwork. As demos are rather complex any helping hand is welcome. Each scener provides the team with different skills. Graphicians and musicians create suitable pieces of art, the programmers fit all the parts together in an extensive amount of detail work to finally make it an executable program: the demo.

> The sceners don't necessarily have to physically meet each other at all during the whole process. Usually they meet in chatrooms and share their latest work over the internet. Most sceners live in Europe but you can find them almost everywhere in the world.
>
> http://www.demoscene.info/ (2019)

Machinima began to emerge when creators were able to start recording game footage, using such as *Disney's Stunt Island*, and share edited footage on electronic bulletin board systems (BBSs), from which it progressed to other games now associated with the emergence and early stages of the development of machinima, specifically *Doom* and *Quake*. The potential of the in-game tools was first noted by German academic, Uwe Girlich, who created a tool for *Doom* that recammed demos, later badged the *Little Movie Processing Centre*. This was the original concept of what would later become *Keygrip*.

By way of a technical note, a demo file (.dem) was used to record the movements and text on the screen at that time. When completed, all the game could do was simply replay this file. Games and .dem files did not have the capability to add or store voiceovers because the only functionality was as a means to generate playback footage, much like playing the same exact game of chess after clearing the board. As early as 1992, however, with BBSs, viewers of *Disney*'s *Stunt Island* did not require copies of the game because the file was transferred as a self-contained movie package with all the assets built in. This meant that all that was required was a mini-player to play back the visuals.

It was *id Software's Doom* that introduced gameplay recording of multiplayer matches from the player's point of view. *Doom's* successor, *Quake* provided a 360-degree viewing space with the freedom to introduce an interactive camera system. In the game, the camera *was* the player and, with a sprinkling of a few magical cheat codes, some interesting effects could be generated, such as the 'look at me I can fly and nothing can hurt me!' scenario, often used to acquire the perfect shot of game action. Later on, new content creation tools included the addition of custom assets such as graphics, sound effects, levels (sets) and voiceovers. At that point, the game was changed in ways most people at the time could not imagine. But the tools themselves had earlier foundations in *id Software's Wolfenstein3D* game (see Vignettes 2.6.1: *Wolfenstein3D*, 2: *Doom* and 3: *Quake* about these games).

As intimated above, Girlich's role in the development of machinima was instrumental. He was already recognized as an authority in *Quake* movie making and had identified that its demo format enabled console commands to be added to files which made their conversion to video file formats eg., MPEG, possible (Girlich, 1996). Having previously written code for the *Little Movie Processing Centre* editing tool for *Doom* and other games, he then wrote an editor for *Quake* on its release which was, in turn, picked up and developed by David Wright. Wright then wrote the *Keygrip* and *Keygrip2* programmes which subsequently became the most used tools for editing and post-production of machinima works (Lowood, 2006).

With this review in mind, it leads us to an interesting question: if machinima was already being made in 1992, why is *DoC* (1996) considered the 'first machinima' film?

2.3 About DoC

Quake allowed development and expansion using an early form of production technique: firstly, multiple players could play individual parts; secondly, a multiplicity of additional camera angles could be used; and thirdly, each player had control of his/her own puppet (or avatar) independent of others playing the game. However, there was a lack of voiceover or vocal track capability. *DoC* was produced with the stock game/product (*Quake*) output. Whereas *Quake* is a first-person point of view (pov) game whereby characters' own eyes are used to show how weapons are viewed, such as guns (over the barrel) or an axe and whether it is held in the character's left or right hand, *DoC* was shot in third person using one of the characters as a camera.

DoC is widely considered by the community of practitioners and followers to be the first machinima film because it was the first example of a computer game used to craft a solo project with a simple story. There were five players or, in this case, actors who moved their characters into different positions much like traditional actors performing in positions and 'speaking' and/or targeting and hitting their marks by unleashing massive firepower of the game assets. By modifying (aka modding) the game code, *DoC* showed alternative views and allowed the players to traverse the game in ways not originally permitted. The sixth player was the cameraman/director who recorded the action unfolding using the game's built-in recording function to a demo file (.dem). Subsequently, *DoC* (run time 1 min, 36 secs) was shared by the early internet sites and BBSs.

DoC was the only film known at the time taking a real-time 3D computer game to use it in a theatre/puppet style instead of for its original gameplay purpose. There was no comparator – it was the first known example of this new artform or technique. Much like the Silent Film era in cinema, it is an example of machinima's 'silent era' albeit the stock sounds from the game environment itself could be heard in the film as an ambient soundscape.

As with prior gaming platforms from *id Software*, the community of players would in the future develop and enhance the game to add to it the ability to use voiceovers and more powerful camera and editing capabilities. First examples are *RangerCam* and *KeyGrip*, some of the most powerful tools in the *Quake* period of machinimating. It was just a month after the release of *DoC* that *3DFX* released its first consumer-level 3D graphics accelerator video card which completely changed the visual representation of what could be seen. Accelerated graphics were used to redefine how features such as lighting could be used in a 3D environment, effectively creating new visual effects (e.g., lens flare light intensity, translucent water, etc.). It was these effects that enabled the possibility of telling richer and more detailed stories through visualizations.

Today, *DoC* remains a film that is available on various social media platforms as well as the Machinima Collection on the Internet Archive (https://archive.org/details/DiaryOfACamper), with millions of views since it was first released in October 1996.

2.4 What's the storyline?

As a story goes, its tale was deeply embedded within game culture specifically related to the *Quake* community. *DoC* occurs entirely within the *Quake* map DM6 (*The Dark Zone*). Its short format storyline was about a team of *Rangers that after exploring an area in the game, decide to send two members of the team, Sphinx and Pyoveli, to scout ahead. After teleporting into the new area of the game, the two members are ambushed by a *Camper, as confirmed by in-game text messages that appear on the screen. Following the carnage, the three remaining Rangers – ColdSun, ArchV, and an unidentified member – realize their comrades' fate and return fire from a distance, launching an all-out attack on the Camper's position. The Rangers' attack was successful and the camper's remains were then examined.

In a twist of the tale, these remains were determined to be that of their foe, John Romero (one of the co-creators of the *Quake* game).

Figure 2.1: Screencaps *Diary of a Camper*.

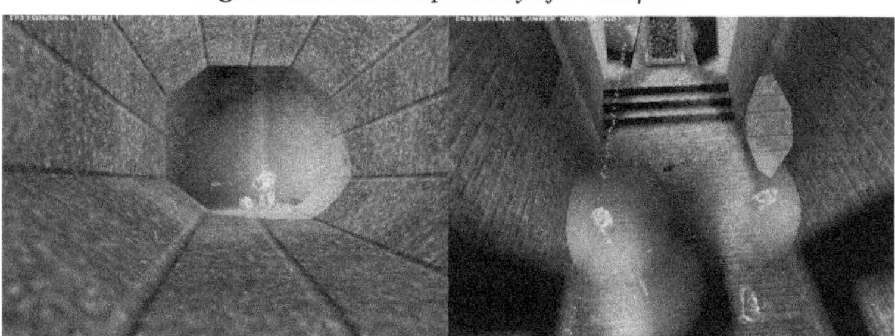

Source: *United Rangers Films*, 1996.

*A Ranger was a common term used to describe a *Quake* game player, or clan member. A Camper is a player who does not move from a position that has a powerful 'power-up' and is therefore able to kill and prevent other players from getting the same power-up. This kind of game strategy provided an unfair advantage to a Camper, hence becoming a play target.

The *Rangers* were a clan with a deep passion for the *Quake* game, leading to one member having a closer association with *Id Software* as a contractor working on the mod, *Capture the Flag* (*CTF*). Another member, Heath 'ColdSun' Brown, noted how *DoC* came to be made:

> One night after one of their many 6 hour games in DM6 [the *Rangers*] were discussing making demos of their playing to show off to people. It wasn't really any serious discussion, just some way for *The Rangers* to make a bigger impact on the community. One of the members made a joke, saying something along the lines of 'wouldn't it be cool if we could make a movie out of a demo.' *The Rangers* sat for a second in Internet Relay Chat as the wheels turned in their heads. ColdSun's creative desire suddenly reared up as he talked excitedly to his clan about the prospects of being able to pull it off. ArchV volunteered to hack the demo files to place their own story text in them. *The Rangers* then created the first *Quake* movie (and arguably the first in-game cinematic ever made), *Diary of a Camper*, filmed by UnknownSoldier. It was a comedy, and not a very good one. It was something new and the community loved it.
>
> Heath 'ColdSun' Brown (correspondence with authors, 2008)

Thus, from small talk began a big idea, where its ripples can still be seen!

2.5 Reflections of the Impact and Influence of DoC

The story of machinima is in many ways indelibly tied to the development of games and computer technologies just as much as it is to those early ground-breaking filmmakers. As demand grew for more cinematic experiences by gamers and machinima creators, the direct impact of machinima is firstly most evident in games development. As time passed, engines such as *Quake* began to incorporate in-game cinematics, level packs and mods (eg., *Zerstorer – Testament of the Destroyer*), often by drawing heavily on the enthusiastic gamer fan base as well as commercial projects such as *Ritual's Sin* and Romero's *Daikatana*. This meant that for the relatively low cost of developing camera and editing tools for the game, machinima creators did not have to rely on expensive and outsourced computer-generated imagery houses to create pre-rendered cinematics (see, e.g., Hancock and Ingram's *Machinima for Dummies*, 2007).

In the early years, the impact of *DoC* was profound on a small group of creators whose own work then became the foundation for the machinima movement. As John Romero, co-founder of *id Software*, publisher of *Doom* and the subject of *DoC*'s plot twist said:

> It hasn't really influenced anything I've done but I know it's made other developers add custom camera controls into their games to enable machinima... I thought it was funny when I saw it. In deathmatch, some players have an attitude that if you're sitting and waiting for someone to come around the corner or teleport to your location that it's called Camping. They called me a camper, when in reality it's just tactics. So, the first machinima was a joke about my camping.
>
> John Romero (correspondence, 2020)

Academic authors such as Henry Lowood (2006; 2008; 2011), Michael Nitsche (2005; 2011) and Lev Manovich (2011) among others years later have attributed the emergence of machinima and its longevity as a unique new media production method. They position machinima as the convergence of emerging gamer culture with 'high performance' play, such as speedrunning and observation of performance capture (e.g., esports) and its alignment with filmmaking and theatrical production techniques more generally.

In more recent years, the impact of machinima has been apparent when Hollywood directors started using the creative techniques in pre-visualizing their films, as highlighted in our Prologue interview with Kim Libreri. By using 3D games as real-time animation tools to scope out a scene, machinima films were used to test script ideas before they were translated to real-world action scenes, where considerably more money was to be spent. Examples have been cited as Steven Spielberg, who used the techniques when making *Saving Private Ryan, A.I.*, and the *Indiana Jones* franchise. Peter Jackson's use of game technologies in making the *Lord of the Rings* war scenes is also well known. More recently techniques have been used to create the *Star Wars* series, *The Mandalorian* (see Chapters 3 and 7).

It is not surprising that some from the community of practice feel that machinima as a creative medium would have happened in any event as a simple consequence of the game development trajectory. Bryan Henderson (aka 'CrustaR') and founder of one of the first machinima production studios in 1999, *P1mp Slap Productions*, for example, commented:

> ... I personally do not think Machinima was significant overall; I believe it was a small community that was just having fun at the time. I think game cinematics would still be where they are today, that's just kind of where it was all going. It makes sense to be able to render in real time and not have to go pre-rendered for cutscenes.
>
> Bryan Henderson (interview, 2020)

Tracing the history of machinima, others also comment that similar creative forms were evolving simultaneously, such as speedrun films generated in

Doom, Disney's Stunt Island films and those that emanated from the demoscene. Whilst member of the *ILL Clan* and later co-founder of the influential *Academy of Machinima Arts & Sciences* body (*AMAS*), Paul Marino (2004), commented that what distinguished machinima from other creative forms of its day was its generative 3D format, reflecting the *Quake* game engine design. Henry Lowood (2005), curator for History of Science and Technology Collections and Film and Media Collections in the Stanford University Libraries, differentiated it on the basis of its storytelling rather than documented gameplay. Irrespective of these comments, it was machinima that gained attention among an ultimately very broad community of followers as a production methodology. In later years, it became better understood as a brand which enabled *Machinima.com* to become one of the most influential websites of its time, with millions of unique hits per month. We discuss this development trajectory specifically in Chapter 3.

As to its foundational film, years after *DoC* had been made, one of *The Rangers* clan, Brown, wrote in the *Machinima.com* forum:

> I was reading *Yahoo* tonight and lo' and behold I see a story about Machinima. You see, I hold a special place in my heart for the subject. I was thrilled to see this article and even more thrilled when I saw the single paragraph on '*Diary of a Camper*'. I made that movie with my clan, *The Rangers,* way back when. I'm ColdSun. I'm not sure anyone remembers me but I just wanted to thank you for making Machinima what it is today with your wonderful site. We Rangers still exist, in a secluded corner of the internet - all of us are still together... It's great to see our *Ranger* movies still exist and have a home for all to see them even though they are very dated.
>
> Heath 'ColdSun' Brown (*Machinima.com*, 2005)

Notwithstanding his comment above, Henderson (*P1mp Slap Productions*) had always been an enthusiastic follower of *The Rangers* in the 1990s and he himself became a key influencer in the development of machinima during the early period of its development, having produced the *Rick Jones* series (1998-2000) in *Quake II*. He was particularly interested in *The Rangers'* efforts to extend storytelling in *Quake* which they did in their subsequent release of *Ranger Gone Bad* (*RGB*, changing their name to *United Rangers Films*) some five days after *DoC* had been released, and later films in the following couple of years (see Figure 2.2).

Figure 2.2: Screencap *Ranger Gone Bad II: Assault on Gloom Keep.*

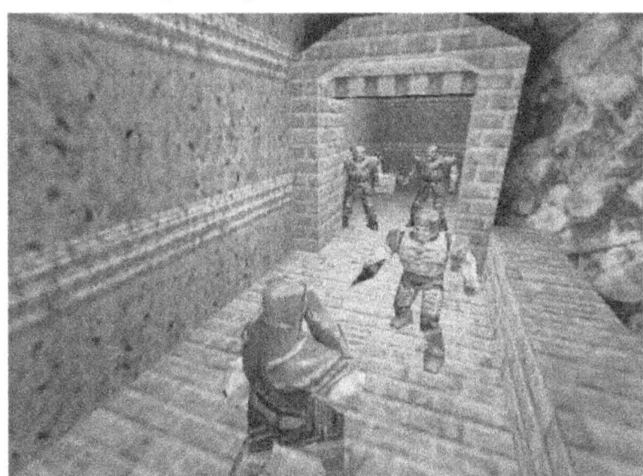

Source: *United Rangers Films,* 1997.

Reflecting both on his own creative endeavours and that of the burgeoning machinima community, Henderson commented on how and why machinima had evolved in an article in 2016 that:

> Right after the *Quake* demo was first released there were mods for it… The mods instantly increased the longevity of the game because there were so many things you could do with the engine; it was no longer about the game out of the box, it was what people could do with the game.
>
> Bryan Henderson (in Craddock, 2016).

Figure 2.3: Screencap *Devil's Covenant.*

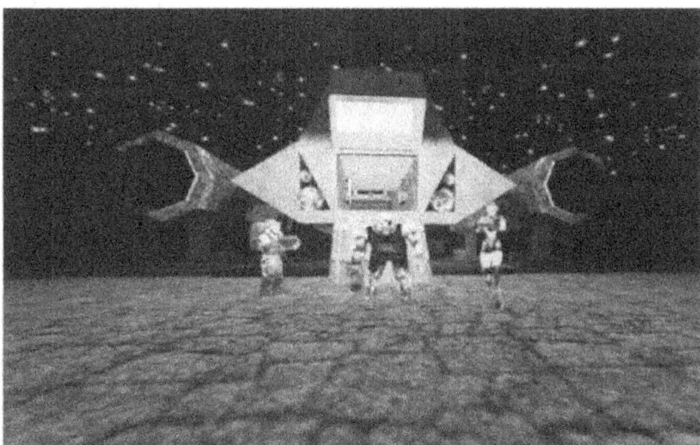

Source: *Clan Phantasm/Starfury Productions,* 1998.

Thus, the *Rangers'* films *DoC* and *RGB* paved the way for numerous other series of *Quake* movies, ultimately leading to the first full-feature in-game film, *Devil's Covenant* (by *Clan Phantasm/Starfury Productions,* 1998 – see Figure 2.3). At 2 hours 5 minutes in length, it is this film that became the cult hit which enabled others in the community to engage more fully with the phenomenon. *Clan Phantasm/Starfury* also produced different versions of the storyline (in

1999, 2000) and *Starfury* (as a solo creator) completed a side-project editing and experimenting with the *Quake 2: Late Nite Talk Show* series.

In the meantime, *United Rangers Films,* discontinued their creative works and splintered as a consequence of a failed experience in showcasing their latest *RGB* film at the second annual *QuakeCon* in 1997 (see Craddock 2016 for the backstory). The *RangerCam* they had made so much use of in their machinima was, however, picked up by the then start-up, *Valve Software.* Two of the clan (known as Bond and Guthrie) also contributed to such games as *Half-Life, Half-Life 2* and *Left 4 Dead* whilst another clan member (David 'Zoid' Kirch, Bond) created the *Capture the Flag* mod for *Quake* and yet another of the clan (Steve 'Blue' Heaslip, Guthrie) founded *Bluesnews.com.* This was a popular site of the time which subsequently evolved from its *Quake*-centric news origins to include gaming news more generally.

With this beginning and developmental trajectory in mind, Henderson commented on what he felt the legacy of *DoC, RGB* and machinima more generally has been since its earliest days:

> The biggest legacy that machinima left behind, at least from my perspective, was the memories of all the crazy short films everyone created. This was back in the late 90s and early 2000s, when the gaming community was still fairly small. Everything created felt significant, special somehow, like you could be heard even if you didn't produce something all that great... Machinima did seem to spark a few profitable ventures, most notably *Machinima.com* and *Rooster Teeth. Machinima.com* initially was about game engine movies, but then it turned into a commercialized venture that didn't really have much to do with in-game cutscenes at all.... The *Ranger Gone Bad* films definitely sparked everyone's interest. All of that was treated like real film sets – these were game cinematics with real actors. Without that, I think machinima films would have still popped up, but they would have been a bit different, maybe a bit more scripted like the in-game cutscenes we see today. I'm pretty sure Red vs. Blue wouldn't be around without *Diary of a Camper* setting the table with that type of film making. Or maybe someone else would have thought of the idea, and we would have had a different kind of game cinematic initially created.
>
> Bryan Henderson (interview, 2020)

Others at the heart of the evolutionary development of machinima, whose sphere of influence continued in a range of creative industries, are also explicit in their view of *DoC*'s contribution.

By the time *Quake II* was released in November 1997, there was already demand for creative works made from the game. It was the *ILL Clan's Hardly Workin'* machinima (released 1998) that demonstrated to a much broader audience that high-quality production values were possible from machinima such that the original game aesthetic was barely even noticeable (see Chapter 3).

The *ILL Clan* (founded 1995) was a creative production team made up of professional filmmakers, with prior careers in the film industry. Paul Marino, who was co-founder of *ILL Clan*, became one of the most recognized producers of comedic machinima from the outset. He commented on their own role in machinima using the *Quake* game as a jump off point:

> ...we saw that we were a bit more passionate than others about what we were doing in *Quake*... *Quake* at the time seemed to be the go-to for anything that resembled [Hugh Hancock's] term 'machinima'.
>
> Paul Marino (interview, 2020)

His co-creator and co-founder in *ILL Clan*, Frank Dellario, comments on the role of *Quake* and its considerable impacts on their creative practices:

> Our game clan, *ILL Clan*, was made up of media professionals (I was a grip and AD, Matt an artist, Paul a 3D modeler/animator, Manu an audio engineer and backend coder). We met at Manu's office Friday nights to play *Quake 1*. While he set up the LAN we watched demo file videos where we saw the first rocket jump and then, of course, *Diary of a Camper*, and others like *Babalicious* and *Operation Bay Shield*. Our response was immediate: 'We can do this!' A few months later Apartment Huntin' came out and the rest is history... Working in machinima led to producing machinima and then 3D CGI, usually meant for game industry marketing. We were usually hired by ad agencies. Each Fall we produced a more elaborate Intel spot based on a AAA game title due out for Christmas. The characters in the game complained about how good the players were because of using an *Intel* processor. We produced little machinima bumpers for a video game centered show on MTV/VH1 and a year-long proof of concept for the *Xbox*. Ultimately, we began producing our live animated improv shows with *Lenny and Larry Lumberjack*, totally out of a misunderstanding by a client regarding what 'real-time' meant in machinima. But we didn't complain. We ended up performing a live show at Lincoln Center and in the UCB theater...
>
> The most significant thing about it and where [machinima] came from was that it bubbled out naturally out of pent-up creativity that just wanted to get out. It also showed that when an industry (the game industry in our case) embraces this type of non-commercial use of their IP, it can build serious grassroots marketing. I think this has led to a lot of similar changes in other industries. Look at *Star Trek Continues*, a fan-based recreation of the *Original Star Trek* funded by *Kickstarter*. It's won

> many awards. Look at the use of User Generated Content (UGC) videos in marketing (usually from a YouTube channel review). *Dr Who* used a fan-based CGI creation of their opening credits for the Capaldi *Dr Who* episodes… Ultimately it has kinda led to game engines being used by animation houses to render tests in real-time (vs waiting overnight for a render) and more. A huge LED screen was used for the backgrounds instead of greenscreen on the *Mandalorian. Unreal Matinee* was used to render those animated backgrounds in real-time while filming the actors in the foreground. That is just insane and so wonderful to me at the same time.
>
> Frank Dellario (interview, 2020)

Ultimately, it was the development of games engines and their increasing complexity that influenced how professionals such as Marino and Dellario progressed their filmmaking careers. *Quake* had merely been a beginning. Dellario comments:

> Over time, game engines became more and more complex and producing machinima harder. It's tough to use a game engine no-longer supported by the game developer (like *Source Filmmaker* where it's wonderful to produce in but impossible to import your own models into unless you have a seriously talented and dedicated 3D modeler with export/import experience)… Machinima was just a production technique that in and of itself didn't become a big thing but did lead to other avenues. For example, I produced full 3D CGI commercial spots for Intel that were meant to look like machinima (using the character models supplied to use from the game developer such as *Hellgate: London* and *FarCry 2*). *Rooster Teeth* started with the *Halo* series *Red vs Blue* but have gone on to produce comics, web series, cable and a feature film.
>
> Frank Dellario (interview, 2020)

With the release of *Quake III* in 1999 (see Vignette 2.6.3), *Tritin Films'* Joe 'Wreck' Goss, came to the fore, spending a notable five years creating content in the engine and effectively laying the foundations for a future *YouTube* platform. Goss' interest had been piqued particularly by *Devil's Covenant,* and he notes that it was his skills as a modder that enabled him to make machinima. He comments:

> I was always in the pak files and messing with everything and anything you could with the *Quake* engine. Once I saw people were making cinema with it like *Devil's Covenant,* that's where I shifted gears into wanting to make movies. And it was tons of fun! … I also wasn't a huge fan of the camera control in 90s machinima. I wanted to be able to pan or move the camera like it was on a crane. I felt I had more control of

> what I was doing for my movie if I could control the camera myself and add cool effects in post after… I was the one that was doing it differently. If you were to search out machinima movies today, mine may not be that noticeably different because the viewing platform in 2020 for all old machinima movies is most likely *YouTube*, BUT back then you couldn't watch a movie I produced in the game. So it really took a side-seat to 'real' Machinima. Yes, we modelled maps, worlds, skins, characters, and we even shot the movies 100% in-game engine live, but the ultimately definition of 'machinima' to me is that the computer is using the engine to view the programmed movie in real-time. In that sense, I was doing it differently. I was more in the *Red vs Blue* crowd.
>
> Joe Goss (interview, 2020)

Reflecting the influence of the emergence of machinima production studios, he goes on to say:

> While the professional game developers had already established their methods (pre-rendered), the art and even the term machinima was coined by the little people. If you asked anyone in the gaming community in the 90s what 'machinima' was, most could tell you or list a few small internet studios made up of teenagers or people in their early 20s that were developing these movies that you could watch right in your game console. That is cool to me… Machinima piqued my interest because groups like *Clan Phantasm, P1mp Slap* and *ILL Clan* were aggressively working to make movies that ran live in the game-engine. I know that today 90% of cutscenes [in computer games] are now running real-time. Processing power is finally able to achieve this, and it is a machinima legacy at the highest level.
>
> Joe Goss (interview, 2020)

With enhanced graphic quality, another of the pioneering creators, Leo 'Dr Nemesis' Lucien-Bay, was also influenced heavily by *Devil's Covenant,* particularly in his quest for storytelling. Lucien-Bay founded *Binary Picture Show* and co-founded *Sudden Death Productions*, producing more than twenty *Quake* films using a host of mods between 2000-2007 that enabled them to develop films. Beyond simply re-camming scenes in the game, their films emphasized storytelling. For example, of his film *Life on the Edge,* Lucien-Bay described the plot as a "*kind of a take on death matching, and romance, from a poetry angle*" (Grussi, 2008). It was however in later films, when other platforms and tools started to be used that demonstrated bespoke cinematic capability (such as *CrazyTalk* and *iClone*), that creators were able to focus more on storytelling than modding a game to achieve creative goals. Such became his skill at this that in 2008, Lucien-Bay began work for *Bioware* (Canada) as a lead cinematic designer, working on games such as *Mass Effect, Star Wars* and *Dragon Age.* In 2019, he joined a start-up with another of the *Bioware* team he had collaborated with over the intervening years. Of the influence of early machinima works on his own storytelling practice, Lucien-Bay commented:

> I was studying biology, chemistry, and maths when I found machinima. The next year I stopped and switched to English lit, classical civilizations, and media studies, all so I could learn to be a better story teller… I just remember being blown away by everything in [*Devil's Covenant*]. At the time, my best friend and I watched so many times while trying to work out how we could do something on a similar scale… Machinima gave us the chance to be creative in ways we'd never thought… *Quake* movies were niche but to us we were as big as Hollywood directors and actors… Today I'm working in the videogame industry... I owe all of that to machinima.
>
> Leo Lucien-Bay (interview, 2020)

By December 2001, *id Software* released the source code for *Quake II,* allowing creators to delve even deeper into the game. A number of mods were subsequently created which further extended the life of the game by enabling it to be integrated with newer videographic technologies which thereby facilitated a groundswell of community interest in developing stories.

In the next chapter (Chapter 3), we explore more of the growth of machinima from these early beginnings as *Machinima.com* took shape. In Chapter 4, we focus on the story of *Rooster Teeth,* which became the most successful machinima production studio of all time.

2.6 Vignettes

Vignette 2.6.1: Wolfenstein3D

Figure 2.4: *Wolfenstein3D.*

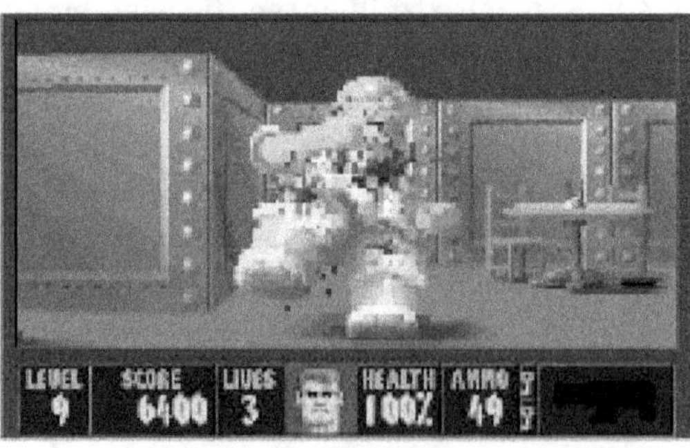

Source: Grussi, 2008.

Released 5 May 1992, *Wolfenstein3D* changed the PC gaming world by redefining games as a medium where anything was possible and rules are meant to be broken (often). It was created and released by *id Software*; players were pitted against a powerful Nazi regime and several bosses that packed plenty of firepower.

One of the first game machinima tools was the demo playback system it used to show off the game and its various play levels. Unfortunately, the code and tools to record demos were not released or revealed to the public. Nonetheless, *Wolfenstein3D* was a starting point for the first game modifications (mods). Mods are the changes to the game that make it different from the original game. The scope of these mods was anything from making the player unbeatable, to being able to move through the game faster than the World's fastest runner, to changing the original art of the game to something completely different. One of the most infamous characters to be imported into the game was *Barney the Purple Dinosaur*. *Wolfenstein's* older generation player-base had grown tired of this character's singing and were able to take their revenge in the game. This unofficial movement of game modding would eventually become a major force in the gaming industry, surpassing game developers in their creativity. The skill became central to the machinima community, with the ability to modify a game being essential to achieve desired effects, scenes and views.

Vignette 2.6.2: Doom | Doom II | Doom III

Figure 2.5: *Doom.*

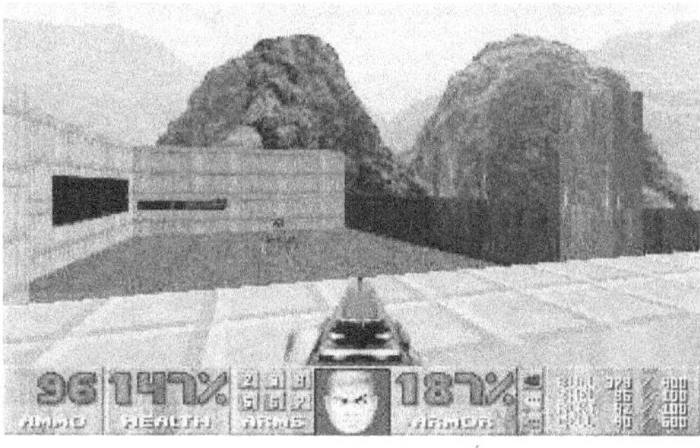

Source: Grussi, 2008.

On 10 December 1993, *id Software* released *Doom* on the back of its success with *Wolfenstein3D.*

Doom was a milestone in the computer gaming industry much like *Wolfenstein3D.* Its engine featured some of the first uses of machinima even before the term was coined. When it first started up, the game played back a pre-recorded demo of a player running through a level to illustrate the kind of world that player was going to encounter. This has been noted previously in the *Wolfenstein* entry except in *Doom* the game allowed players to record their own demos with its internal demo recording/playback module. This enabled player-recorded demos to be swapped over pre-internet systems (Bulletin Board System aka BBSs), allowing them to 'show off' their individual or team skills. Though simple, this mechanic would sow the seeds for the future of machinima.

Furthermore, modifications (mods) continued to gain notoriety since *Wolfenstein3D* after *id Software* realized the potential their community could have if they were provided with more access to the game's inter-workings. The community of players were able to make their own tools to create the unthinkable or impossible.

Doom II was released October 1994; Doom III was released on 3 August 2004, presenting new possibilities for machinima. This version of the game included considerable complexity, restricting modification and effectively preventing adaptation for machinima making. Creators therefore moved on to different games that better facilitated storytelling and offered easier routes to the outputs they wanted to share with the growing community of practice and followers.

Vignette 2.6.3 Quake I | Quake II | Quake III

Figure 2.6: *Quake.*

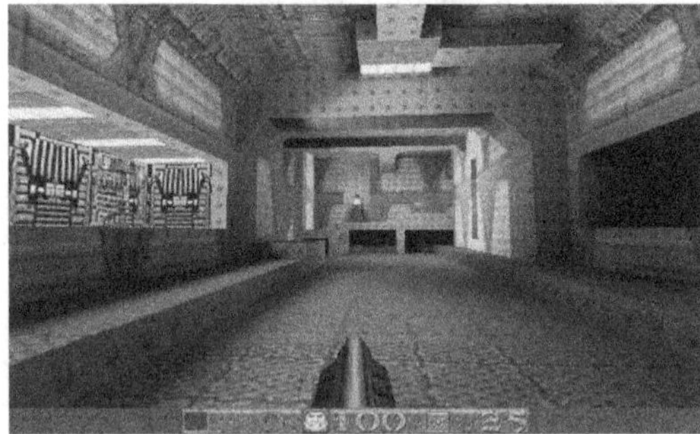

Source: Grussi, 2008.

Released on 22 June 1996, *Quake* seemed to not have the punch that *Doom* brought to the world 3 years earlier, but the game still had a strong player-base that would allow it to evolve to be more fun and challenging for years to come. Machinima came to the forefront with the *Quake* engine when the first homemade '*Quake-movie*' entitled *Diary of a Camper* was released in October 1996. *Quake* subsequently became the platform for movie distribution with over 30 hours of films and cutscene action.

Figure 2.7: *Quake II.*

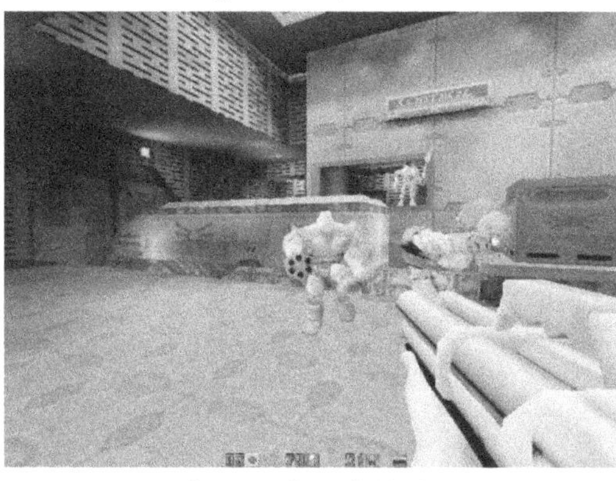

Source: Grussi, 2008.

Quake II was released on 11 November 1997 and was welcomed by players eager to see what kind of movies were going to be created. Along with new features and graphical effects, *Quake II* also provided the potential for higher quality visual effects.

In this engine, two notable films were released: the *ILL Clan's Hardly Workin'* (1998), which showed how machinima could be produced so that the underlying game engine would not be noticeable, and *Anachronox: The Movie.* This was a film that was first developed as cut-scenes for the *Ion Storm* role-playing game of the same name. *Anachronox: The Movie* came into existence when the project's cinematic director (Jake 'Strider" Hughes) cut gameplay elements from the game to create a feature-length film that did not require the game to be played to understand the story but yet provided cinematic quality. *Anachronox* subsequently won four awards at the first annual machinima film festival, held in August 2002.

On 22 December 2002, John Carmack (*id Software's* Lead Programmer) released the source code of Quake II to the gaming community. This allowed players to explore more deeply into how the engine rendered graphics. Several engine modifications with names such as *BeefQuake, Q2Max,* and *Quake2Evolve* were created by the community which enabled the games' engines to be used with contemporary technologies of 2003-2004 such as *Shaders* and *Bump-mapping.*

Quake III Arena was released on 3 December 1999. This game and its underlying engine were further developments of graphics and gameplay, however, machinima was not really invited with this one. Although built to be multiplayer only, due to *id Software's* determination to make this a fair and enjoyable game (by preventing cheats and hacks) tools could not be updated for this new engine, effectively crippling machinima development. However not all was lost: several films were still produced with this technology, notably by a group known as *Tritin Films,* headed by Joe 'Wreck' Goss. Goss created three films and two shorts with this engine.

Chapter 3

Machinima! [.com]

Machinima.com is a curatorial proposition. Whilst Philip and co have changed the focus of the videos they curate, they are still about curating.

Hugh Hancock (interview, 2014)

3.1 Introduction

In the previous chapter, we highlighted how machinima pre-dated the word, evolving from gameplay modding in the early 1990s. With Anthony Bailey and Hugh Hancock coining the term, the obvious next step was to develop a website – so *Machinima.com* began life in 1999, launching in January 2000. Hancock is largely attributed with catalyzing the community, as Ben Grussi (the website's community manager from its inception to 2006) stated in an interview in 2008:

> I believe that if *Machinima.com* did not exist the community would not have progressed as fast as it did – you need a base of operations for people, in a virtual world especially, you need a place for people to congregate and express themselves...
>
> Ben Grussi (interview, 2008)

Thus, *Machinima.com* became the grassroots of the phenomenon. It was a place where all machinima films and conversations about creative content were posted, technical achievements were discussed, and where stories of creators' successes beyond games were captured and shared by the growing community of practitioners and followers.

As time progressed, the website was successful in shifting attention to broader video-game culture, comic books and fandom more generally. Its lifespan totalled 19 years, albeit, from 2004 onwards, its original community ethos changed as it became part of *Machinima Inc.* and the foundation of *YouTube* phenomenon under the auspices of the DeBevoises and later part of the *Warner Bros.* stable. Its ultimate demise was sudden and surprising – in many ways, a victim of the corporate machine that overcame it.

In this chapter, we set out the evolution of the *Machinima.com* website and Hancock's influence, including its *Machinima Inc.* days, and its impacts and influences beyond machinima, beginning with its backstory.

3.2 Backstory

Machinima.com's story begins some time before its launch in 2000. Its founder, Hugh Hancock, had started the machinima production house, *Strange Company*, on 22 July 1998 with Gordon McDonald. The previous year, Hancock had become more aware of *Quake* movies having been involved in the scene since *QTest* (1996, see Gestalt, 2000) as a *Quake Movie Library* forum manager. He had been an enthusiastic fan of the sci-fi author and cyberspace theorist Bruce Sterling's work for some time (McDonald, private correspondence, 2020), particularly in relation to his views of a perceived general malaise in the gaming sector, reflected in Sterling's comment:

> I think we face a digital industry with some serious creative problems. Though *Nintendo*'s about as big as Hollywood, I don't think that computer entertainment has ever managed to reach its potential, commercial, artistic or otherwise. The gaming industry seems to have fossilized into shoot-em-ups, car chases, beat-em-ups, and aircraft simulations. It's amazing how boring and predictable computer entertainment is, given the well-nigh permanent state of technical revolution in its industry. The same creative properties are re-numbered, re-released and recycled over and over, with a few more bells and whistles added as the platform advances and the chip gets faster... Occasional breakouts like *The Sims* and the online version of *Ultima* indicate that there is some huge, bizarre potential there, but the industry as a whole seems stymied.
>
> Bruce Sterling (Blog, 2000)

This sums up Hancock's ethos well and, inspired by weird horror and pulp fiction writer H.P. Lovecraft, who had also inspired such authors as Stephen King, Hancock began directing *Eschaton: Darkening Twilight* in *Quake* having taken it over as an abandoned film project from another producer.

The project was completed on a network of 20 locally connected PCs in Edinburgh's first video game café, *Reality-X*, owned by Paul Younger, who commented on the experience:

> At the time, we thought [Hugh] was a little mad... his vision was right up our street and our customers were eager to help... I have fond memories of Hugh shouting across the room telling the 'actors' to stop throwing grenades while he was trying to set scenes.
>
> Paul Younger (in Cockburn, 2018)

Hancock was particularly drawn to Lovecraft's creation of whole worlds of horror with interconnections between characters, lore and tropes, which had been referred to as *Chthulu Mythos* (Derleth in Schweitzer, 1972) – meaning 'shared fictional universe' – and which in Hancock's mind reflected the virtual reality of a 3D computer game.

He met McDonald when making the second *Eschaton* production, *Eschaton: Nightfall,* in 1998. A version of the *Eschaton* series was subsequently showcased at the Edinburgh Festival Fringe in 1999, ostensibly demonstrating the machinima filmmaking technique, by which time Hancock and his production colleagues had developed a new lip-synching tool, *Lippy.* This provided a means to further animate characters, enabling them to show emotion and blinking (see Figure 3.1), and underpinned Hancock's lifelong commitment and contribution to machinima and filmmaking. In part, this was driven by his frustration both with the filmmaking industry and his desire to showcase his creative works once made. At the launch of *Machinima.com,* he wrote:

> ...I made some of my dream films. I made them part-time. I don't have any debts at all. I know I'm a good writer because a fuckload of the 20,000 plus people who've watched the *Eschaton* series have told me. I'm living in paradise as far as film-making is concerned. And so is everyone else in machinima. We've got the potential to change the entire future as far as art goes. For the first time in more than a hundred years since films were created, they're a thing of possibilities, a place in which anyone can bring to life their dreams, their hopes, their stories that they see inside their heads every night and share them with other people. No longer do people have to suffer the ... inverse snobbery of "low-budget" and "indie" films, where the hideous limitations they're suffering under have been internalised to such an extent that the community looks down on anything which isn't set in one location, shot on grainy 16mm, and entirely consists of three characters talking about their mother. Sure, you can still make that, but you can also make *The Matrix. Star Wars. Neuromancer. Sandman. Beowolf. The Lord Of The Rings.* Any story you can imagine, you can create... Machinima isn't just a toy. It isn't a poor cousin of rendered animation or 'real' film. It's one of the first Veridian technologies. It's something that will change peoples' lives. It might be the thing that finally turns film-making into an artform.
>
> Hugh Hancock (*Machinima.com,* 1 January, 2000)

It was while Hancock had been with another of the *Quake* movies community in 1999, Anthony Bailey, co-founder of the speedrun clan *Quake Done Quick,* that the machinima term was devised. Ultimately *Strange Company* worked in a range of game engines, including *Quake* (and *Quake II*), *Antics, Half Life, Neverwinter Nights* and others, but it is Hancock's vision for the use of machinima as a filmmaking technique and method that led him to develop *Machinima.com.*

Figure 3.1: Screencap *Eschaton: Nightfall.*

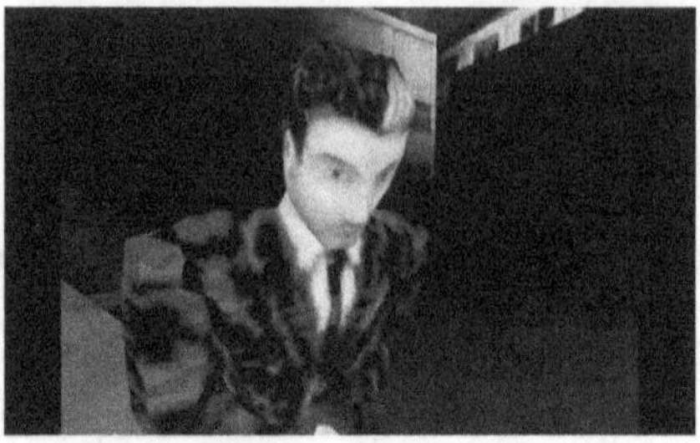

Source: Strange Company, 1999.

Machinima.com was established primarily to shine a light on the creative content generated using game technologies, as well as feature articles and content about film and technology. This was partially as a consequence of *id Software's* announcement, in December 1999, that it was not going to allow its new *Quake III Arena* game to use facilitated cheating for its multiplayer game modes, which effectively made machinima difficult to create on this particular platform. That said, it still actively supported content being made with earlier versions of the game (*Quake, Quake II*), primarily because it had the effect of lengthening the lifecycle of the games, as we highlighted in Chapter 1.

Machinima.com's aim was, therefore, to encourage production of content using games other than *id Software's Quake,* with *Quake* having previously dominated the machinima scene. *Machinima.com* publicly launched on 2 January 2000 with a series of articles, tutorials and interviews that extended the creative practice beyond *Quake,* acquiring exclusive releases of latest productions by creators.

Machinima.com was never made a separate formal company by Hancock, and its success as a website relied entirely on the goodwill of those involved in creating works. It had been established as part of *Strange Company,* but it quickly became its own entity. In fact, *Strange Company* was originally set up as a charity with a view to spring-boarding the new art form but the associated bureaucracy of charity formation in the UK was eventually outweighed by the impetus to just get on and create (McDonald, 2020). On 3 January 2000, Hancock set the scene for future of the website, writing:

> In short, Machinima is a new type of animated film, using computer graphics techniques similar to those used by films like *Toy Story,* but with refinements taken from the world of computer gaming to allow almost anyone with a home computer to create these films, rather than needing expensive equipment to do so. Many or most of the films that have been created so far have actually been created using computer game engines, but that is changing fast... If you're asking whether you

> can watch any of these films straight away, the answer is 'Yes'! Whilst many of these films require some software to be installed on your computer prior to watching the film, to allow the Machinima to be generated on your computer at detail levels and quality far beyond that of any conventional video format, we are converting many of these films to conventional video formats, to allow newcomers to the world of Machinima to get their first taste of the medium.
>
> Hugh Hancock (*Machinima.com*, 3 January 2000)

Alongside this, an oft-hidden part of the machinima story is that of its site manager. Ben Grussi (co-author of this book) had been involved in the *Quake* movie scene almost since it began. At the point that Hancock developed *Machinima.com* (and also *Strange Company*), Grussi volunteered and took on the unofficial role of site manager, making sure the site ran and the links worked. In addition, he also made sure appropriate quality content was uploaded and correctly described, tagged and recorded – in effect, he became the curator of *Machinima.com*. His role was instrumental in the site's development and continuity for the first five years of its existence, not least because Hancock was spinning two plates simultaneously, focussing unsurprisingly more on his creative energies with *Strange Company* than that of the evolving website.

Augmenting his curatorial role, Grussi's attention to detail made him the perfect keeper of records for the community: from the outset, he captured and recorded information about every film, event and major news report that impacted the development of machinima and its growing community, focussing particularly on *Machinima.com* – someone that Anthony Bailey referred to as machinima's own Wikipedia (Bailey, 2006). Previously unpublished, we have drawn heavily on Grussi's records of machinima in writing this book, a 1,700 plus page document that we have fondly come to refer to as 'Ben's Tome' was a major source for this text.

Machinima.com's popularity grew throughout 2000. This was not least because other game engines and new tools, such as *Unreal Tournament* (see Vignette 3.7.1) and video capture technologies were now coming to the fore as media for creative practice. Thus, driven (and fronted) by Hancock and with a community ethos underpinned by Grussi's curatorial skills, it is a trinity of factors that led to the development of the website: firstly, demand from game players for more than just the game; secondly, the availability of skills and demand for tools to do more with the game; and, thirdly, the creative storytelling capacity of the gamers themselves.

It is, however, the outward-facing nature of *Machinima.com* that took games beyond their immediate communities of players – beyond game – and positioned machinima as something unique of its time.

3.3 Evolution of Machinima

One of the first machinima releases on *Machinima.com*, on 2 January 2000, was *Quad God* by *Tritin Films* (Figure 3.2), ironically made in *Quake III Arena*. Interestingly, *Tritin* had converted the file to a conventional video format making it more accessible to a non-game playing audience. It was the first alternative format machinima film made which led *Machinima.com* to become known as both a hub and a platform for game content. The film received press coverage before it was released, with an article in *Spin Magazine* (December 1999) as well as after, with a mention on *ZDTV's Internet Tonight Show* – it had been made by the clan for a Katherine Anna Kang contest but was withdrawn in the process. The contest had called for creations that demonstrated '*the coolest thing with Quake III Arena and its logo as the topic of focus*' (Kang, 1999). *Tritin* had misread the instructions although later learned their entry would have been valid after all.

Figure 3.2: Screencap *Quad God*.

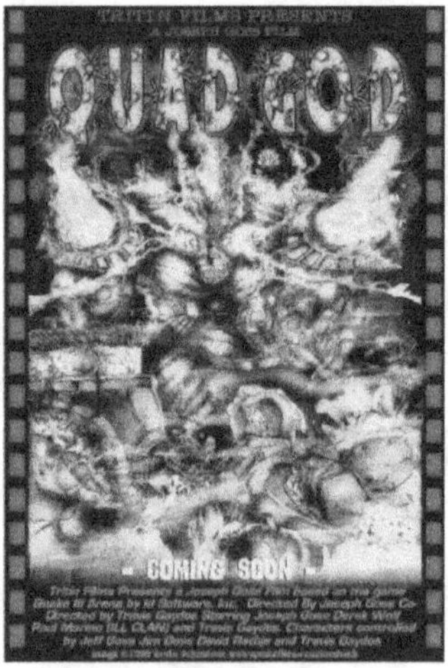

Source: *Tritin Films*, 2000.

On 4 January 2000, *ILL Clan*'s website joined *Machinima.com*, positioning it yet further as a hosting site for established as well as up and coming artists. *ILL Clan* had been founded in 1995 by a comedy improvisation troupe from New York, all with varying degrees of professional backgrounds in filmmaking. *ILL Clan* comprised of Paul Marino, Matt Dominianni, Frank Dellario, Manu Smith, Paul Jannicola, John Clavis and Patrick O'Shaughnessey (see http://www.illclan.com/

bios.htm with the *Wayback Machine* for details of their respective early careers). Their comedy *Quake* film, *Apartment Huntin'* (1998, see figure 3.3) achieved the top of the *Quake Movie* producers' ranks that year, and their subsequent film *Hardly Workin'* (released on 27 August 2000) made in *Quake II* also received much critical acclaim within the community. In between, the clan had focussed on live performances and skills development, participating in workshops and writing about machinima. Their involvement and alignment with *Machinima.com* was therefore an obvious development. It is their credibility in mainstream media which helped to underpin the trajectory of the website. On 12 February 2001, they received Best Experimental Short and Best of Show awards at the USA's *Showtime Network Alternative Media Festival* and by May that year, were the subject of broader entertainment media reports.

Figure 3.3: Screencap *Apartment Huntin'*.

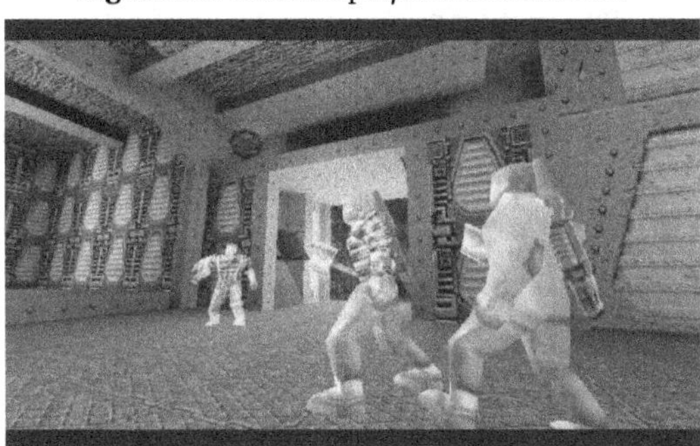

Source: *ILL Clan*, 1998.

In *Time Out New York*, on 7 May 2001, a feature article (Wisniewski, 2001) covered the backstory and emergence of machinima as a creative medium, highlighting the main characters and their substantive roles. Roger Ebert, the film critic who had become the first to win a Pulitzer Prize for Criticism in 1975, is quoted as saying machinima is the wave of the future:

> ...[machinima as] affordable, accessible animation is on the way... and the key thing about it is there is much less of an apparent gap – to the audience – between the production standards of desk-top studio animation than between low-budget and professional live action.
>
> Roger Ebert (in Wisniewski, 2001)

This statement pre-empted the aesthetic qualities of games as they evolved, albeit this does not fully recognize the very different skillsets required to make the content, which is firmly rooted in games and gaming – what Henry Lowood in 2006 referred to as 'high performance play'.

On 7 July 2001 *Entertainment Weekly* magazine covered a story mentioning both *ILL Clan* and *Strange Company*. In the article, machinima is referred to as a new film method: a means to make animated films, highlighting that by using software from common computer games 'upstart directors are flocking to the web to learn it' resulting in 'net-nerdy flicks' (GG, 2001)!

Katherine Anna Kang, who married John Carmack co-founder *id Software* in January 2000, was CEO of machinima production company, *Fountainhead Entertainment*, and an avid machinima fan. She was director of business development at *id Software*. *Fountainhead* had been founded also in January 2000. It was later that year, announced by *Machinima.com* on 6 December 2000, that *Fountainhead's* film *Sidrial* was slated to become the first commercial big screen machinima, for which it had developed the *Machinimation™* tool. The tool was subsequently launched separately for the community in 2003 although failed to gain a significant footing in the market.

The following year in 2004, Kang's film *Anna* was released and was thereafter listed as one of the top machinima films of all time (Hancock and Ingram, 2007). Ironically, it was also made in *Quake III Arena*. This film is astonishing because its visual aesthetic is completely unrecognizable from the original game, telling the story of a flowering plant as it seeds, grows and dies (see Figure 3.4).

Figure 3.4: Screencap *Anna*.

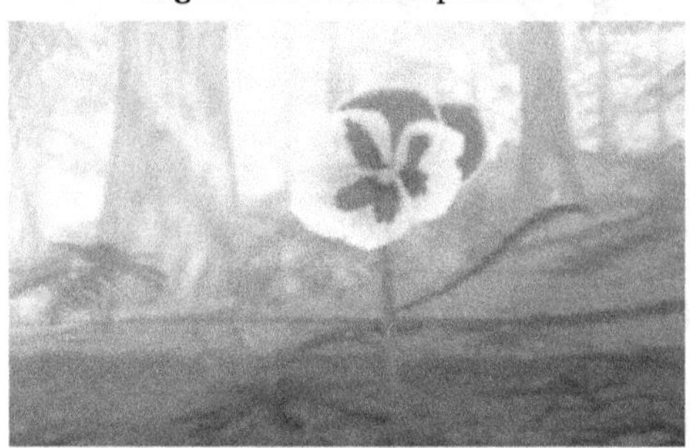

Source: Katherine Anna Kang, 2004.

Kang, Marino and Hancock working with Anthony Bailey (by then an independent filmmaker) and Matthew C. Ross (one of the *Fountainhead Entertainment* members) collectively co-founded the *Academy of Machinima Arts & Sciences* (*AMAS*) on 14 March 2002. Ben Grussi was appointed its official historian, a role that aligned with his pre-existing involvement in *Machinima.com*. On 11 July 2002, *AMAS* was formally launched with another prominent website, *Machinima.org*, and a mission to 'promote, organize and recognize the growth of machinima filmmaking and filmmakers' (*Machinima.org*).

Machinima.org was positioned differently to *Machinima.com* as the body for a professional filmmaking community, reflecting primarily Marino's background in the industry (with an Emmy award to prove it). To further help position its credibility in professionalizing machinima production methods, *AMAS* created and supported an annual awards ceremony, reflecting Hollywood's own film academy and Oscars in its 'Mackies' (machinima awards). At its launch, *Machinima.org* broke the news that *Nvidia* (video card chip designer and manufacturer) would be sponsoring the first annual *Machinima Film Festival*, which would take place at *Quakecon* in August that year. Working with Hancock and Marino, Kang hosted the inaugural annual *Machinima Awards* at the 2002 *Quakecon* event. *Quakecon* had previously hosted workshops involving the production teams of both *ILL Clan* and *Strange Company* in 2000 and 2001 respectively.

Eleven days later, on 22 July 2002, the first mainstream news story about machinima appeared in *The New York Times* quoting Hancock and Marino, and also highlighting the interest that had been generated in machinima as a new media form by the *American Museum of Moving Image*'s (New York) then curator, Carl Goodman.

Goodman had acquired a number of machinima films for the museum's archive, including *ILL Clan's Hardly Workin'* (2000). The article highlighted how machinima enabled both the dream of becoming a filmmaker and the challenge it presented for viewers with wide variation in quality of content produced. In it, Goodman stated: "*The stuff that rises to the top is certainly entertaining... [but] what enables them to do all this is also what limits them in the end*" (Mirapaul, 2002). He predicted machinima would have limited life as a creative or streamed form for viewing audiences. Hancock disagreed, and instead raised some concern that it may become professionalized too quickly. Indeed, just a few days later, on 26 July 2002, Charlie Stross, the British science fiction and space opera writer, wrote of machinima:

> I can't exaggerate how big this is going to be. It's going to be huge. I mean, you don't often stumble across a new media form that amounts to the next generation of computer animation before it hits its second birthday, but the signs are clear: this is something new, and freakish, and out of control because suddenly instead of needing thirty painstakingly rendered frames per second, 90,000 frames per hour, drawn using *Renderman* or *Softimage* using CAD systems to model the components, now you've got VR systems to do the donkey-work. I think it's going to have the same impact on CGI that the cassette tape had on popular music. The MPAA aren't going to die of *Napster* and P2P networks; they're going to be nibbled to death by a horde of bedroom machinima runaway hits. Punk meets CGI.
>
> Charlie Stross (Blog, 2002)

Together, the two websites became the catalyst for the growth of machinima: *Machinima.com* focussed on community content whilst *Machinima.org* on legitimizing the community beyond gameplay. From their perspectives, Goodman, Hancock and Stross were each right. Goodman pinpointed the key problem of getting good content seen above the plethora of user-generated content, long before the term UGC emerged to describe an internet phenomenon that is well known today. Hancock effectively predicted the challenge that would be faced when using machinima as a professional tool, which is what happened when *Machinima Inc.* bought *Machinima.com* (see below) in 2004. Stross highlighted the significance of its impact on both audiences and creators.

In 2003, *Quakecon* hosted another machinima workshop, aptly entitled 'The Machinima Momentum: The Rise and Rise of a Medium', by which time *Machinima.com* reported it was serving 4M page views and 200,000+ films to the community (*Machinima.com* press release, 17 July 2003). The same year, Stuart Brown (*Artery Productions*) directed and produced a broadcast TV documentary on machinima, focussing on the production techniques used to make the *Eschaton* series and featuring *Strange Company,* with commentary from *ILL Clan* and others (see also Chapter 6). In this documentary, Hancock (figure 3.5) stated that the originality of the machinima technique would lead him to become a multi-millionaire within five years. Much ridiculed by the community's grassroots members, he was ultimately entirely correct in his prediction about the financial viability of the medium, albeit he was not personally the one to gain the millions. Nor was the capital a consequence of the film sector's direct interest.

Figure 3.5: Hugh Hancock.

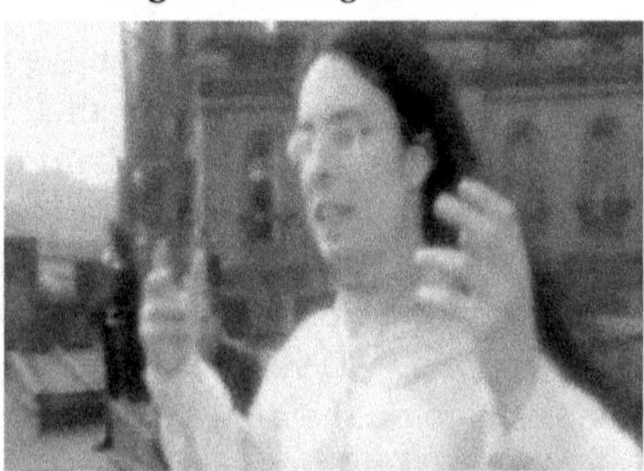

Hugh Hancock filming the Artery Machinima TV documentary on location in Scotland. Image used with permission, source: AMAS ©.

What Brown's documentary perfectly demonstrates, however, is the huge amount of creative endeavour involved in making machinima films at a time when mobile phones were not smart, chatrooms were text based, cameras were standalone devices (except when they were actually the game) and big hair was *de rigueur.* Far from being a quick process with a speedrun through a game engine, filmmaking involved extensive research and planning, scripting, storyboarding, acting and filming, as well as technological wizardry in manipulating gameplay using either locally connected computers to generate the content or via multi-player recordings from the internet which was then edited into a finished artefact. That said, Frank Dellario (*ILL Clan*) stated that by using machinima techniques, film and TV production could be speeded up by 30-40%, making it a very real proposition for the professional sector not least as a pre-production method, resulting in significant potential budget savings over traditional approaches.

To capitalize on the growth within the community and among the viewing public audiences, and in part pre-empt the challenge identified by Goodman, *Machinima.com* made use of channels. These channels focussed on the broadening number of game engines that were being used to generate content. *Quake* movies were of course a central theme among *Machinima.com's* community but as early as June 2000 the films made available for viewing on the rapidly evolving platform were already being listed separately by game version as well as different engines and conventional media formats.

As machinima making studios began to proliferate, so they were identified as 'affiliate' members of *Machinima.com.* Affiliates were largely selected on the basis of their professionalism and community impact (Grussi, 2020). In February 2002 for example, the *Quake Movie Library* website began pushing all machinima-related activities towards *Machinima.com* and by December that year, its functionality and *'QMunity'* had been completely absorbed by the site (see *QML*). Other websites either took their lead from *Machinima.com,* developing their own style, communities and content, such as *Pysk's Popcorn Jungle (Machinima Encylopedia),* or merged with *Machinima.com* and closed eg., *The Cineplex* (Lum, 2000). By September 2002, the likes of *Clan Phantasm, Quake Done Quick* and *Zarathustra Studios,* among other well-known studios, had become affiliates and the list thereafter increased exponentially month on month.

At this point, films were now listed and tagged by genre such as comedy, action, horror and video file format such as .avi, Quicktime, .exe, etc. Shortly thereafter *Machinima.com* would provide rankings based on viewer ratings. This was not represented as the number of 'likes' but as percentages calculated using an average of ratings. What this review process therefore appears to have, perhaps unwittingly, promoted was the endorsement of, typically, affiliate-related content and material that had been on the site the longest. Undoubtedly, this strategy underpinned its stickiness for the community who clearly earned their chops over time, in much the same way that reviews of content on streaming platforms (eg., *Amazon Prime, YouTube* and *Twitch*) now gain kudos through up voting and likes over an extended period. In many ways, it also provided a pathway for others to follow to gain profile, encouraging them to create and share more content in order to build their reputation in the community. This community-focussed ethos was ultimately the key to the longevity of the site: by late 2004, Hancock wrote to the community, highlighting an increasing focus on serializing machinima shows, which he described as "*a great way to build the artform's audience up, by putting out regular content that people keep coming back for*" (Hancock, 2004).

The website had also become increasingly dedicated to providing file and server space for the community, attracting alongside its increasing content a growing number of machinima advocates among game, tool and audience developers including creator competitions. For example, by September 2002 it had already a bandwidth of 400GB per month, significantly more than other websites at the time which perhaps averaged 50-100GB. By February 2003 demand exceeded its bandwidth capacity and the site temporarily suspended downloads!

Machinima.com had become a central hub for all things machinima – and the early adoption of new technologies beyond game and filmmaking were a particular hallmark of the community. For example, video blogging (vlogging) which became popular for the masses on the launch of *YouTube* was previously used by the community to report machinima releases by using machinima content about in-game activities by *ILL Clan* (*Grid Review*), Chris Burke (*This Spartan Life*) and others. Hancock's introduction to the website now stated:

> There's a revolution going on in film-making. But you knew that already. DV, DVD, Internet Distribution, *Blair Witch*, blah, blah, blah. I'm talking about a different revolution. Beyond the bleeding edge of film there's things going on that could reinvent storytelling. There's bedroom hackers and new-wave garage auteurs taking technologies developed for computer games to make a new kind of computer-generated film. They're creating virtual worlds and virtual actors, using their imaginary worlds to create in a bedroom what others can't create using $100,000 sets and cameras. They're shooting their films, but they're shooting them in worlds that will never exist, using actors who never lived - and because of the technology they're using, they aren't painstakingly animating these films frame-by-frame, they're filming fast, cheap and live. They're using Machinima - shooting film in virtual reality. *Machinima.com* is the showcase and the hub of the revolution. We're providing machinima creators with the space to show their films and the publicity to get them seen. We're collating, archiving and listing, putting the whole world of Machinima where you can get at it. And we're covering the revolution ourselves…
>
> Hugh Hancock (*Machinima.com*, 26 October 2002)

Thus, it was as a consequence of the site's convergence of game, play and creator communities, the use of new technologies combined with tagging content, affiliate and advocacy programmes, and promotion of game titles that aligned with the *Machinima.com* mission, that its usage skyrocketed – by mid 2004, the site was averaging 70K unique viewers per month, uploads of 60K files per month and some 450K page views per month (Gordon, 2020). It is therefore not surprising that *Machinima.com* attracted attention not just among community members but also media moguls, would-be platform competitors who recognized its potential as a burgeoning media streaming technology innovation, as well as media theorists and artists who saw it as a cultural turn (eg., Jenkins, 2006; Lowood, 2006, Clarke and Mitchell, 2007; Lowood and Nitsche, 2011; Lowood et al., 2011; et al).

Beyond Game

The growing *Machinima.com* and *Machinima.org* teams were focussed on content, striding towards professionalization in line with Hancock et al's shared vision of aligning the filmmaking technique with other emerging animation processes. These included CGI, stop motion, claymation and anime (Salen, 2011). Hollywood had indeed become aware of machinima, with the likes of George Lucas' *Industrial Light & Magic* using machinima to storyboard *Star Wars* movies and Peter Jackson using it as a fight simulator in the making of *Lord of the Rings* and *King Kong*. Cliff Plumer, chief technology officer at *LucasFilm* stated:

> Machinima is a great new technique for creating cost-effective animated stories… our initial use is for pre-visualization for our feature film work (but) we envision eventually using it for all our productions in movies, games, television and on-line.
>
> Cliff Plumer (in Pasha, 2005)

Although game-based films had been of interest for some time, the failure of the game-based film *Final Fantasy: The Spirits Within* (Sony Research, 2001) at the box office had apparently 'left a bad taste in the mouths of movie executives' (Gitesh Pandya, editor of *BoxOfficeGuru.com*, in Pasha, 2005). That said, its critics were far more positive, particularly of its aesthetic qualities and achievements, as well as its reflection on science fiction storytelling. Roger Ebert commented:

> The reason to see this movie is simply, gloriously, to look at it… I want to see more movies like this, and see how much further they can push the technology… In reviewing a movie like this, I am torn between its craft elements and its story… the look of the film is revolutionary… it exists in a category of its own, the first citizen of the new world of cyberfilm.
>
> Roger Ebert (2001)

Animation studios such as *Pixar, DreamWorks* and *Disney* heavily (at least explicitly) resisted what they saw as a potential threat, claiming cost was less of a factor than retention of aesthetic values, even at pre-visualization stages of filmmaking. Tom Sito, who was president emeritus of the *Hollywood Animation Guild* and had worked on such films as *Aladdin* and *Shrek*, commented 'real-time performance-based animation will never replace traditional methods' (in Biever, 2003). Gabe Newell, from the game developer *Valve Software*, disagreed stating that whilst machinima was still primitive, its developmental trajectory was tied to computer-based technology and it would not only catch up with traditional methods but eventually overtake them (Biever, 2003). Indeed, Paul Marino (*ILL Clan* and *AMAS)* compared the animation qualities of machinima as early stage in its development and akin to *Toy Story* (1995) as an early example of CGI animation.

Machinima had also attracted the attention of the music industry. Several machinima films were ultimately produced as video accompaniments, with *Machinima.com* receiving its first request for content in January 2002. It was, however, 5 February 2003 that *Fountainhead* worked on what would become the first machinima music video to air on *MTV* (in March 2003, see Robertson, 2003). The video was for *Zero 7*'s *In the Waiting Line* (on its *Simple Things* album) and was made in *Quake III* using the studio's *Machinimation* tool (figure 3.6). It was produced by Tommy Pallotta, a US film director who worked extensively with Richard Linklater, notably on *Waking Life* (2001) which was itself the first independently financed computer-animated feature film, and subsequently on a number of Philip K. Dick inspired films. Pallotta's adoption of innovations in filmmaking, such as machinima, was noted by *Microsoft Research and Development*, for whom he worked for a short while on an interactive experience project that was ultimately never released (IGN FilmForce, 2006).

Figure 3.6: Screencap *In the Waiting Line.*

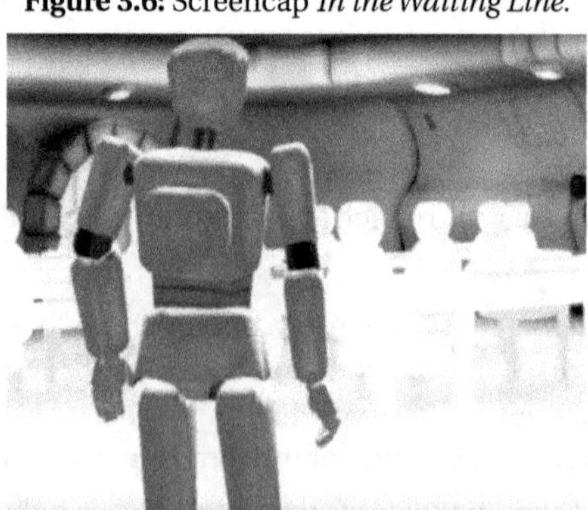

Source: Pallotta, 2003.

In the meantime, *3DTV* began to emerge with a focal interest in machinima, beginning with a group called *3DiTV*, a new channel was developed in February 2002 seeking to become a dedicated machinima TV station, albeit this never gained ground. By mid-September 2004, *MTV*'s side channel, *MTV2* aired a new series called *Video Mods*. *Wired Magazine*, on 30 September 2004, summarized well the convergence that was becoming evident between film, music, comic book and games, encapsulated by machinima. *Video Mods* was described as being dedicated to showing machinima music videos drawing on games such as *The Sims 2*, *Tribes: Vengeance*, *BloodRayne* and others. Its executive producer, Alex Coletti, said:

> I know that our audience, when they're not watching music videos, they're playing video games. Here's a way to do both.
>
> Alex Coletti (in Wired, 2004)

The show aired for two years from 18 September 2004 and was produced by Tony Shiff of *Big Bear Entertainment*, with a pilot for the series having been underwritten by *Electronic Arts* in December 2003 featuring its *SSX3*, *Sims* and *Need for Speed* games. What they had produced, however, was not so much music videos celebrating the music with game-based stories but advertisements for games set to popular music, some of which had not even been released to the market at the point they were used, and where game characters were seen in novel and unexpected environments (Shiff in *Wired*, 2004) (see Figure 3.7). What is interesting is that Shiff gave an interview to *Nzone.com* in mid-September 2004 in which he stated that the *MTV2* show was aiming to reflect the convergence of animation styles between games and TV (Shiff, 2004), which partly explains why *MTV* did not clear rights beyond those for its TV airings to use the music (Wired, 2004).

Figure 3.7: Screencap *MTV Video Mods*.

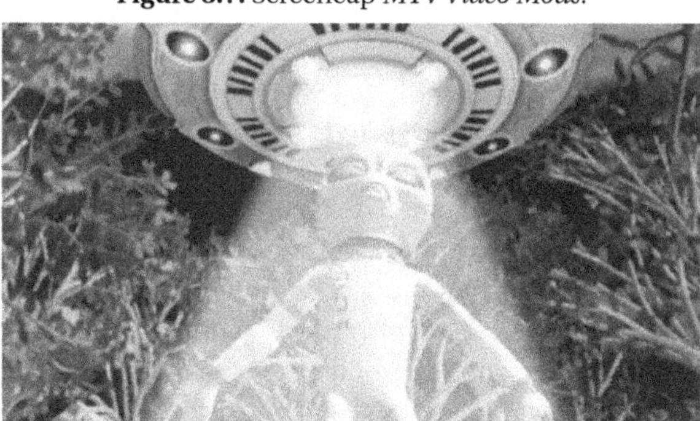

Source: @RebelTaxi, 2020.

In dealing with the thorny issue of intellectual property rights, Hancock's approach was to work closely with the games developers to solve what he referred to as the EULA problem (end-user license agreement) through a strategy of professionalization of content creation. This effectively enabled creators to work directly with games developers for a common goal. Hancock called for more creatives to become involved in the production of machinima in an attempt to meet growing demand for content, especially with games organizations (Hancock, 2004). Around this time, however, some of the games developers and publishers were becoming resistant to their assets being used for anything other than originally intended gameplay. Whilst a number of games developers had informal arrangements with the machinima community, such as *Quake, Sims, Halo,* et al., the issue was rapidly coming to a head with an increasing number of attempts to commercialize creative works. The problem was first formally aired on *Machinima.com* on 13 October 2003 by Hancock. In his article, he wrote:

> If you make commercial Machinima in most commercial engines, you're outside the law. The good news is that there are a number of ways around this problem. First of all, you can use a Machinima engine whose license allows you to create commercial work. That generally either means using a professional tool with Machinima capabilities, or using an Open-Source game engine. In the future, there will also be the option to use a dedicated Machinima production environment, but so far there are no commercially-licensed Machinima suites available.
>
> Hugh Hancock (*Machinima.com,* 13 October 2003)

Whilst noting the numerous available animation tools, most of these were unaffordable for many within the community. Importantly, Hancock went on to note at that point that the first machinima production suite, *Antics Linear,* would be available later in the Autumn 2003, having been worked on partially by *Strange Company.* Whilst games increasingly integrated filmmaking tools into their play assets (see also Chapter 4) as machinima began to become more of a mainstream gameplay activity, new games that centred on machinima creation also emerged. For example, *The Sims* was released in 2000 and its second version in 2004 (see Vignette 3.7.3). The following year, *The Movies* was launched (see Chapter 5, Vignette 5.6.1). These were followed by a series of more bespoke machinima creation products whereby assets, scenes, sets and stories could be devised from a library with no actual gameplay to hack or modify. In 2005, having worked closely with *Nvidia, Reallusion's* marketing director, John C. Martin II, launched its *iClone* avatar generation product. Following a chance meeting at a trade show that year, Martin and Marino (*AMAS*) began discussions with the machinima community that would then lead to the launch of the *iClone* product at the 2006 *Machinima Film Festival* (Martin, 2008). In 2007, at the *European Machinima*

Film Festival (12-14 October, Leicester), *Moviestorm* pre-launched its machinima film making product, officially launched in November that year (Kelland, 2008) albeit the company had been working with the community to create the software since 2005.

By the end of 2005, however, machinima had become a global phenomenon, encompassing a broad cross-section of games created by a growing community of filmmakers. For example, *Lionhead's* (*The Movies*) community site reported new machinima films were posted at a rate of one per minute by December (Matlack, 2005). This was the consequence of a confluence of factors including: the curation and scope of machinima on *Machinima.com* that had become a platform not just for content but for all things creator related; the legitimization of machinima underpinned by the efforts of *Machinima.org* with its often sponsored annual film festival, as well as its professional and community outreach activities; the growing success of *YouTube* as a viewing platform for the masses as well as a place for new content; the emergence of increasingly professional machinima content, including the influential *Red vs Blue* (*Rooster Teeth*, discussed in Chapter 4) comedic series and a few key films that generated unusual attention (some of which are discussed in Chapters 5 and 6).

Community groups, each with their own websites, began to emerge around the world, notably in Germany where *Machinimag* an online magazine was produced, in France where *Machinima.fr* became a catalyst for French-speaking content, with both later becoming part of a loose European collective unified by a love of games and film (Gras, 2008). Other notable groups emerged across the US, in Russia and Mexico. Numerous animation, film and web-based festivals around the World began to include machinima film sections in their programmes, including *Sundance, Slamdance* (US), *AMD* (Canada), *Bitfilm* (Germany), *Mediamatic* (Netherlands), as well as games developer competitions by *Valve, EA/Maxis, Rockstar, Epic, Sony, Linden Labs, Blizzard Entertainment, Bungie, Lionhead* and hardware developer competitions such as *Microsoft XBox*, with the backing of sponsors such as *Chrysler, Honda, IGN*, et al.

In gaining momentum, machinima now faced three significant challenges related to capacity, relationships and creative absorption of the community into the gaming sector.

The first challenge, capacity, was a direct consequence of its success as a filmmaking technique: the *Machinima.com* platform was unable to cope with the volume of content and through-flow of online traffic. Server capacity became a major issue for *Strange Company* and ultimately not only did it struggle to host the material but it also needed to update its image, reflecting the rapidly changing virtual environment. In his announcement to the community on 1 December 2004, Hancock commented on plans to include *Bittorrent* downloads to combat bandwidth issues as well as streaming on the platform. Games developers showed increased interest in machinima, many of whom had now realized its significant potential as a marketing tool for their own core gamer audiences, leading to competition from game-owned community channels. Furthermore, big media companies such as *Google* and *Yahoo* were predicting that aggregation of video content would become the new programming opportunity, whereby the lines between professional and amateur produced content would be blurred as content would be streamed alongside relevant advertising using a combination of editorial selection, algorithmic analysis of viewed content and search results (Fritz, 2006). This necessitated development of the way machinima films were tagged and categorized. Ironically, it also coincided with an advertising crash which resulted from the availability of many different outlets for marketing promotion, driving earnings possible from advertising revenue to a minimum for platform owners such as *Machinima.com*. *Machinima.com* therefore began to come apart at the seams.

With this as context, next, we discuss the second and third challenges in the following sections, respectively relationships and community absorption.

3.4 Becoming Machinima Inc.

With the rapidly evolving context in which *Machinima.com* operated, during 2004 Hancock struggled to raise the capital he needed to refresh and rebuild the site that would take it to the next level of sustainable growth. His creative endeavours and search for commercial outlets for his own work produced by *Strange Company* had, however, enabled him to have access to the richer Hollywood scene. In time, this led him to Allen and Philip DeBevoise (brothers) who were venture capitalists with a background in film and television media production, having founded and sold *Creative Planet* for a reported $100M. Allen DeBevoise also had a background in computer animation, having worked on the original *Tron* movie (Pollack, 2013). For an undisclosed sum, Hancock transferred the machinima brand (logo), ownership of the *Machinima.com* domain and copyright of text-based materials that were hosted on the site to the DeBevoises in Autumn 2004. Copyright of the machinima works themselves remained with their original creators, as they had done throughout the development of *Machinima.com* as a hosting platform.

A new registered company, founded and owned by the DeBevoises, was established in October 2004 in the US State of Delaware, citing its business as twofold: *"(1) the Network business, which builds, scales and monetizes a global audience of core gamers and young adults and (2) the Content business, which develops, produces, licenses, and acquires original programming that it can promote, distribute, and monetize via its online distribution network"* (*Machinima Inc.*, 2012). Hancock became a minority shareholder and remained part of the newly formed *Machinima Inc.* team as both editor-in-chief of *Machinima.com* and a consultant/advisor, whilst Grussi, the site's curator, remained in position as a contractor.

The period between October 2004 and February 2006 marked a major shift change in the site's operation and community focus as the DeBevoises began to exert their control over the platform and its content, and as they began to develop the business proposition. Spending some time to learn about machinima and its community of creators, they began to refocus the platform. For the community, notably, they revised machinima upload terms for content creators which included a loose takedown statement, where previously there had been none: "*Make sure your show has the proper clearance for any copyrighted content! Please note that any show that receives a rights-related complaint will be immediately removed until it's in compliance*" (*Machinima.com*, February 2005). In January 2006, they appointed Paul Marino (*AMAS*) as Acting Creative Director of the organization to advise on creative direction and community engagement as well as another of the long-term community members, Johnnie Ingram, as content editor. They also appointed a webmaster and software developer.

Hancock resigned as editor-in-chief on 30 January 2006 with an announcement to the community:

> Well, I assume that most people are of the 'single-rip' school of *Elastoplast* removal, and I also figure most of you have read the title of this article… I guess, if you've got any questions now, they will either by 'why?' or 'who will you be handing it to?'… I'm getting stale. I've been doing this for an eternity in web time, and I'm starting to feel that I'm losing my edge and my enthusiasm for my current role. I want new things to do and new challenges to face, and *Machinima.com* needs new blood and enthusiasm from people like Johnnie Ingram, our new site editor. It's time for me to move on…
>
> Hugh Hancock (*Machinima.com*, 30 January 2006)

Hancock goes on to explain his preferred focus for his creative work at *Strange Company*, and his disclosure that advancements over the year had been due to *Machinima Inc.'s* investment, including streaming content, new file server, games channel pages, and web redesign. However, he also noted his various disagreements with the DeBevoises:

> As you'd expect from any relationship like this, I've not always agreed with the decisions that *Machinima Inc.* have made, even when they've turned out to be good ones (like the games channel pages, for example). Over the last year, I've come to the conclusion that my approach – both in business and vision terms – to *Machinima.com* differs significantly enough from the folk at *Machinima Inc.*'s approach that it isn't useful

> for me to continue working on the site. It's better that I devote my energies toward other projects, both for myself and also for the success of machinima as a whole... At this point I think both machinima and *Machinima.com* are big enough and hard enough to stand on their own. John Carmack said a while ago that the best way to help machinima to grow is to make great machinima films. I'm planning on doing that now.
>
> Hugh Hancock (*Machinima.com*, 30 January 2006)

The creeping control over content became a significant bone of contention for the community. This was coupled with a lack of attention to obvious detail, such as pornographic spam advertising that began to proliferate in the forums, making the site unusable for young audiences and unrecommendable for older audiences. Despite these matters being brought to the attention of the growing corporate *Machinima Inc.* team, the issues remained unresolved.

Thereafter, the commercial trajectory of the platform began to take shape, influenced by the new owners, who it transpires instead of developing the platform itself, instead scraped its content and uploaded material directly into a new *YouTube* channel. *Machinima Inc.* did not ask the creators' permissions to do this, and neither did it notify them that it had done it. As a consequence, the site's forum became a flame war zone, followed by a period of censorship. Many of the established content creators on whose work the reputation of *Machinima.com* had been built asked for their films to be removed from the platform and *YouTube*.

The second significant challenge was therefore the souring of relationships between the creative machinima community and the *Machinima.com* platform.

For Grussi, the difference of opinion in community ethos that had evolved during this period of change resulted in him stepping away from his association with *Machinima.com* on 15 February 2006. In Grussi's view, the years of building trust between creators and the platform had been utterly destroyed. Whilst Hancock had stood down just a few days before this, he remained an active contributor to *Machinima.com* until 3 May 2007, at which point he wrote on its forum:

> It's with great regret that I have to follow Phil Rice in asking for my films to be removed from *Machinima.com.* I find both the recent and less recent activities of the site administration to be sufficiently disturbing that I no longer want to be associated with or promote this site in any way... To the few people who still have intelligent debates on this forum, I've enjoyed our discussions, and I'll be sorry to miss them. I'll be actively posting and commenting on *Machinima Premiere*, amongst other sites. Hopefully, I'll see you there...
>
> Hugh Hancock (*Machinima.com*, 3 May 2007)

Ingram and Marino stepped away in 2006. Thus, the creative community that had previously been involved with *Machinima.com* diverged and coalesced around new platforms and ventures. *Machinima Premiere* (*MPrem.com*), which had been launched on 23 September 2006, is one site that those who had previously connected on *Machinima.com* naturally migrated to (Grussi, 2020). Other sites were *3dfilmmaker.com* and various community and game brand sites, along with *AMAS*'s legacy of an annual community awards programme, *MachininaExpo.com* led by Ricky Grove, US actor (e.g., *Army of Darkness, Point Break*) and long-time machinima fan, et al.

The DeBevoises, however, sought out new audiences beyond *Machinima.com*. To achieve this, *Machinima Inc.*'s *YouTube* network channel partner (NCP) strategy was notable and hugely successful in developing the reach of the brand, albeit with entirely different values to its original brand.

Over the next fifteen years, from take-over to closure in 2019, *Machinima Inc.* raised a total of $91.6M in funding over seven rounds of investment (Crunchbase), largely on the incredible size of its audience and its ability to convert audiences to marketing revenue for games developers and publishers. *Machinima Inc.* reached its 1B video view in March 2010 (Takahashi, 2010) using a combination of *Machinima.com* and its *YouTube* channels.

By November 2010, *Machinima Inc.* had moved all video content to *YouTube* and by 6 December 2011 reached 1B monthly video views (Takahashi, 2011). Content now comprised gaming news, culture, events and trailers, with episodic series and professionally produced material. Of this achievement, Allen DeBevoise said:

> As we expand our base of core gaming-oriented programming, by producing and distributing more long-form, premium content, our global audience of millions of highly engaged young males continues to grow and spends more time watching *Machinima*... our reaching one billion monthly video views is a watershed event in the growth of online video. This scale, coupled with our deep audience engagement, has shown that we're leading a third wave of video programming brands that are emerging online.
>
> Allen DeBevoise (Takahashi, 2011)

As the dominant channel on *YouTube*, *Machinima Inc.* became part of *YouTube*'s premium channel initiative in October 2011, whereby content was streamed, on-demand and paid for, with revenue earned from audiences and advertising shared with the platform (Kramer, 2011). By the following March (2012) *Machinima Inc.* became the top non-music content publisher on *YouTube*, hosting 347M videos with 1.3B monthly views (Roettgers, 2012). It was, however, now recognized mainly for its core gamer viewing audience rather than its content creator audience (Takahashi, 2012), achieving partnerships with games developers to support game releases with engaging marketing campaigns.

Machinima Inc.'s aggressive approach to audience acquisition and marketing revenue generation had not gone without note by the original and growing network channel partner community. *Machinima Inc.* had approached *YouTube* channel partners whose content they felt was a good match for its brand and offered them partner contracts with the organization. It asked the typically young male gamer audience to sign extensive legal agreements which bound them as partners to *Machinima Inc.* in perpetuity, even when the content they as partner creators made moved beyond machinima and game-related material. News of this began to circulate in September 2011 which to most channel partners came as a total shock. As one wrote at the time:

> Here's the thing that I keep coming back to. I am one of the strongest supporters of this massive *YouTube* community, according to multiple people I respect and look up to. When I joined – and until tonight – I had this ever-present naïveté about the way this new media world worked. I really believed that people were in the business of fostering creativity and entertainment that could not only launch careers, but unite and inspire people around the world. Hell, I still DO believe that. But I've now seen a small glimpse over to the other side of the online video world. The grass isn't always greener it seems… What shouldn't have a place is shady marketing of a 'sweet partnership deal' to kids who aren't even of age.
>
> Ben Hughes (2011)

This had very little influence on the growth trajectory of audience views and new network channel partner participation. By December 2012, *Machinima Inc.* had farmed around 6,000 channel partners, reported 2.6B video views with 14.4M unique views of videos on one day alone – the 2012 E3 Convention (Pollack, 2013). As Dan Rayburn, business analyst at Frost and Sullivan consultancy stated:

> [*Machinima Inc.* had] done a great job of taking the value of the Internet, targeting a specific group with a specific kind of content, and monetizing it.
>
> Dan Rayburn (in Pollack, 2013).

By now, *Machinima.com* had become simply a placeholder linked to a number of *YouTube* channels, including *Respawn* (first-person shooter games), *Realm* (fantasy and role-playing games), *Sports, VS* (competitive gaming), a channel for trailers and beyond gaming, it also hosted *Prime* (original entertainment, including content made with Ashton Kutcher's production company, *Katalyst Network*).

The contractual agreements with partners saw a number of them begin to kick back and desert the platform, however, culminating in *Machinima Inc.* having to rethink its content development strategy. With a background in TV production, the DeBevoises had apparently come full circle, and their approach to producing machinima now was to focus on premium content, using a subscription-based business model (a la *Netflix)* which it launched in July 2013 (Ingraham, 2013).

In the process of developing this strategy, it made a number of its staff redundant in 2012. This proved to be a surprise to the media, given its phenomenal success in tapping what the DeBevoises had described as the lost boys of cable television. Staff it jettisoned were those associated with its more traditional *Machinima.com* days, such as the *Inside Gamers* producers, leaving it room to focus on high-quality series based on games and well-known terrestrial brands, such as *Battlestar Galactica.* In effect, *Machinima Inc.* was now positioning itself as a TV network rather than a multichannel *YouTube* network. This had probably been its strategy from the outset, given the adoption of *YouTube* as a platform and its use of the community of machinima and other creators as a pipeline for income generation derived from programming and advertising.

Machinima Inc. had already established content partnerships with *Warner Bros.* and *Paramount* and in May 2012 it was announced that *Google* was investing some $35M to underpin what it described as the future of TV (Popper, 2012), valuing the organization at $200M. With its sights now firmly set on production of TV quality content, the following year *Machinima Inc.* partnered with Ridley Scott's production company, *RSA,* to produce twelve sci-fi short films. These would be distributed not just via *YouTube* but also on other social media and mobile platforms including *Facebook* and *Twitter. RSA*'s list of directors at the time was impressive and included Kathryn Bigelow (*Zero Dark Thirty, Hurt Locker*), Martin Scorsese (*Goodfellas, The Departed*), Sam Mendes (*American Beauty, Skyfall*), Joe Carnahan (*Smokin' Aces, The A-Team*) and Neill Blomkamp (*District 9*). DeBevoise said of the new partnership:

> By combining this unique incubation model together with our powerful partnership of established creative talent and scaled distribution to millions on *Machinima,* we believe new Sci-Fi franchises will be born.
>
> Allen DeBevoise (Ong, 2013)

It quickly became evident that significantly more funding was needed to achieve the DeBevoises' vision (even though the deal with *RSA* was reported to have fizzled because of scheduling difficulties, Chmielewski, 2013). In June 2013, *Machinima Inc.* was reported to be seeking a mega round of funding, estimated to be $70M, to support its content and platform development as a subscription channel in what was described as a 'bellwether for YouTube and its ambition to take on TV' (Kafka, 2013). It was clear that its intention was to seek alternative channels beyond *YouTube* such as its own defunct *Machinima.com* site as well as new channels such as *Microsoft's Xbox* and others. *YouTube*, which had been owned by *Google* since October 2006, was however more than happy with its current advertising-based business model. Indeed, by the end of 2013, *Machinima Inc.* had acquired some 10,000 partners albeit its monthly views were slipping back, reported at the time to be around 2B (Takahashi, 2014a).

By November 2013, the content funding plans had fallen through and the DeBevoises moved away from their roles in the organization. It was announced that Allen DeBevoise would become its chairman once a new CEO had been found (Lawler, 2013). *Machinima Inc.* had already laid off 10% of its 206 staff in September and the DeBevoises had been reported to be considering a sale of the business among other options in their search for funding. The following March (2014), *Warner Bros.* invested $18M (Weber, 2014) and *Machinima Inc.* made a further 42 of its staff redundant from mainly sales-related positions. As an acquisition alignment, this made sense: *Warner's Interactive Entertainment* business already had gaming interests making both *Batman* and *The Lord of the Rings* games (Takahashi, 2014a). Furthermore, *Machinima Inc.*'s advertising market was beginning to face increasing competition, with the likes of *Steam* and *Twitch* forging ahead in the channel stakes, particularly for live-streamed content. *Twitch* was a spin-off of *JustinTV* and had launched in June 2011. It was subsequently acquired by *Amazon* for a reported $70M in 2014. At the time, it was rumoured to have been targeted by *Google* for $1B, but it emerged there were antitrust issues given that the organization already owned *YouTube* (Mac, 2014). Thus, *Machinima Inc.* restructured itself, drawing on *Warner Bros.* distribution expertise and appointing the former chief operating officer of *Ovation TV* network, Chad Gutstein, as its new CEO in March (Takahashi, 2014b).

In 2014, *Warner Bros.* led an investment round of a further $24M, with *Machinima Inc.* reporting 3.7B monthly video views in the process (up 70% since 2013) – for a summary of its investments, see Table 3.1. The new CEO, Gutstein, had achieved this by refocussing on its creator network and repositioning its brand in the digital video marketplace, which by mid-2015 had reached 32,000 creators producing 32,000 hours of content per month (Jacobs, 2015). Of this approach, Craig Hunegs, *Warner's Television Group* president of business strategy, stated:

> *Machinima* continues to grow as a key entertainment destination for millennials. With its enormous fan base, *Machinima* is an important exhibition partner, providing content creators, including *Warner Bros.* multiple platforms for distributing and monetizing digital content and programming brands.
>
> Craig Hunegs (in Takahashi, 2015)

In fact, *Machinima Inc.*'s strategy was now to integrate mobile platforms for streaming on-demand as well as facilitate communication between creators and their audience: it launched its first mobile application in June 2015. This was made possible when 4G communications technology on *Apple's* popular *iPhone* and *iPad* models began to proliferate, making persistent interaction through a range of social media platforms possible, such as *Facebook*, *Twitter* and *Snapchat* (Terbeek, 2015).

Its strategy was described as 'windowing' (Jacobs, 2015), which means that its highest-quality content (e.g., its professionally produced *Robocop* spinoff and *Mortal Kombat: Legacy* shows) was used as a sampler across multiple networks in order to capture audiences at every opportunity. *Machinima Inc.*'s market position, whilst grounded in its *YouTube* presence, was beginning to be encroached by competitors such as *MakerStudios* (acquired by *Disney), AwesomenessTV* (acquired by *DreamWorks Animation*) and *Fullscreen (AT&T).* Thus, it required new audiences and relationships on emergent streaming platforms (such as *Vimeo* and *Vessel*), as well as new markets eg., China (via its *Sohu* platform, the Chinese equivalent to *YouTube* which had been banned in China since 2009), with Gutstein arguing that creators and audiences were moving across multiple channels and so should *Machinima Inc.* (Spangler, 2016a). As he stated: *"In a world of infinite choice, the curator is king"* (Gutstein in Jacobs, 2015).

At the same time, *Machinima Inc.*'s focus on quality content saw them reach a high-profile deal with Justin Lin (producer of *Star Trek Beyond* and *Fast & Furious* films) for a *Knight Rider* digital series which was originally forecast to release in 2017 but has so far not happened (July 2020). The deal followed its incredible success from series to date (*Battlestar Galactica: Blood & Chrome, Mortal Kombat: Legacy, Mortal Kombat: Legacy 2, Street Fighter: Assassin's Fist, Street Fighter: Resurrection,* and *Halo 4: Forward Unto Dawn*), which *Machinima Inc.* claimed had generated over 300M views across its range of platforms.

It is no surprise, therefore, that *Warner Bros.* acquired full control of the organization on 17 October 2016 citing its strategic fit as a distribution network, albeit options to acquire it had expired in Spring 2016. *Machinima Inc.*'s reported value of $100M was therefore $50M lower than its value at expiry (Spangler, 2016b) and $100M lower than its valuation in 2012. *Warner's Digital Networks Group* already owned a number of digital businesses, including *Stage 13*, a start-up focussing on short-form video; *Boomerang*, a cartoon subscription streaming service; *DramaFever*, a Korean drama subscription service; LeBron James' *Uninterrupted* and Ellen DeGeneres' *Ellen Digital Ventures* (Patel, 2017).

At the same time, *Warner Bros.*' parent *Time Warner* had agreed to be bought out by *AT&T*, which would effectively put *Machinima Inc.* in the same corporate stable as its competitor, *Fullscreen.*

Table 3.1: *Machinima Inc.* summary of key investments (2004-2019).

Date (reported)	Who Invested	How Much	Reported Audience	Reported Revenue Streams
Oct 2004	DeBevoise Bros. (acquired Machinima.com from Hancock/Strange Company and started Machinima Inc.)	?	Pre-sale stats 60K videos per month (70K unique monthly visitors)	None identified
6 Nov 2008	MK Capital and private investors	$3.85M	30M videos per month	Advertisers eg., EA, HP, Intel, Sega, Universal Studios, Warner Bros, et al
26 Nov 2009	MK Capital (add on to 6 Nov 2008)	$1.7M	60M videos per month	'Inside Gaming' series – a new video game awards; producing premium content and contracting independent creators
14 Jun 2010	Redpoint Ventures (Geoff Yang)	$9M	127M videos per month (27M unique monthly visitors)	Strengthen marketing platforms, including new channels (Machinima Sports and Respawn); producing 25 original shows
May 2012	Google Capital	$35M	2.6B videos per month	Advertising and content partnerships, primarily through YouTube channels
May 2013	Private equity (Triangle Peak Partners & Raine Investors)	?	3.4B monthly video views	Advertising and content partnerships, primarily through YouTube channels
Mar 2014	Warner Bros. (with MK Capital, Redpoint & Google)	$18M	??? monthly video views (??? subscriber)	Content production, platform development (beyond YouTube)
Mar 2015	Warner Bros. (with MK Capital, Redpoint, Google, Coffin Capital & Ventures, Allen DeBevoise)	$24M	3.8B monthly video views (430M subscribers)	Content production, platform development (beyond YouTube)
TOTAL INVESTED		**$91.55**	**reported**	
7 Oct 2016	Warner Bros. (acquired)	$100M (sale)	3.8B monthly video views	Content production, multi-platform distribution

Various sources, Crunchbase, collated by authors.

This trajectory and turn of events undoubtedly presented challenges to the future of *Machinima Inc.*, at least in its focus on both creator content and multi-platform streaming and distribution. Its revenue models were becoming squeezed and its expertise across different platforms stretched. In March 2017 new management was announced by *Warner Bros.* Russell Arons, who was *Warner's Interactive Entertainment* senior vice president of worldwide marketing and previously the head of marketing for *Electronic Arts' EA Play* division, as well as spending time at *Mattel*, stepped into the role of general manager. Her gaming experience was considered a good match with *Machinima Inc.*'s creator community and worldwide audiences, which was now reported to be 3.8B views of 19B minutes of video served per month (Takahashi, 2017), as was her marketing revenue focus. Spending a year to redevelop *Machinima Inc.*, taking it back to its gamer roots and also aligning it more closely with the *Warner* brand, in February 2018 Arons launched a revised strategy, focussing on the intersection of gaming culture and entertainment, with a renewed emphasis on its talent network. Importantly, she also announced that *Machinima Inc.* had begun to provide business intelligence for other parts of the *Warner* stable, commenting:

> With so many of the changes coming out of *YouTube*, how do you insure safety for your brand partners? We have been doing a deep dive to understand every one of our channels and think about how it is fitting into our vision for our talent network.
>
> Russell Arons (in Jarvey, 2018)

This was a strong hint of what was to come.

With proliferation of streaming channels, reportedly over 100 in August 2018 (Perez, 2018), as well as convergence between traditional TV and digital formats, content that merged games with film and fan-based material, *Machinima Inc.*'s market position became increasingly competitive and its revenue harder to earn. Alongside this, *Warner Brothers Digital Network*, which included *Machinima Inc.*, was acquired by *AT&T* in 2018, as part of its takeover of *Time Wa*rner. With significant restructuring and paring down of digital media assets, *Machinima Inc.* was subsumed under *AT&T*'s *Otter Media* organization. *Otter Media*, which already owned machinima producers, *Rooster Teeth* (see Chapter 4), thereafter folded *Machinima Inc.* under the *Fullscreen* brand, and in the process made 84 of its staff redundant (Weiss, 2018). Its remaining staff was focussed on internal projects, but far from being the end of machinima, *Otter*'s CEO Tony Goncalves stated that changes had been made *"to optimize the effectiveness of our brands, services and teams. These changes will make our business more focused, competitive and profitable"* (in Weiss, 2018).

On 18 January 2019, however, *Machinima Inc.* set its video content to private and on 1 February 2019, it officially ceased operation. This was almost a year to the day that Hugh Hancock had passed away, having suffered a heart attack at an event in London on 5 February 2018. His *Strange Company* was formally dissolved on 7 April 2020, ironically as we wrote this chapter of the book.

The outpouring of frustration at *Otter Media's* treatment of *Machinima Inc.*'s community was very evident in the heated exchanges that ensued across social media platforms. Reported in *Wired Magazine* on 27 January 2019, machinima creator Jeremy Azevedo, its former director of entertainment programming, summed it up thus:

> For those of us that truly helped build that company, it's a pretty huge disappointment that *Otter Media* would make private, or delete, thousands of videos from *Machinima*... Hundreds of creators have, in some cases, had years' worth of work eliminated in a snap. Some of the programs we're talking about here, like *Inside Gaming, Sonic for Hire, Battlefield Friends,* and many others, had tens of millions of views each. This isn't like one of the other MCNs [multi-channel networks] that acted as a bush-league talent agency. *[Machinima]* was a brand with dozens of genuine hit shows that were watched by hundreds of millions of people over the years.
>
> Jeremy Azevedo (in Onanuga, 2019)

Whilst gut-wrenching to witness, it is apparent in the events described in this chapter that Hancock, through various interstices and the auspices of many stakeholders over the nineteen years of *Machinima.com*'s existence, had achieved what he set out to do back in 2000 at its launch. Furthermore, the ever-popular machinima series, *Red vs Blue* (*Rooster Teeth*) prevails, along with a number of others that have since been reprieved (see Chapter 4). Few of the original or later community members expressed sympathy on the demise of *Machinima Inc.*'s channel network partner business practices.

3.5 Legals and Creative Absorption

Although legal issues had always been a challenge that machinima creators have navigated – because they use some intellectual property created by games developers, as we have said – the legals first came to a head as a significant problem after *Machinima.com* transferred ownership to the DeBevoises in November 2004. This coincided with the early developments of *YouTube*, which launched on 14 February 2005, first allowing users to upload content on 23 April of that year, and quickly becoming a popular place for home film makers to upload content, streaming over 100M videos a day by mid-2006 (Fritz, 2006). *YouTube* was sold to *Google* on 13 October 2006. Reflecting the stringent approach to copyright protection taken by the music industry on creative works (see also Chapter 7), *YouTube* attempted to apply take downs of any works that included copyrighted content from other sources. Its considerable dilemma by mid-2006 was that much of the content on *YouTube* was in fact machinima material, nearly all of which used assets derived from other sources.

A number of machinima creators successfully negotiated arrangements with the games developers to support their creative content, notably Shiff's *Video Mods'* series and *Rooster Teeth* with *Halo*'s developer and publisher, respectively *Bungie* and *Microsoft.* Others had, however, faced significant challenges with attempts to develop cross-media distribution channels for their creative work. For example, Phil Rice, founder of *Zarathustra Studios,* a prolific and another well-known *Quake* movie-making studio from machinima's early days, found he could not take his work to the next level. He had been approached by the US *The Tonight Show* (hosted by Jay Leno) in 2006. Despite content, music and general content being cleared, *Electronic Arts,* owner of the game in which the film they wished to showcase had been made, refused to give permission to show the work (Rice, 2020). Both *EA* and the TV channel lost out to online in their decision – the film became the most viewed *Sims* machinima on *YouTube* (*Male Restroom Etiquette* is now in the *Guinness World Records Gamer's Edition,* 2009), and has over 6.6M views on *YouTube* alone (as at April 2020), where it is still available to see.

The frustration among community members with some of the games developers' apparent refusal to explicitly support machinima by revising their end-user license agreements was ultimately summarized best in a machinima film produced by Phil Rice of *Zarathustra Studios,* working with *Krad Productions* (figure 3.8). The film provided a satirical review (using *Halo 2*) of what could and could not be used to create machinima stories.

Figure 3.8: Screencap *[COMPANY]Rulez!*

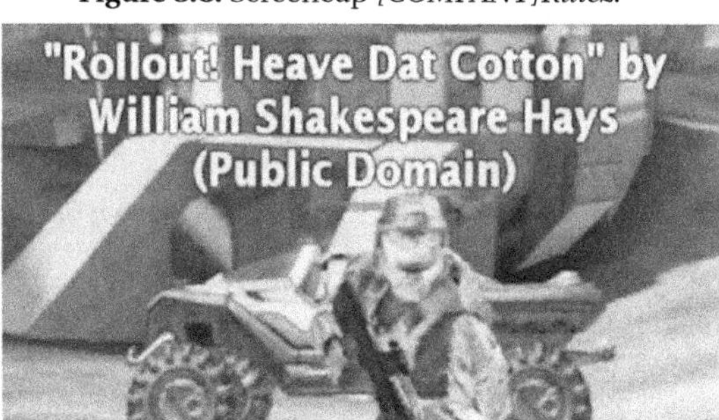

Created under *Microsoft's* Game Content Usage Rules using assets from *Halo 2.*
Source: *Zarathustra Studios* and *Krad Productions,* 2007

This was despite what Marino stated was the secret desire of many games developers:

> [Games developers] turn a blind eye... quite a few games developers really like it when they see machinima made with their game because it means a certain thing: our game has so embraced that people want to use it to creatively express and as a way to tell stories. They feel so enthused and engaged, connected to our game that they want to do that - it means games companies have won people over... [it's the reason why games developers] give you tools to make machinima. And then if you read the end user license agreement you don't own it!
>
> Paul Marino (interview, 2008)

Thus began an extensive debate involving various stakeholders such as academics, lawyers, copyright owners and creators on what constituted originality, authorship and ownership in machinima – a debate that is unresolved and ongoing today, when many more types of creative practice use content derived from other sources (see eg., Reid, 2008; Bittani, 2011; Harwood, 2011; Krapp, 2011; Harwood and Garry, 2013; et al). Indeed, the last official machinima community event that Hancock participated in, at the *International Machinima Convention* in Leicester (UK) in 2016, was partly about this very issue.

Some games developers did adapt their end-user license agreements, including *Blizzard* (*World of Warcraft*), but a number sat back and waited. As Jo Twist, CEO of the association for the *UK's Interactive Entertainment (UKIE)* industry association saw it some years later, stated:

> There's no point in punishing your fans – the games industry has always had a different track record when it comes to copyright infringement than the music or film industry does because we have a better relationship with our fans.... We live or die by how the community gathers around the game... it's a relationship, it's not a top-down thing, it's a mutual, beneficial relationship.
>
> Jo Twist (interview, 2014)

Nonetheless, many were nervous about the potential for unsavoury content such as porn, racism and defamation to be created. As Marino commented in an early interview:

> [games developers are] leery of any adult content since *Rockstar Games* got clobbered in the media for the sex scenes in *Grand Theft Auto: San Andreas*... Game companies are terribly worried that they might get sued just for making it possible for kids to create X-rated mods, let alone X-rated movies.
>
> Paul Marino (in Gladstone, 2006)

Thus, content moderation by brand appointed community managers was more about brand protection than copyright per se.

Whilst copyright was largely addressed by the DeBevoises through their strategy of contracting with games developers to create content that promoted games, ultimately the issue was superseded by *Machinima Inc.*'s avarice. It is this that led to the development of contracts which exploited the creators and made them part of the corporate marketing machine, as highlighted above.

In 2013, this came to a new head as another of *Machinima Inc.*'s then high profile network channel partners raised the issue of its 'in perpetuity, throughout the universe, in all forms of media now known or hereafter devised' contracts by denouncing his relationship with the organization in a *YouTube* video. Whilst the video was deleted as a consequence of legal discussions, the creator did eventually leave. At the same time, other digital video media organizations were attempting to renegotiate contracts that increased their percent share of advertising revenue and take ownership of intellectual property of works created (Marsden, 2013; Stuart, 2013). Many felt this corporate behaviour unreasonable and greedy but organizations, including *Machinima Inc.*, did it nonetheless in what can only be described as a content land grab which enabled the exploitation of its extracted digital oil through advertising. Some creators took their grievances to court (e.g., @Jericho, 2019). Moreover, its behaviour was clearly endorsed by its investor, *Google* at the time. Its sharp marketing practices, however, came under US Federal Trade Commission scrutiny when in 2015 *Machinima Inc.* was found to have paid influencers who could guarantee high numbers of views (17M+) to post *YouTube* videos endorsing *Microsoft's Xbox One* and a number of games (*Microsoft* was later absolved of responsibility) (Makuch, 2016).

The third significant challenge in the development of machinima as a creative practice was, therefore, the absorption of the creator community into the corporate marketing machine. This absorption is alluded to in the description of events relating to the evolution of *Machinima Inc.* and was clearly two-fold. Firstly, this was achieved by direct means, as explained in the development of contractual arrangements with creators as network channel partners. Secondly, indirectly by the increased focus on professionally produced content. Although *Machinima Inc.*'s aim in its earliest years was to compete with TV and film rather than grow game audiences, the recruitment of machinima creators for making content had a profound impact on the creative community at large. A number of filmmakers were recruited to work on machinima productions, working closely with games developers to make series (see, e.g., *Rooster Teeth* in the next chapter) but many ultimately joined the staff of games developers – their second love was game, not film (which industry had apparently rejected machinima production techniques in the early days, although we discuss this further in Chapter 7). Well-known creators and community advocates such as Hancock (*Machinima.com*) and Marino (*AMAS*) were stymied by their own contractual arrangements with *Machinima Inc.*, which effectively altered their creative trajectory. In an interview with one of the authors in 2014, Hancock reflected:

> … there are an awful lot of starving film makers who have decided to make ends meet by attempting to use their machinimating skills in whatever way they can. As a result, people tend to massively under value film making ability and technical ability and therefore machinima contracting doesn't pay that well. Additionally, machinima is seen as a lower cost, lower production value way of making corporate videos… The only exit for machinimators, aside from *Red Vs Blue* [machinima series] and myself… for most people the exit has been 'you're quite good at making cinematics for computer games, lets hire you to make cinematics for computer games'. *Bioware* obviously hired a load of people, *Blizzard* hired a load of people… it's still happening – I saw an ad for more machinima guys from *Blizzard* a little while ago. It works out for people who want to get into the games industry – I find it upsetting on a personal level because quite a lot of the good machinima people, who I wanted to see more machinima films by, …. well, it's never going to happen any time soon.
>
> Hugh Hancock (interview, 2014)

For Marino and various others active in the community from the outset, their creative skills were quickly absorbed by games developers who made use of their cinematic skills in developing the next generation of triple-A games. For example, Marino became creative director of *EA* owned *Bioware's Mass Effect 2* in 2007 which, after years of work, launched in 2010 to critical acclaim (Castillo, 2010). In an interview in 2008, Marino had commented:

> It's definitely the case people are looking at machinima as a way to generate profit and commercialize production… it does take away from people that are just passionate about their work… There are a number of games companies out there who are supporting creation of machinima using in-game tools, a mod pack or tool set, and they know that they are getting value out of the game, additional value that's not packed with the game, to build the sale of the game beyond its box so I see that as an exploitation of end user work. I also think end-user film makers see also the potential for their content to be turned into something that can be commercially exploited… [this] saddens me a little bit because previously it was more about passion and now it's about high-end visualization.
>
> Paul Marino (interview, 2008)

As Brian Mayberry, co-founder of *Dead on Que* studio which worked with games such as *Half Life* and *Unreal*, reflects:

> *Machinima.com* pretty much forged the path for my development as a professional creative. I simply do not know where I would be today without this community's influence on me during my formative years. The networks developed through *Machinima.com* allowed many of us to explore real careers within the game development industry. For a time, Mike [co-founder of *Dead on Que]* and I were able to work side-by-side as 'Machinima Pros', creating in-game cinematics for the PC MMO: *Star Wars: The Old Republic* in 2010-2011. I had the great fortune to do this again myself for the action game *Defiance,* which came out in 2013 on *PS3, XBox 360,* and PC. Today Mike works with *Rooster Teeth,* while I continue to make games as a part-time indie dev with *Steamburger Studios.*
>
> Brian Mayberry (interview, 2020)

One of the key applications of machinima techniques within games is that of cutscene making. Hancock felt that machinima creators were well-positioned to create these because of their keen eye for narrative storytelling, albeit the method takes play away from the game player and he heavily criticized its over-use:

> Cutscenes are useful to a very limited extent. They are sometimes a very powerful tool for showing what is happening in the game, however, over using them is something that almost everyone does – it's a terrible idea... I'm of the opinion, and far from alone in this, that 99.95% of the time you are better off telling the story through an in-game mechanism. *Dark Souls* is one of the big stand out successes of the last few years in computer games and that tells its story mostly on the loading screen actually, but does not use, actually no it uses them very briefly to show a particular part of play but not involving the player. Any time you have a cut scene where control is taken over from the character and the character wanders around doing things you would not do or saying things you would not say is highly risky. It has worked for some famous games, eg., *Mass Effect,* but I would say that the future of games lies in no cut scenes rather than loads of them.
>
> Hugh Hancock, (interview, 2014)

This is reflected in comments by actor/presenter James Hamer-Morton (actor and voice of *Stitch* in *Disney*'s Lilo & Stitch), who was another of the original team working on the *Machinima.com* website from its inception:

> I was offered work creating cinematics and level design for some video games, no doubt based upon the 'work' I had made, and the fact that so few other people were doing it within the *Unreal Engine*... Eventually, paid work and further studies led to less time and less motivation to make more of what I was doing to earn money on the side.
>
> James Hamer-Morton (interview 2020)

Unusually, Hancock remained a committed and passionate independent filmmaker, exploring creativity in other creative forms as well as expanding his machinima portfolio, releasing a Lovecraftian comedy-horror short in 2015. Of his own creative practice development, he said:

> *YouTube* is a terrible, terrible route to monetizing anything video-based, particularly if you have a massive IP incumbent… so, unfortunately, game-based machinima, it's not dead but it is wicked limited and certainly I doubt I will do any more game-based machinima. Having said that, procedural content generation is coming on leaps and bounds and the growth of the independent gaming scene means there are enormous libraries of 3D content being made available on a commercial basis because, unlike web series creators, machinima creators, independent game developers tend to want to get paid. So I think there is a parallel route for it and that's the route I'm going down. Yes, triple-A stuff is probably going to be out of our reach forever but it is becoming increasingly irrelevant anyway.
>
> Hugh Hancock (interview, 2014)

But as highlighted by Gladstone (2006) in his article for *Computer Gaming World* magazine, many games developers were mostly interested in machinima filmmaking skills for game promotion, citing Paul Della Bitta, *Blizzard*'s (*World of Warcraft*) community manager:

> We batted the idea [of employing machinima makers] around for a while but ultimately decided that we'd be better served by running contests to encourage fan films.
>
> Paul Della Bitta (in Gladstone, 2006)

Such a view in many ways missed the point. Machinima is as much about creative process as it is about the outcome, as we discuss in some detail in Chapter 7. Ever associated with innovation in filmmaking, before his death, Hancock was especially proud of *Strange Company's* seminal virtual reality horror roleplaying game (*Left-Hand Path*) which drew on machinima roots to use room scale tracked motion technology and contemporary headsets (at the time *Oculus Rift* and *HTC Vive*). This indie game was released in November

2017 and was one of the first virtual reality experiences on *Steam*. As *Strange Company*'s co-founder, Gordon McDonald, commented:

> [Hancock] got involved in the whole VR scene so that he could use the controller for digital puppetry… the jump from writing a good [fantasy] game to creating a VR game wasn't a massive one for him because of his experience hacking games... I think he could have done some really amazing thing there if he'd had more time.
>
> Gordon McDonald (interview, 2020)

And similarly, others abandoned machinima to focus on game-related careers. For example, Alexander Winn, founder of *Edgeworks Entertainment* and popular *Halo* based drama series, *The Codex*, commented:

> While we were making *The Codex* and then *The Heretic*, I was involved every day on forums and groups. I was making a series, but it was also important to me to stay connected with the fans. Since then, I've pulled back because machinima was a bit like a drug for me: it allowed me to tell the huge, epic stories I wanted to tell, but it did so in a copyrighted medium that I couldn't actually build a career on. We tried so hard to get a license from *Bungie*, the same way *Rooster Teeth* did, but they weren't interested. So in the interest of not getting seduced by the fun-but-not-helpful world of machinima, I pulled back and focused on building my career.
>
> Alexander Winn (interview, 2020)

Thus, creative absorption by corporates was inevitable for many yet for the pioneers, independence remained a driving force.

3.6 Reflections of the Impact and Influence of *Machinima.com*

Whilst acknowledging the role of *Machinima Inc.*'s network channel partner strategy in popularizing machinima (its 'dead' *YouTube* network still had 12.1M subscribers as at 10 April 2020), Hancock, founder and originator of *Machinima.com*, was critical of both the commercialization of machinima and the exploitation of machinima creators:

> It was doing fine before *YouTube* and will do fine after *YouTube*. Obviously it is, actually I despise the phrase UGC [user generated content] because its ghettoizing low budget production, but it is not studio created and it is not, by and large, created by people who are comfortable going to a distributor and saying 'hello, I've got this 36 part series would you like to show it?'. So, if all of the self-distribution channels disappeared over night and bandwidth became exponentially more expensive say by the FCC doing something stupid in 120 days' time, then I think machinima would suffer quite a lot. Having said that, there is always a way. I think it falls into

the wider sphere of ultra-low budget film making, the same sphere as 'let's play' and all these other things that have been enabled by the fact that you can make a film and show it to thousands of people and not spend thousands of dollars on it.

Hugh Hancock (interview, 2014)

Others mourned the loss of community, which had been rough-shod over as the site became more commercially oriented:

[When] *Machinima.com* changed hands and became more commercially viable… I both loved the expansion and hated the feeling of our original community being overrun by what we wanted all along; a mainstream audience.

James Hamer-Morton (interview, 2020)

It was a fairly clear case of a couple of individuals coming in a bit late and trying to monetize, with very little concern for the legacy of the form or the community. They were fairly successful at that, so good for them, I suppose, but I don't think they did any favors for anyone that came before them. I have been involved in a number of early-adopting scenes in which a glitch in the programming of some software or other allows an entry by a small number of people who notice and take advantage. Hackers, circuit benders, chiptune musicians and visualists and the like. In each scene, there was a familiar scenario that repeated itself every few months in which some outsider would jump in, send a bunch of the people who were producing the work an email saying something like 'Hey! I want to make you guys all rich!' or 'I have been watching what you're doing and I KNOW what you are missing!' Then they would suggest we sign on to their thing which always amounted to little more than a way to cash in on a trend. It was always laughed off and pushed aside by the people actually producing the work. In this case, though, [*Machinima Inc.*] was able to connect to a large number of producers who were young enough that they didn't yet know how to protect their interests. And sadly, a large number of them were taken advantage of.

Chris Burke (interview, 2020)

For some who had not been involved from the very first day, Machinima.com had become an important part of their development as creators. Joe Falcione, founder of *Reliant Films* and producer of award-winning machinima film, *The Outcome* (*Machinima Film Festival* 2003, Best Editing):

In 2006, I was hired by EA to make three game films for *Battlefield 2142* and I also helped produce footage for an *Intel* Web series in collaboration with other machinima filmmakers and developers [*Sir Community, Team Ten24* and *Combat Studios*]... [following this period, *Machinima.com*] became corporatized and literally was not accepting anything that was less than 'professional' and that was such a turn off for me. Even though I had been hired by *EA* and others to create, by the time I was considering making something else, there was no more creative space for me. Being a part of the community with so many contacts, I no longer felt welcome and it was not surprising at all to hear that the website and community were pretty much shut down... What killed *Machinima.com* was whoever took it over in the later years, missed out on what the community was all about. It failed at its core by changing it to a business model when it wasn't yet an established industry. I respect so many for trying to get it there but, fundamentally, it needed a different voice or presence so that developers would see the future and benefits of such an industry. It's not too late, but it is too late for *Machinima* [as a brand]. I felt for a time, it was going to take off as developers were starting to see the benefits of allowing people to use their games to make films – it was like free advertising.

Joe Falcione (interview, 2020)

and Damien Valentine, founder of *Bathtub Productions*:

I was working on my first series *[Consanguinity]*, a *Buffy the Vampire Slayer* inspired story created with a heavily modded version of *Neverwinter Nights*. I'd read about machinima in gaming magazines and I thought maybe I should share it with the community. I didn't expect much of a response – here was this new guy bringing a pretty rough series that so far only had two episodes to an established community with people far more talented and experienced than I was. It turned out, I was wrong about the response. While I was right, there were a lot of talented people using *Machinima.com*, they were so welcoming. They didn't care that I hadn't made anything before, they liked what I was doing, wanted to see more and offered me advice on how to get better results with the game and software... You can see the jump in quality with episodes three and four as I incorporated the suggestions being made. They taught me a lot... [It was] the encouragement from Hugh [Hancock] and from the community that made me continue making machinima... I don't think I would be working on my current projects if I hadn't signed up and started posting on those forums. Sadly I think this era of *Machinima.com* will be forgotten except those of us who were present for it, which is a great shame because it was such a great community that was all about creativity and encouraging people to tell the stories they wanted to tell and make the films they wanted to make but had no other means to do so.

Damien Valentine (interview, 2020)

Some others saw it as a mutant media form, hard to pin down but inspirational in its potential. Ricard Gras, film producer/director and machinima maker as well as European member of *AMAS*, commented:

> [Machinima is one] of the many things that you can find in a very fragmented and varied media landscape. Personally, I do have a love for [machinima] but… it changes all the time and it really escapes all my attempts to pigeonhole it. It started as a media trick in the 1990s when people started to record themselves very timidly and then it's now moved into a new production method which is attracting the attention of VJs and is the only way of documenting virtual worlds. It's a very flexible tool [but importantly] machinima has this relationship with the audience that is given by the pre-existing game and the scenario in the game.
>
> Ricard Gras (interview, 2008)

Thus, platforms that focussed on social exchange such as *Linden Labs' Second Life*, which had launched in June 2003, were using machinima as an embedded part of community cohesion because it recorded user activity. This was explicitly endorsed by the organization and moreover it was clear that, at least in *Linden Lab*'s case, it had no intention of monetizing its relationship with creators beyond its resident/player subscription model. Ebbe Altberg, CEO of *Linden Labs*, explained:

> We've never had issues with machinima getting out in the world, no one ever has discussed the concern that machinima is spreading around the world that was created in *SL*, it's a great thing. It ends up being more between users and users than between us and users. If you have created an experience in *SL* that you feel you have the rights to and then I create a machinima that includes your experience, whether as a background or the scene takes place, and then I go and monetize that machinima, what are you going to say as content creator about the other users using your content for their monetary gain? I'm very comfortable with the fact that I'm not going to use it for direct monetary gain. Obviously I have to promote the service, so I want to be able to show your experience to the world to bring in more users to the service, but not to be sold or resold by myself. Whereas between users it gets more complicated, and that ends up having to be a negotiation between the users... What we can do is to help the distribution and production and ultimately also help bring traffic back into *SL* to create a strong cycle of content being created, bringing users in, more content being created…
>
> Ebbe Altberg (interview, 2014)

Evidently, a number of established games did likewise whilst others saw it as a means to develop their marketing strategies.

So, beyond the boom and bust of corporate greed evidenced in the *Machinima Inc.* years, what is the lasting legacy of *Machinima.com*?

For many of the original community, there remains tangible bitterness emanating from the role *Machinima Inc.* played in its evolution. One active community member who had written a popular tutorial series (*Filmmaking Tips for Machinima Directors,* 2004) and attempted to take her skills into the new organization, summed it up:

> I think most of us were expecting it would be something more robust and useful in the machinima community. However, [the DeBevoises'] initial goal was to cash in on the thousands of non-narrative gaming videos that were becoming a trend. This was not really what (we) the community wanted as it did not highlight the skills and creativity that the narrative films showcased... Everything was a conflict, not just of the goals of the company vs. the original community, but the goals of the company with every conflicting decision they made about it.
>
> Ingrid Moon (interview, 2020)

Nonetheless, it is the community ethos and creative storytelling methodologies which stand out. As Marino stated:

> It was a 'Wild West' of sorts – pioneers venturing into new territory, sometimes successful in their endeavours, sometimes not – but learning all the way.
>
> Paul Marino (interview, 2020)

His comments are also reflected in those made by Ken Thain, who created another popular machinima website, *3dfilmmaker.com*, and was the first of the original machinima community to become part of a triple A game developer in 2006 as a cinematic designer at Bioware:

> I will always remember it as the grassroots website that pulled a bunch of ragtag creatives together and built a passionate community around a new medium for storytelling, that even today, 20 years later still has barely hit its full potential... Many people from the early days of *Machinima.com* went in many directions and went on to do incredible things, and I can't help but feel the site was a beacon of hope for a bunch of creatives that wanted their chance to tell the stories that would have not been possible without the site, community and support of each other... It was like everyone saw the power and potential of 'real-time filmmaking' but it was a matter of the tools and technology catching up to our vision and dreams.
>
> Ken Thain (interview, 2020)

Tawmis Logue, machinima creator of long-running and popular series *Neverending Nights* (2004-2013), described *Machinima.com* aptly as the Grand Central Station of machinima, commenting:

> You could get opinions and suggestions in your own thread about your machinima series by folks who were sincerely wanting you to grow. It was also a hub for people looking for small bit pieces of voice acting which I had also done through the forum to be on other machinima out there… where all these 'would be' film makers could come together - work with one another, whether that's providing advice or seeking talent to be in their series. It was a great community when it first started.
>
> Tawmis Logue (interview, 2020)

Of its creative influence, Ingrid Moon went on to comment:

> Machinima should be remembered for its storytelling capabilities, the rise of many talented people in the games and animation industries, and pushing an envelope not previously explored. It seems to endure mostly in independent art, but because some developers like *Epic* made their engine more open, people in the games and film industries used these tools to previsualize shots and create in-game cinematics. People have used it to create 3D demos of products. I used it to make a fly-through of a *Disney English* site (schools in China run by *Disney).*
>
> Ingrid Moon (interview, 2020)

Marino also summed it up well in his statement:

> *Machinima.com*'s legacy has been a huge influence on my life. It gave me a platform to show off my work, it provided answers in times of need, it forged friendships that I hold to this day and it legitimized my working with game-tech to create films. I don't think I'm overstating it when I say it changed the entire trajectory of my life. I can't thank Hugh enough for that and do wish he were around so I could express that to him directly.
>
> Paul Marino (interview, 2020)

Importantly, he also highlights its ongoing relevance as a creative practice for contemporary technologies which are being used in both games and film making, such as special effects, virtual and augmented reality production:

> Recently the term and practices around 'virtual production' are making waves across film, VFX and animation studios. And unfortunately, because *Machinima.com* became more affiliated with 'game videos' its original intent of 'a platform for filmmaking using virtual spaces afforded by games' was somewhat the victim to its success. But one only needs to review the history of *Machinima.com* to see virtual production's roots are

> directly linked to it. That, to me, is how impactful the site was. It provided practices and language to a creative process before that process had fully formed. History should honor the site's foundation and how its grassroots filmmakers had nurtured this innovative approach that's causing fundamental shifts in how stories are now being told.
>
> Paul Marino (interview, 2020)

This is also evident in comments made by music video producer, Tony Shiff, who explained why *MTV* had first bought his machinima video series, *Video Mods* in 2004:

> My background is music videos – I was very comfortable with that; I'd sold my company in the 90s to *Warner Music* and I knew how the business worked and I just thought games technology was a very good fit. The reason *[MTV]* actually bought it, and this is a very important point, was the games industry and music industry overlapped very well… so anything the games companies were interested in, *MTV* had to be interested in.
>
> Tony Shiff (interview, 2020)

and following its success (it only stopped because the *MTV2* channel ceased), Shiff had been approached for a similar style of content by *Yahoo Music:*

> My concept was to put music into games but what about if we do the reverse and put musicians as games characters? So we turned artists like Lil' Wayne, JohnPaul, Disturbed, Tommy Lee into game characters in game environments. That was probably the first time on a regular basis – I did about five of them for *Yahoo* – and it was the first time that anyone had made original music videos, as music videos, as machinima, in that style. *Yahoo Music* ran them on their front page, like once a month.
>
> Tony Shiff (interview, 2020)

It is clear the broader media industry, however, struggled to understand the convergence in the early days. Shiff again highlighted this:

> A lot of times in the music industry though, at the label level, they couldn't understand it: 'like, how can we add value to this, how can we make this pay?'. It a dilemma that goes on now: the music industry is threatened by games but at the same time attracted to games.
>
> Tony Shiff (interview, 2020)

But, despite its different cinematic aesthetic qualities, the application of machinima beyond game is evident:

> It was the wild west in graphic technology, full of potential with only one's imagination limiting the possibilities. With every new machinima film, we would all believe even stronger in the medium and come closer together as a community. It still exists today in every video game, every CG film and in many high-end films.
>
> Ken Thain (interview, 2020)

And Tony Shiff expanded on this:

> I had a friend that was a CG [computer graphics] artist at *ILM [Industrial Light & Magic]* and she came over and watched one of the shows. She nodded politely – because it was beneath *ILM* – whereas nowadays game art, like *Red Dead Redemption* and I've just been playing *Half Life Alyx*, that's the state of the art. It's more interesting than another *Marvel* cinematic visual effect. It's replaced it. I think you look at what *Unreal* is doing, 4.2 and above releases. I think they're creating a whole production pipeline that's fantastic. Its state of the art for doing [machinima]. They're doing all the right things, using all the right systems. I do think VR/AR they're all just tools. *Unreal* is now the one to watch in terms of making that content.
>
> Tony Shiff (interview, 2020)

Commenting further on the challenges in different creative industry sectors, Shiff stated that it is largely a lack of vision that is currently the main difficulty:

> It's like rap music, it's derivative but it's original. [Games are a lot of more flexible than the music companies] the problem is that they're always scared of destroying what little revenue they have, because it got destroyed once before with *Napster* and then suddenly, as someone said to me, there's still the lights on in the building but there are fewer floors in the building every year! Then with streaming, they're finally coming back to seeing more stuff and - actually the reason I got into VR and some of the stuff I'm doing now – in the music industry it's always just what if we do it, and it turns out to be the deal that destroys it again. When you're employed by a large multinational your timeline is always driven by this quarter's reports. It takes an exceptional leader. There used to be (in the 1980s and 1990s in the music industry), it was intensely profitable, you had these kind of wild raconteur entrepreneurial types that drove the industry, but those guys have gone.
>
> Tony Shiff (interview, 2020)

The potential of machinima for mainstream filmmaking was summed up by Tony Dyson, creator of the *R2D2* robot in *Star Wars: The Empire Strikes Back* and an Emmy nominated film special effects designer whose work also included *Superman 2, Moon Raker* and *Dragon Slayer*. Dyson, who passed away unexpectedly in March 2016, was an avid machinima fan who worked on his own machinima-based virtual storytelling projects:

> When we think about CGI, computer-generated images, you have to have very technical people doing that. They put the frames together for a director or writer – it's very time-consuming because those people have to relate to each other. With machinima the whole thing changes: everyone can learn it very quickly which means they can really show their creativity – they are actually inside the computer, the programme that produces the machinima. It's a very strange thing but remarkable. I've never seen that before. When you go into a virtual world or game, you can use it rather like a creative studio. The framework has been built by thousands of dedicated people and you can just customize it to your own liking – you can then film at the same time, which means you don't have to be writing or creating. You are basically cutting out the middleman, the technician who has to put all those figures together using a very complicated and expensive piece of software… Machinima will not go away, it will just grow and grow. There are a lot of techniques to learn, I'm learning all the time, how to make it all come together for the outside world. Film schools aren't really on to it yet – it's such a shame because it is so creative: we have thousands of images created in these virtual worlds all for sale at incredibly low prices, many can be adapted or modified, it's possible to build anything you want, as far as the imagination goes.
>
> Tony Dyson (interview, 2012)

It is only in more recent times, however, that machinima techniques have been actively integrated into contemporary filmmaking methods at the scale hinted by Dyson – and it also continues to be used to document a range of emergent virtual, augmented and digital interactive experiences. As John Romero (*id Software*) commented:

> The biggest legacy [of machinima] will be movies of the future being entirely digital, actors and all. James Cameron's *Avatar* was shot entirely in the digital *Pandora*, and I qualify that as machinima. Hollywood has been using far more digital effects lately, and is experimenting with digital actors. We already got a digital Peter Cushing and Carrie Fisher a couple years ago.
>
> John Romero (correspondence, 2020)

This is well summarized by Hamer-Morton:

> Its impacts are probably more subtle and larger than most people realize. *Disney* use machinima techniques in their theme parks to create amazing live puppeteering effects. The film industry uses machinima to show directors live previews of their multi-million dollar visual effects on set. News channels create virtual sets and dramatic weather effects using machinima techniques which will go over the heads of the majority of their audience, and of course game engines now have in-built machinima tools to allow video games use machinima in ever more elaborate ways to make their games more immersive and cinematic. As computing power has increased, it has become easier and easier to do this in more interesting ways, but *Machinima.com* was the hub that allowed us all to experiment and hopefully sped up its development by bringing us all together.
>
> James Hamer-Morton (interview, 2020)

Demand is a consequence of the convergence of a number of key influences: technology platforms are now becoming feasible to use as a consequence of developments in processing speed, capacity, etc.; developments of game aesthetics now enable increasingly photorealistic content; audience demand for game inspired content; and, the need to reduce time to market and budget spend. For example, on the launch of *Disney's Lion King* (2019), Kevin Kelly, founding editor of *Wired Magazine*, former publisher of *Whole Earth Review*, writer, photographer, conservationist and enthusiast of digital culture, wrote on his blog:

> Today live-action action movies are often completely sketched out in a rough crude 'previs' (pre-visualization) stage before they are filmed… The movie *Avatar* pioneered in creating totally artificially constructed worlds, but in that movie the actors were 'live-action' or real. In *Lion King* the actors are animals that are not real. *Ready Player One* also had virtual sets and virtual actors, and it was filmed by pushing a virtual camera through the virtual set, but the world they inhabited was not quite photo realistic in the same way or detail that *Lion King* is; here nature looks real down to each blade of grass… The new way of movie-making uses a virtual production process which employs a video game engine to create the landscapes and characters, including animals. Each object, scene, character is computer generated to look so convincing that most people can't tell they are not real except the animals may speak, or humans fly. *Lion King* is the cumulation of four strands of new filming: 1) CGI, computer special effects, 2) wholly animated movies like *Pixar*'s *Coco* or *Up*, and 3) the 'pre-vis' multiplied by a 1,000 and 4) VR and video games…
>
> Kevin Kelly (kk.org, 2019)

In a review of *Industrial Light and Magic*'s video effects process for *Star Wars: The Mandalorian* series (distributed through *Disney+* in the US from November 2019), Jon Favreau, executive producer, discussed their use of *Epic*'s *Unreal Matinee* game engine to create scenes in a novel way by creating a computer game. He commented:

> We have been able to see through a few firsts that I think are going to have a lot of impact on the way television movies are made moving forward. In partnership with *ILM* and *Epic*, we have put together a system whereby which we can have game engine real-time render and video wall technology coming together to create a backdrop for the big beautiful world of *Star Wars*... this is not just greenscreen!
>
> Jon Favreau (*ILMVFX*, 2020)

As Frank Dellario (*AMAS*) commented of *ILM*'s technique in relation to machinima's legacy:

> A huge LED screen was used for the backgrounds instead of greenscreen on *The Mandalorian*. *Unreal Matinee* was used to render those animated backgrounds in real-time while filming the actors in the foreground. That is just insane and so wonderful to me at the same time.
>
> Frank Dellario (interview, 2020)

Favreau's colleague, Hal Hickel, *The Mandalorian* animation supervisor, commented from a filmmaking perspective:

> It's incredibly impressive when you first walk out there because it completely surrounds your peripheral vision. You really quickly forget that you are indoors, you are out on some planet's surface, it feels like a real three-dimensional environment surrounding you – because it is a three-dimensional environment!
>
> Hal Hickel (*ILMVFX*, 2020)

They, and others involved in the series production, noted the significant positives of being able to create scenes quickly, move scenes when they need to during production, and generate in-camera shots that incorporate computer-generated imagery. And all of this with actor performances that incorporate lighting effects also taking account of parallax effects when moving cameras. These developments represent a fundamental shift-change in the way films can now be made to achieve realism in fantasy environments (see also *Unreal*, 2019). Well, it is certainly true the scale-up may be their own invention, but the use of games to create film? That has clearly been around some time – something we revisit in Chapter 7. Moreover, rising demand as a consequence of the COVID-19 pandemic lockdowns on film production studios has led to even lower prices for LED studios – for example, whilst at the beginning of 2020, there were fewer than a dozen such stages in the world, by July the number was double (Steigrad, 2020).

In summing up, it is evident that *AMAS* (and *Machinima.org*) was also ultimately successful in professionalizing machinima as a filmmaking method, albeit this happened outside of the original community's immediate sphere of influence and many of the original creators have not been part of the process at the end. Thain commented:

> I think *Machinima.com* is a special place that had a time and a place for a burgeoning creative medium that was well ahead of its time. I often tell the stories of the early days with *Machinima.com* as people are interested in learning about the history of using game engines as storytelling tools. I also believe as much as *Machinima.com* should be remembered as a pillar in the early scene, Hugh Hancock was the face of *Machinima.com* with his non-stop drive and creativity in making it a valid and respected new medium.
>
> Ken Thain (interview, 2020)

There is also still a clear desire to see a platform for emerging creators whereby games and game-based technologies are used as tools to hone storytelling, filmmaking and interactive experience design skills, supported by collective knowledge and a community ethos. Phil Rice, founder of *Zarathustra Studios* commented:

> The earlier days, it seems to me, were rich with bold storytelling and technical innovation. I feel like capital M – *Machinima.com [Machinima Inc.]* – drowned that out with a sea of noise, hi-jinx, and creator-exploitation. Is there anyone left even using it in those old ways anymore? How in the world do we find them, if they exist? I would love it if little m – *Machinima.com* – twenty-some years on were still a haven for innovation and creativity, even if the popularity for that content naturally waned over the years. The Mecca for independent real-time machinimators, that's what *Machinima.com* could have been. I'd still be involved at *Machinima.com;* I'd gladly take on the 'wise old man' role today that Ricky Grove took on back then, hoping to shepherd more vibrant and daring and interesting choices for the medium.
>
> Phil Rice (interview, 2020)

3.7 Vignettes

Vignette 3.7.1 Unreal Tournament | UT 2003 | UT 2004 | Unreal Engine 4

Figure 3.9: *Unreal Tournament (Epic Games).*

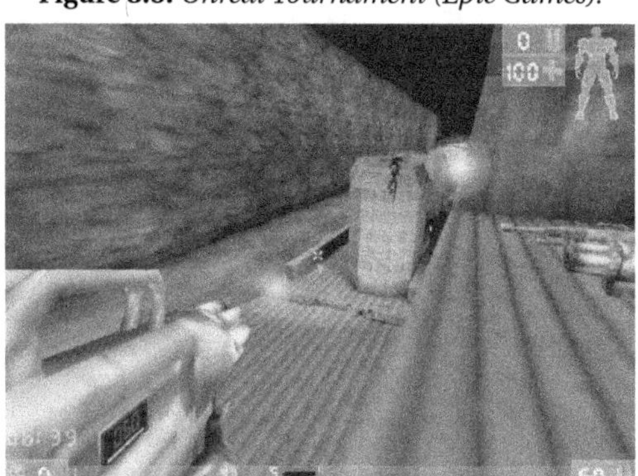

Source: Grussi, 2008.

Released on 23 November 1999, *Unreal Tournament* was developed as a multiplayer game using Unreal Engine 1. Machinima development did not, however, happen quickly and very few films were produced until a free movie-making tool developed by *Internet Team Reactor4* called *Real-Time Movie Studio* (*RTMS*) was released. This enabled players to have better control over producing movies that were mostly shot to be action-oriented. There are no notable machinima movies made in this engine. Conversely, however, a version of the game was used by professional special effects filmmakers, *Industrial Light and Magic* by director, Steven Spielberg, helping him to visualize storyboards for a scene in the 2001 film, *A.I.: Artificial Intelligence* (Mirapaul, 2002).

Figure 3.10: *Unreal Tournament 2003*, released 30 September 2002.

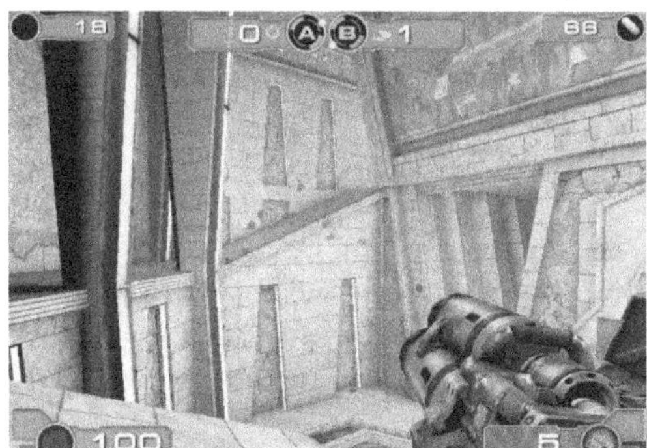

Source: Grussi, 2008.

Figure 3.11: *Unreal Tournament 2004*, released 16 March 2004.

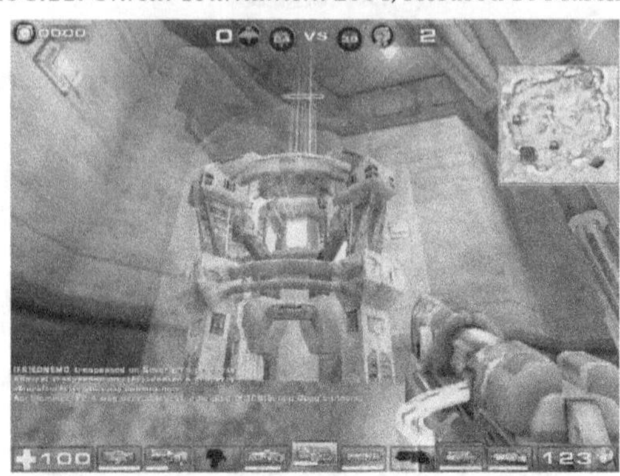

Source: Grussi, 2008.

Unreal Tournament 3 (*UT 2003*) was built in *Unreal Engine 2* with machinima enthusiasts in mind, with a new prepacked cut-scene producer and editor, referred to as *Matinee*. Few films were, however, produced with this new tool, beyond *Epic Games'* team. In an effort to stimulate the creation of new content using *Matinee*, *Epic* launched a large-scale machinima contest for *UT 2003*, called the *Make Something Unreal Contest* (*MSUC*) through which it promoted the development of user-made content ranging from new models and levels to new gameplay genres. *Epic* (the game and engine developer/publisher) also included a category for machinima productions under the title of *Non-Interactive Movie*. Later competitions, after 2007, required mods/movies to be made in *UT 2004* (*Unreal Engine 2.5*). Despite much hype, *Unreal Tournament 4* was cancelled in December 2018.

Unreal Engine 4, which began development in 2003, was control released in 2012 and released in 2014 with a royalty-based subscription model. It was made freely available to schools and universities. In addition to its use as a platform for games, it has since become an important toolkit for filmmakers, primarily because of its modular design. Its Matinee module in particular facilitates cinematic editing (see Chapter 3, Impacts).

Vignette 3.7.2 Half-Life (1 & 2)

Half-Life is a first-person shooter game, by *Valve* first published in 1998. It has strong presentation of single- and multi-player modifications. Machinima using the game has tended to comprise in-game cutscenes from the main game and small cutscenes in single-player add-ons made by the community. Notable machinima examples are by *Dead on Cue* (their award-winning *Fake Science* film) and *Strange Company's* *Matrix 4x* series. The game inspired a number of fan-made games, including *Counter-Strike*, *Day of Defeat* and *Sven Co-op*.

Half-Life 2 was released on 16 November 2004 and included some machinima making tools but these were not easy to use. The most interesting machinima was created with many actors in the game which were filmed as a massive battle scene (*Lord of The Rings*) and put to a score. Others include Randall Glass's *Halo's Warthog Jump* and a scene from the movie *A Few Good Men* entitled *A Few Good G-Men. HL2* was followed by a series of episode releases and *Half-Life Alyx*, which is a virtual reality version of the game, was released in 2020.

Figure 3.12: *Half Life*, released 18 November 1998.

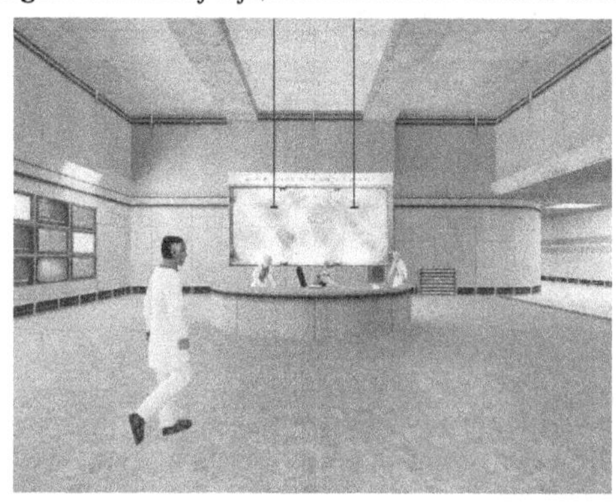

Source: Grussi, 2008.

The *Counter-Strike* source portion of *HL2* led to *Red vs Blue* (*Rooster Teeth*) style comedy machinima, the first being a serial, *Over the Counter-Strike.* Another notable machinima was a piece made for a presentation at the 2005 *Sundance Film Festival* by Paul Marino of *AMAS.* This was a music video in *HL2* with *G-Man* lip-synced to words of *So Cold* by *Breaking Benjamin.* This also subsequently appeared in *MTV2*'s *Video Mods*, season 2 premiere. Others include *G-Worx Pictures*' *Militia II* and *Clan Wars.*

Vignette 3.7.3 The Sims (1 & 2)

Sims is a virtual sandbox style of game. It was first released on 4 February 2000, developed by *Maxis* and published by *Electronic Arts.* Its open-ended play format with characters immediately attracted the attention of machinima creators.

Sims 2, was the most anticipated machinima game after *HL2. Sims 2* enabled the community to make *Sims* lives and movies were made using the game's toolset. *Maxis* helped to seed the machinima community by making several promotional movies with the same tools that creators could use in-game. Seven months after release, *Sims 2* had resulted in a steady stream of creative work which *Maxis* pushed further by supporting film contests to challenge skilled Sims 2 film makers. Notable films were created by *Atlas Productions* including

The Missing which won *Maxis' Halloween Horror* film contest. Other work *Atlas* produced contained elements that had not previously been presented in machinima, such as religion, child adoption, companionship and love.

Figure 3.13: *Sims 2*, released 14 September 2004.

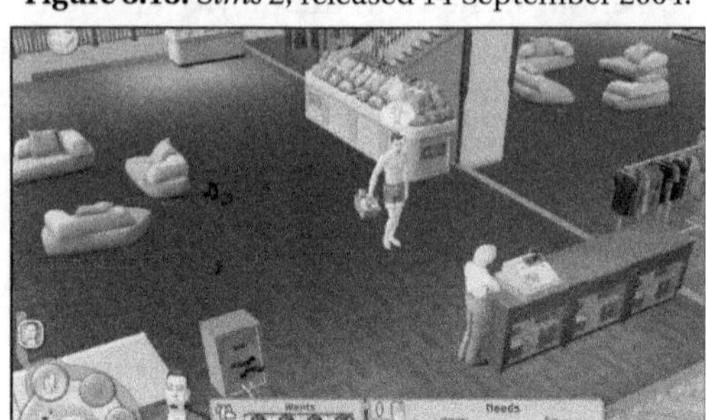

Source: Grussi, 2008.

Vignette 3.7.4 iClone and CrazyTalk (Reallusion)

iClone is not a movie-making game or sandbox, but it is a tool by which 3D animations can be rendered in real time, specifically for use with digital photographs and other assets. It was first released in December 2005 and was based on its *CrazyTalk* 2D facial mapping animation software that had been released in 2001. It is particularly useful for generating lip-synced animations which enabled film makers to devise new ways to see game-based characters. It became popular with machinima makers, having been released at the 2005 *Machinima Film Festival*, hosted at the *Museum of the Moving Image* in New York by *AMAS*. *Reallusion*'s commitment to the machinima community saw them sponsor the 2006 *Machinima Film Festival* (along with others).

Figure 3.14: Screencap *Beast* demonstrates *CrazyTalk*.

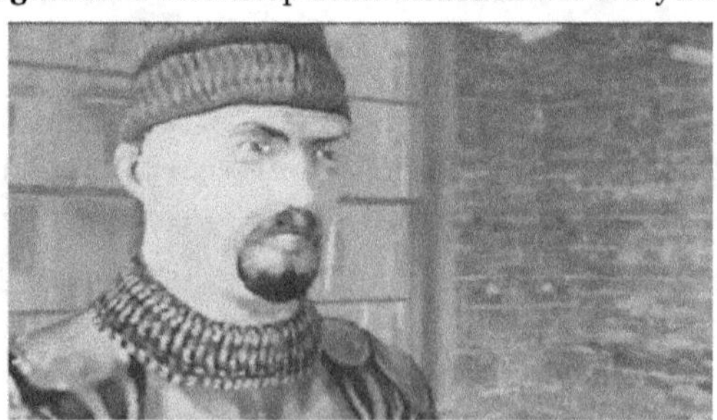

Source: Binary Picture Show, 2006.

Notable machinima films created with *CrazyTalk* include *Binary Picture Show*'s (director, Leo Lucien-Bay) *Beast* (2006).

iClone has since gone through various stages of development, and is currently in version 7 (released 18 November 2019). Its facial recognition tracking software has received considerable mainstream media attention.

Vignette 3.7.5 Moviestorm | Moviestorm First Stage

Founded by the UK's *Short Fuse Limited, Moviestorm* is a software toolset that enables machinima creators to make films from its catalogue of scenes, sets, avatars and related assets. It was first established in 2003 and pre-launched at the 2007 *European Machinima Festival* before the main launch in 2008. Tens of thousands of videos have been made with its toolset, many shared on its dedicated community site. *Moviestorm* also actively supported numerous machinima contests over the years, not least by enabling filmmakers to own their creative works. It updated regularly with new character and set assets over the years, with a major version update in 2014. In February 2020, *Short Fuse* released *Moviestorm First Stage*, a digital pre-visualization tool for film, TV, animation, theatre and games production, motion capture, architecture and interior design, as well as immersive VR experience design.

A notable film, receiving several machinima awards at animation festivals, was *IceAxe Production*'s *Clockwork* (producer/director, Iain Fryer), inspired by the film *A Clockwork Orange*.

Figure 3.15: Screencap *Clockwork*, used *Moviestorm* (and *iClone*).

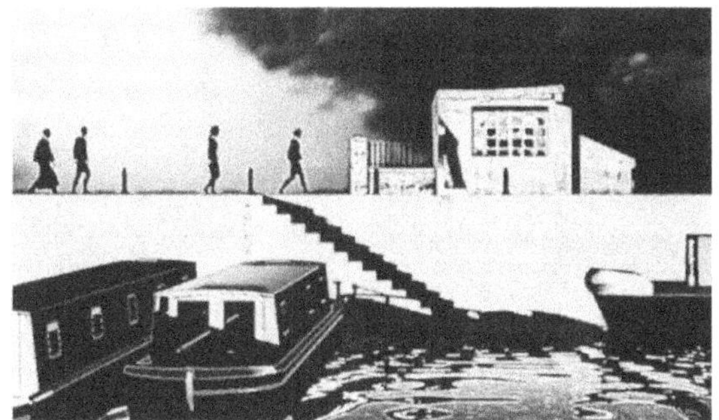

Source: IceAxe Productions, 2007.

Chapter 4

Rooster Teeth Bites

> It's one of the more unforgettable moments in recent film history: the opening shot tracks slowly up a cliff face, so tight you can't tell what exactly you're looking at, until it reaches the top and reveals two sci-fi soldiers clad in futuristic armour standing at the edge of the precipice, laconically discussing the eternal question: 'Why are we here?'. You know this style, this mood, but you can't quite place it; could be Beckett, could be Tarkovsky. Then it hits you: This is Halo for the fucking *Xbox.* And bam, like that, you've entered the world of machinima…
>
> Julian Dibbell (2005) on *Red vs Blue: The Blood Gulch Chronicles*

4.1 Introduction

This chapter examines the most prolific and financially successful machinima production team: *Rooster Teeth Productions.* Best known for its infamous *Red vs Blue* series which began in 2003, we consider its approach to professionalizing machinima creative practice. Its story is not exclusive from other machinima creative works and producers but it is intertwined with that of *Machinima.com, Machinima Inc.* and *Machinima.org* discussed in the previous chapter. Together with the *Academy of Machinima Arts and Sciences* (*AMAS*), *Rooster Teeth*'s story unfolded alongside the emergence of the digital cultural practice of other active community members such as Paul Marino (*ILL Clan* and *AMAS*), Hugh Hancock (*Strange Company* and *AMAS*) and numerous others, and it has been a significant source of inspiration to a breadth of creative communities, including machinima. *Rooster Teeth*'s contribution has, however, extended well beyond the reach of the immediate machinima community, and for that matter, games development more generally, and we therefore examine its sphere of influence as a global fan-based phenomenon.

We begin with the backstory to its development, then examine how *Rooster Teeth Productions* developed, considering its breadth of content creation products, before focusing on its impacts on the community and beyond.

4.2 Backstory

Following the likes of animated television series such as *The Simpsons,* the *Rooster Teeth* producers began as a collaborative team of game reviewers with an alcohol-infused twist. The team consisted initially of Burnie Burns and Matt

Hullum, who had first worked together on projects during their student days at Texas State University. Although Burns had originally been enrolled into a pre-medical programme, he had changed his major to computer science and found he had more time on his hands than he knew what to do with. Burns created a show called *Sneak Peek* at the University's student TV station, *TSTV*, which he produced between 1993-1996 (the show remains on air and has become the longest-running TV show produced by students in the world). His TV show concept was to acquire free movies, ostensibly for reviewing purposes but mainly because he was interested in watching the films.

In his development of the show, Burns had been heavily influenced by Robert Rodriguez' (film director, *Desperado, From Dusk Till Dawn, Spy Kids*) one-man film crew and *Mariachi* style of filmmaking. Rodriguez had also been a student at the University of Texas but had failed to make the grade in its film school. His feature-length directorial debut film, *El Mariachi* (1992) was made with a miniscule budget of $7,000 primarily for a Spanish-speaking Mexican audience yet became a national hit, winning numerous awards. It has since been recognized as the lowest budget film grossing over $1M (Lynch, 2015).

Subsequently, Burns expanded his interests by attempting to make a live-action film for which he had no formal training. He had learned editing skills in a couple of days in the *TSTV* studios which gave him the confidence to proceed. Ultimately he put out a call for help which reached Hullum, a film studies student. As the concept came to fruition, the two connected with actor Joel Heyman, who was Hullum's roommate, and together they made *The Schedule*. Their greatest challenge and ultimate frustration, however, was in distributing the film which involved sending copies of it to festivals and distributors as a way of getting the film shown to audiences. They struggled to get traction for the movie and it has never been released in theatres.

Thereafter, they extrapolated the concept of the *Sneak Peek* TV show to an online forum that focussed on reviewing games that had also been acquired for free (years later this became *The Drunk Tank Podcast)*. As their review concept progressed, other members joined the group, including Geoff Ramsey (formerly known as Geoff Fink) and Gustavo Sorola, and collectively they created a website called *Drunkgamers.com*. Providing a novel approach to game reviews, the *Drunk Gamers'* aim was to review whilst inebriated. Their first review, focussing on the game *Conker's Bad Fur Day*, took place on 9 March 2001 (with two of their team and two others, 2001). As a team that identified themselves as drunk, their challenge was that few games publishers/developers would provide them with games, sponsor their reviews or indeed were happy to see their game having been reviewed by them.

Despite this challenge, their comedy improv and laddish parody style of reviewing became popular with a relatively small number of fan-subscribers to their website, numbering approximately 550 by 2003. In one session, however, two of the team (Burns and Sorola) parodied a gamer perspective on a PC versus Apple Mac advertisement which generated high levels of attention. The film was downloaded thousands of times from the internet in a period of less than 24 hours. Burns only realized this after the fact, when one of the *Drunk Gamers* team brought it to his attention the following day. Burns identifies this as a seminal moment in which he realized the internet had the potential to overcome many of the distribution challenges experienced when attempting to reach an audience with *The Schedule*.

As the team's general goofing around and riffing each other in the process progressed, it led them to develop increasingly complex plots, team and game-based in-jokes. Burns, Ramsey and Sorola began creating voiceover-enhanced gameplay videos for their website. As avid fans of *Bungie's Halo*, they discussed the role of the *Warthog* automobile in the game which ultimately sparked the *Red versus Blue* (*RVB*) web-based series. With an eye to a longer storyline, Burns created a trailer for *RVB* which was released on 5 September 2002 on the *Drunk Gamers* website. It received little attention and shortly thereafter they closed the website for unrelated reasons. Their new website *RedvsBlue.com* came into existence on 30 January 2003, but it was not until March when *Computer Gaming World* magazine sought permission to include a different *Drunk Gamers'* video on a compact disk to be circulated with its April edition that the team sought to exploit their *RVB* work. They launched the *RedvsBlue.com* website on 28 March and re-released the trailer on 31 March 2003. A few days later, on 1 April 2003, they released *RVB* Episodes Zero and 1.

The reason the first episode was separated was not so much related to the storyline (in fact, the episodes contained credits and story separately) but to enable the download of its 80MB files from their server. At the time of the creation of the *RVB* trailer, Burns was working as the president of a technology support company, *TeleNetwork Partners*, based in Houston (Hullum and Heyman had moved to live in Los Angeles following their graduation). Burns had placed the *RVB* trailer video on his office server, but within minutes of its upload, it was being downloaded at a rate of 3,000 videos per second, effectively overwhelming the company's bandwidth.

At the same time, the team also changed their name to *Rooster Teeth*, which was a euphemism for an insult traded in the *RVB* trailer. Its success was such that the *Rooster Teeth* team determined to release an average of three episodes per month. As *Rooster Teeth* came into being it comprised a team of five: Burns, Hullum, Heyman, Sarola and Ramsey. They used *Rooster Teeth* as an umbrella brand for their content, albeit this was largely invisible to their audience. It is this brand, however, that subsequently enabled them to launch other machinima and series-based projects. They justified their name change as a means to provide a veneer of respectability and professionalism to their game reviews, implying they were doing more than simply playing games, and apparently also reflecting that one of the team already had both the rooster and a set of dentures as an ident. In their *RVB* productions, they were joined by Jason Saldana and Dan Godwin, both of whom feature in various episodes from the beginning of the series.

Building on their *RVB* series concept, they began almost immediately creating a shorts series, which they called *Public Service Announcements. RVB PSA #1: Weapons of Mass Destruction* was released on 7 April 2003. Just four days later, on 11 April, *RVB* Episode 2 (*Red Gets a Delivery*) was released, on 18 April *RVB* Episode 3 (*The Rookies*) was released, and on 26 April *RVB* Episode 4 (*Head Noob in Charge*) was released. By the end of April 2003, *Rooster Teeth* had more than 1M downloads of their *RVB* content. Burns described its phenomenal success as one of feeling as though they were 'falling up a cliff' (Burns, 2012) but had quickly realized their next greatest challenge was going to be how to service their rapidly growing audience through the available online media channels of the day. This was a whole different order of distribution problem than the one Burns had dealt with for his first film, *The Schedule.*

As to the creative form of machinima, years later Burns explained how in their development of *RVB* he believed *Rooster Teeth* had invented a new creative format in game-based filmmaking. They had stumbled into creating machinima entirely separately from the growing community that had previously formed around *Quake* and other games (Chapters 2 and 3), many of which they had also reviewed during their drunken podcasts. They were, however unaware of its pre-existence and had wanted to refer to the method as *RenderVision* (Rigney, 2012). As others began to reach out and connect them to the *Machinima.com* community, their practice and approach to developing their own community began to form. This was a different approach from that taken by others such as Hancock and Marino, and even today remains an outlier in the world of machinima and game-based filmmaking. Its success is without comparators: *RVB* became the world's longest-running web-based series.

From the outset, their creative philosophy was to "*only make content that we would want to see*" (Burns, in Brouwer, 2016). Using *Halo* and eventually *Halo 2* as the basis for *RVB*, they describe the plot thusly:

> *The Blood Gulch Chronicles* [2003]: In the time between the Covenant invasion of the outer planets (*Halo*) and the subsequent alien invasion of Earth (*Halo 2*), there was a brief period of civil war among the human marines. Places like Sidewinder, Derelict and Chiron TL34 were the sites of fierce battles where red and blue warriors fought for control of mankind's future. *The Blood Gulch Chronicles* tell the story of the men

> stationed in a desolate outpost as they fight for control of the universe's most strategic dry creek bed in the middle of a box canyon.
>
> *Rooster Teeth* (2003)

Their humour and approach to creating machinima resonated with many of their peer group followers. Content was not about the game or character performance extension, which had been implicit within much of the early *Quake* movie machinima. This was a method of using the game content to create an entirely new sci-fi comedy, a contemporary approach to machinima filmmaking where the game is the source of assets that are repurposed. They were not only prolific creators but their sharp and witty commentary was focussed on current affairs and many of the social and political issues unfolding around them, reinforced by group dynamics that had been honed over an extended period of time.

They have since produced hundreds of thematically different shows: by 2017 they averaged 45 shows per year using various aspects of game-related content. Central to their success is the way in which *Rooster Teeth* reflected and accommodated the socio-cultural perspectives of their growing online fan base and also their can-do-any-how attitude towards emerging technologies, particularly those related to content distribution. They were not so much creative producers of machinima films but cultural icons and influencers in their community of followers: rock stars of game-based playfulness and online digital youth culture.

In the next section, we explore how *Rooster Teeth* cornered a market for online fandom and their fan-based community evolved to include a breadth of media including offline events, alongside the development of machinima creative works. We then consider how the community was harnessed by commercial entities such as *Bungie*, *Halo*'s game developer, and others as the audience grew beyond all expectations.

4.3 Rooster Teeth Grows Up

By the time the *RVB* series was first featured (in *Electronic Gaming Magazine*) on 23 May 2003, two months after it launched, *Rooster Teeth* had released six episodes of their *Halo* parody. Each episode built upon the others and whilst this had been considered to be a generally flawed strategy for TV production, because it required the audience to go back to each episode in order to follow the plot, it is a strategy that specifically helped *Rooster Teeth* retain and build its audience online. Indeed, the approach enabled them to take their audience with them as their concepts evolved, many of whom remain with them today.

Content was described as a sci-fi *Rosencrantz and Guildenstern*, where *Halo* characters discuss their lives when they are not fighting in the game, as

Thompson (2005) commented: "*... as it turns out, they're a bunch of neurotics straight out of 'Seinfeld'... none of the soldiers have the vaguest clue why they're fighting.*" Ramsey, who had spent some time in the Army, responded that it reflected real life in the forces – a lot of sitting around, bored for most of it. It was, however, the combination of regular uploads, series-based content and periodic specials (the *#PSAs*) that drew in such large audiences – light entertainment, designed for the game-playing youth. Eventually, download figures exceeded 1M per episode, which was more than most viewing figures for broadcast TV channels in the USA, using an astonishing 180 terabytes of data per month (*Bungie.net*, 2004).

To enable them to effectively deal with the service and hosting costs associated with this success, which in their first month was calculated at around $13,000, they quickly settled on *Bittorrent,* a P2P sharing platform as a method of download. This enabled costs to be spread across their audience members but importantly helped to reinforce community values of using bleeding edge technology and associated online behaviour around the *Rooster Teeth* and *RVB* brands. The method of viewing, of necessity, was largely social, with friends often seeing their first episode of *RVB* at another friend's home.

Rooster Teeth also realized that their use of fora for feedback enabled them to monitor audience reactions which could be used to help them script subsequent episodes. In so doing, they noticed that there appeared to be a kind of reputational currency in being the first person to comment on an episode – and indeed in general on anything online. The first comments were, however, not prosaic at all but simply the words 'first post'. This led Burns to devise a premium subscription model, which they initially called '*Sponsors*' and later became known as '*FIRST*' reflecting the internet meme. *Sponsors* of the *RVB* series gained early access to content for a relatively small fee of $20 a season, which also included a DVD at the end of the current season and access to branded merchandise such as tee-shirts. There were no advertising pre-rolls with content in 2003 as there is now with *YouTube* and many other online propositions. This was therefore a unique approach at the time, given that the internet had become a global model for free content. They used their model to provide additional content such as outtakes and behind the scenes material (later called '*Sponsor Cuts*'). Burns explained the decision to monetize content some time later:

> What we did with our subscription model was, we built it in such a way that if you paid $20 for the season... you would get a DVD, we would burn all the episodes and send them to you. And you also get early access to the episodes as they aired digitally. So we would put it out on Friday, and then the rest of the public would get it on Monday. We call that 'the economy of first'... it was a nail-biting moment when we say, "Hey, here's the deal, we have to be able to afford the bandwidth cost on

> our server to be able to do this, here's what it's going to cost, if you do this, we'll do this." And then there were definitely some people who were like, "I'm out, bye. Money's involved. Nothing on the internet should cost any money," and they were gone.
>
> Burnie Burns (in Kafka, 2017)

In many ways, the approach was a leap of faith into the unknown and almost prescient of the brand's success in engaging audiences, although their ambition was for *RVB* to be serialized from the outset. At the point they settled on their subscription model with commitments for assets to be created beyond the end of the series, the first series was only halfway through being created. In effect, the model was a forerunner to online crowdfunding, common today but again unique in 2003.

In fact, the model had also settled on merchandise sales, taking its lead from another successful online series (flash-based animation *Homestar Runner*), which became over 50% of the funds they drew upon. The approach generated sufficient income to support their continued strategy for almost weekly releases of *RVB* as well as providing them with the core funding for development and release of a second series (Kafka, 2017).

Another key aspect to the design of their proposition, behind the website paywall, was to develop a points-based system that enabled *Sponsors* to 'unlock' website features, effectively gamifying functionality of the site (*Bungie.net*, 2004). This was also a novel approach and one which was successful in locking fans into their brand.

Whilst content encapsulated their passion for games, fun and parody, there was also explicit acknowledgement of the game on which their content was based. Their short *#PSA* 2 (*Armor Cleaning*), released 13 June 2003, explained why they had not that week released a new episode of *RVB* (they had already released 11 episodes at this stage): it was because this same week *Bungie*'s *Halo 2* had pre-launched and it was their attempt to shine a light, comedically, on a new game version, which of course they effectively asset stripped for their own ends.

In the meantime, their approach had also captured the attention of the games developer, for which they produced an introductory short in May for that year's premiere games industry show, E3 (held in Los Angeles). It was clear that *Bungie*'s attitude to the parody was from the outset entirely supportive, albeit legitimized through their fan-owned site, *Halo.Bungie.org*. For example, the fan site was frequently used by *Bungie* employees, who responded to fan questions, and similarly, *Bungie* often used the fan-site in their own promotion and PR activities. Thus, on 5 April 2003, when *Halo.Bungie.org*'s founder posted about the *RVB* trailer and first episode, *Bungie*'s endorsement was implicit:

> If you're offended by cursing, this might not be for you... but I found it laugh-out-loud funny. If bandwidth gets tight, we're happy to mirror these... so let us and the *RedvsBlue* team know, so that we can coordinate new links. They're planning on doing 3 a month, if they can keep up - releases will be on Fridays.
>
> Louis Wu (pseudonym for Claude Errera, *Halo.Bungie.org*, 5 April 2003)

Just a few weeks later, on 30 April 2003, its endorsement became explicit:

> ... today's new announcement: it is Bungie's great honor to welcome the guys behind the *RedvsBlue videos.* Not only will they be around to sign your girlfriend's breast, but DVD-quality versions of their videos will be playing on the big screen! And here's the kicker: they are working on a special video just for the fan-fest. The premise for this 'special E3 video' is so funny that even the folks at *Bungie* can't wait to see it!
>
> Louis Wu (*Halo.Bungie.org*, 30 April 2003)

Ironically, had it not been for Errera's help in the first instance, *RVB* may never have even got off the ground. He comments:

> I crunched/hosted the *RVB* trailer that started it all ;) They'd made a trailer to show off their upcoming series, but it was huge – a few hundred megs. And their existing site, *Drunkgamers.com,* couldn't host it. So I compressed it to a reasonable level – the tools for that weren't widely held at that stage, in 2003 – and hosted it for them. They secured more robust hosting soon after, but at the start, it was me.
>
> Claude Errera (interview 2020).

Whilst *Halo* developer *Bungie*'s backing was never formally confirmed in those early days, Burns subsequently commented they had been contacted within a week of the first episode release (Williamson, 2006). By August 2003, the backing of *Bungie* and *Microsoft* (*Bungie*'s publisher) was acknowledged with a copyright notice on *RVB* episode 16 (*A Slightly Crueler Cruller*), released 15 August 2003. Their support had been orchestrated by Joe Staten (*Halo*'s creative director) and Brian Jarrard (*Halo*'s community director) among others (Burns, 2017). *Bungie*'s overt approach to *Rooster Teeth* had ostensibly been to find out how they might make the creative process easier for the team (Rigney, 2012). This resulted in a character movement modification and a cease-fire function being added to *Halo 2* before its general release later in 2003, making characters without guns easier to position for filmmaking.

Burns confirmed each episode was cleared by *Bungie* before its release (Williamson, 2006) and with the additional backing of *Microsoft* (Rigney, 2012), *Rooster Teeth*'s success was insured if not assured. Of their support, Burns commented in an interview for *Bungie*'s news web page:

> The fact that the designers went out of their way to add the feature back in [referring to a head movement bug they made use of] was very humbling considering how busy I know everyone was – we cannot thank them enough. I know that everyone who makes narrative *Halo* machinima thanks you as well. The feature that allows you to lower your gun has no impact on gameplay, so adding it for machinima filmmakers just shows how much you guys support your fans.
>
> Burnie Burns (*Bungie.net*, 2004)

Importantly for their future as machinima creators, Burns used the connection he had established with *Bungie* to help *Rooster Teeth* overcome the IP issues that many others using the genre had encountered by seeking permission from the publisher (*Microsoft*) and resolving licensing issues (Sinclair, 2004). Such was their success with this approach that *Microsoft* actively supported them, for example, their *RVB PSA #4* (*Hey, Time Out*, released 12 September 2003) discussed *Rooster Teeth*'s upcoming presence at the *Microsoft Professional Development Conference* taking place in October 2003. Thereafter, they produced a series of commercials for the *Xbox* for game store kiosks (Horiuchi, 2005). Indeed, they became a licensed partner of *Bungie* which extended to its subsequent *Microsoft* studio management team, *343 Industries* (Rigney, 2012). They had, however, signed a non-disclosure agreement which prevented the team from talking about how much money they made from their association with *Bungie, Microsoft* and even their own *RVB* DVD sales. The agreement also precluded them from using images of the *Halo* characters in their merchandise, although names and other details were permitted (Goss, 2004). Ultimately, this strategy whilst protecting the IP of the game developer and publisher also helped to position *Rooster Teeth* as an umbrella brand which would in the future give them a launch pad for new series beyond *RVB*.

4.4 Perfect Storm

On 24 July 2003, the *RVB* and *Rooster Teeth* team participated in the *New York Video Festival* alongside Marino and the *ILL Clan*. It was whilst at Lincoln Centre that Burns realized they were not the first to make machinima:

> We had no idea anyone else was doing this stuff. Then Paul [Marino] told me what machinima was and how many people were working on projects. Up until then, we thought we were so original!
>
> Burnie Burns (in Sinclair, 2004).

They had, however, achieved what others in the community had struggled to do: build a sustainable commercial proposition with a mainstream audience on the back of their creative work, capturing the attention of new media commentators. Graham Leggat, former director of communications for Lincoln Center's film society, described *RVB* as absurdist drama that is 'as sophisticated as Samuel Beckett' (in Delaney, 2004), a comment reflected in Dibbell's quote introducing this chapter. (Dibbell is a US author and technology journalist and fellow of Stanford's *Center for Internet and Society.*)

RVB's first film presentation was a complete sellout at Lincoln Center, and three days later they released a special episode (*New York Video Festival: I [heart] BG*) in which they provided a very dry summary of their New York visit, complete with their definition of machinima:

> [Church]:... It's not exactly a vacation, they want us to come there and talk about pre-rendered game engines for animation purposes – a more efficient way of creating large projects by using established routines to animate individual characters – it's called 'machinima' and it's gonna be a more and more popular way of doing animation projects... [Tucker] Wow, that's the most boring thing anyone's ever said to me...!
>
> *RVB: New York Video Festival Special: I [heart] BG*, 24 July 2003

So successful were they with New York audiences that Lincoln Center booked them for the premiere of their second season – another sellout event on 3 January 2004. In the meantime, ever with an eye to the frustration Burns had experienced with attempts to distribute *The Schedule*, they began maximizing their festival exposure. In September they appeared at the *CinemaTexas International Film Festival*'s *Games Without Borders* event and in October attended *AMAS*' second *Machinima Film Festival* at the *Museum of Moving Image* in New York, where *RVB* won its first awards (Best Independent Machinima Film, Best Writing and Best Picture) among a host of nominations in other categories.

Indeed, the *Rooster Teeth* team segued into the machinima community, which offered established structures with *Machinima.com* and *Machinima.org* (and with the latter, *AMAS*) through which fans could access their work, discuss their approach and appreciate a level of interaction with like-minded creators. Thereafter, *RVB* was showcased at every *Machinima Festival* that took place up to and including the 2008 event – in the US (2003, 2004, 2005 and 2008), the UK (2007) and online (2006) and became a major attractor for audiences worldwide.

Thus, in just a few short months from launch, *RVB* had become the most successful and most recognized example of machinima – the DVD release of the first season went Gold in November 2003, within a month of its release.

Such became their notoriety that by February 2004, Canadian rock group *Barenaked Ladies (BNL)* announced they would be showing two never-before-seen shorts of *RVB* in their music tour (Landa, 2013). So began a creative association between *Rooster Teeth* and various celebrities who would perform cameos in their shows over the years. For example, lead singer of *BNL*, Ed Robertson, appeared in *RVB* as the voice for *Capt Flowers* in several episodes (Robertson, 2005) and again as lead in their *Captain Dynamic* live-action series in 2009 (Landa, 2013); actor Elijah Wood (Jackson's *Lord of the Rings* trilogy) voiced the artificial intelligence *Sigma* in eight episodes of *RVB* Season 10 (Rigney, 2012); web comedy duo, *Smosh*, voiced soldiers in the *RVB* Season 11 trailer, among other things; and actors David Tennant (*Dr Who*), Michael Jordan (*Black Panther*), Dakota Fanning (*The Alienist*), Koichi Yamadera (*Ghost in the Shell*) and Masie Williams (*Game of Thrones*) voiced characters in the 2018 *gen:LOCK* series (Jarvey, 2018; Clarke, 2018).

Building on their early success, *Rooster Teeth* had become a viable commercial entity. As early as November 2003, the team discussed how they may scale, anticipating they would be employing a team of twelve within a few months (Leggat, 2004b). This was an obvious step in their development. Far from being an off-the-cuff comedic riff, each episode was scripted, filmed, edited and reworked over the course of a week – in all, an estimated 50+ hours-worth of work when the team were already in full-time positions with their respective employers.

As the series developed, more characters joined the cast of *RVB*, but their team was also added to by virtue of extended *RVB* activities and new series. Their strategy had from the outset been for *Rooster Teeth* to be a vehicle for other activities and by September 2004, a second series was in the offing, resulting from an approach by *Electronic Arts*. This used *Maxis' Sims 2* as the basis of a sitcom, *The Strangerhood*, coinciding with the launch of the game – again, developed in association with the game publisher (Feldman, 2004).

An entirely different type of game to *Halo*, *Sims 2* necessitated a new website, *Strangerhood.com*, but the attraction for the game developer was the humorous approach to storytelling that was the trademark of the *Rooster Teeth* team. Lucy Bradshaw, executive producer of *Sims 2*, explained:

> The movies we've seen from [*Rooster Teeth*], so far, are amazing. We look forward to showing players out there just how much you can do with our game. The possibilities are endless.
>
> Lucy Bradshaw (in Feldman, 2004).

Albeit content needed to be 'tuned' for the younger audience targeted by the developer, Burns relished an opportunity to create a new machinima series that made fun of sitcoms:

> Well, with machinima, you have to work within this limited world. We can't really go in and make *The Sims* characters fight with guns or anything like that. That's something we can do in *Halo*, but in *Halo* you can't put them on a couch or things like that. Some of the concepts we wanted to make fun of [in *RVB*], things we wanted to parody... we just weren't able to. Now, with the *Strangerhood*, we can make fun of sitcoms, make fun of reality shows, poke fun at stuff that we were just not able to in *RVB*... the way machinima works, you never know. The game's not built to make movies, that's what the creative process is... we try to milk all that out of [the limited palette]. Some things you can do and some things you can't, but that's part of the fun challenge.
>
> Burnie Burns (in Feldman, 2004).

The team also found the game aesthetic and mechanics quite different for machinima filmmaking. With *Halo*, their approach had largely been one of the puppeteering avatars but *Sims* was more like working with real actors and their individual personalities, taking their inspiration from the TV series *Survivor*. Matt Hullum commented:

> Working with the characters in the *Sims 2* is a lot like working with real actors. You have to coach them, get them in the right mood in order to get the shot you want. It's basically machinima method acting. If you want a Sim to act mad, just don't let him go to the bathroom for a while. It's not the most sanitary way of motivating your cast, but sometimes art is messy.
>
> Matt Hullum (in PCGamer, 2005)

> It's rewarding when you try for a long time to get a shot and are finally able to achieve it. It's almost like you work with these characters for so long that when you finally get them to do what it is you want them to do... it's like, ah ha, I've brought you around to my way of thinking! It's almost like you're in the game and are working with a personality... We realized that after we wrote the first couple episodes that we needed to start taking it from the perspective that it's more like a reality series... We get a lot of ideas that the game generates for us in a way.
>
> Matt Hullum (in Adams, 2004).

Their approach with both series in many ways was to adopt TV series-making methods but without corrupting (by hacking or modding content) the nature of the game, which reflects the basis of their relationship with the game developers. The number of episodes per season and storytelling methods largely reflect channel rather than internet origins, adopting the term webisodes to describe the result (Steurer, 2005). They also brought in new actors to ensure *The Strangerhood*'s characters were differentiated from *RVB* and in doing so added more staff to the *Rooster Teeth* team (Kathunter, 2005).

Rooster Teeth's efforts generated considerable mainstream media attention: on 7 August 2003, *RVB* was featured on the *British Broadcasting Corporation*'s (*BBC*) online entertainment review (Waters, 2003). This was the first time machinima had been described in UK mainstream media, defined by the reporter as 'digital puppetry' and the merger of two interests: filmmaking and game playing. Building on the association with the emerging machinima community, and the work of others that had also generated attention in the media over the preceding years, *Rooster Teeth* began appearing in articles alongside Marino (*ILL Clan, AMAS*) and Hancock (*Machinima.com, Strange Company*). Over the next year, they are featured in media production, entertainment, film and game journals and magazines both off and online, focussing on their background and creative work, machinima creative method, their relationship with the games developers and the approach to their audience, with articles appearing in the likes of *The Guardian* (Azhar, 2003), *Filmmaker Magazine, New York Magazine* (Leggat, 2004a), *Daily News* (Leggat, 2004b), *Polygon Magazine* (Sinclair, 2004), *Austin Chronicle* newspaper (2004), *Computer Shopper* magazine (2004), *The Wall Street Journal* (2004), *Xbox Nation* (2004), *USA Weekend* (Louderback, 2004), *Honolulu Star* (Jandoc, 2004), *The Toronto Star, Austin American Statesman* (Goss, 2004), *New York Times* (Allen, 2004), *The Salt Lake Tribune* (Horiuchi, 2005), *Rolling Stone Espana* (2005) and *MTV.com* (Totilo, 2005); technology and film TV shows such as *Pulse* a TV show on *G4TV* (2004), *Unscrewed with Martin Sargent* (2004), *The Screen Savers* (18 January 2005), *Fuse TV's d'FUSEd* (7 February 2005) and featured on *iFilm* (April 2005), a pre *YouTube* website for viral videos, which eventually became *MTV*... and all before *RVB* was two years old.

Furthermore, *RVB* feature-length season videos were shown at local cinemas, such as *The Alamo Downtown*, Texas and *IMAX*, San Jose (Goss, 2004). Their DVDs were found, often playing, in game and toy retailers such as *Target, Babbages* and *Toys R Us* (Errera, 2004). Increasingly, their growing body of fan followers demanded personal engagement with the *RVB* creative team. Many had originated on the *Halo.Bungie.org* fan site (Errera, 2020).

4.5 Building a Fandom

Overcoming their apparent initial reticence with general public engagement, the *Rooster Teeth* team launched on to the fan festival scene with new vigour at *South by Southwest* (*SXSW*) in March 2004, an annual multimedia event that takes place in Austin, Texas – at the time with around 900 bands, a film festival, an interactive media festival and various celebrity appearances. As Hullum commented:

> It's one thing to put something on the Web and get some nice emails about it. It's totally different to be surrounded by thousands of people seeing your work on a huge screen.
>
> Matt Hullum (in Goss, 2004)

Personality and joie de vivre made the team a big hit with attendees – they were living their dreams. In April, they were nominated for both a *Webby Award* in the humour category and entered into the *Internet Movie Database* (*IMDB*). Subsequently, their interaction with fans became embedded into the breadth of their activities.

Rooster Teeth's approach to fandom was to feed the flames of public interest. For example, in May 2004 they released an *RVB* special for fans of the industry games exposition, *E3*; in July 2004 they participated in a *Halo*-focussed 24/7 machinima and clan match event, coordinated by *Bungie*; and, in August 2004, part of the team travelled to the *Australian Centre for Moving Image* in Sydney to present *RVB* seasons 1 and 2. Over the next year, they headlined numerous festivals and events, including *Sundance Film Festival*, where they presented a panel on machinima with Marino and others (February 2005), *JACON* (*Japanese Animation Convention*) in Orlando, Florida (April 2005), *AiggeCon*, the oldest and largest student-run science-fiction convention in the US and the largest convention in Texas at the time, organized by Texas A&M University's *Cepheid Variable* student organization (April 2005), the *San Diego Comic Con* (July 2005), the *Penny Arcade Expo, PAX*, Washington (August 2005); the *Canadian National Expo*, Toronto (August 2005), *GameStop*'s annual managers' conference in Dallas (September 2005), *DragonCon*, Atlanta (September 2005), *OniCon*, Houston (October 2005) and *Reactor*, an anime and comic book convention in Lincolnwood (October 2005). In between, the team attended various invitations to speak, sign DVDs and showcase their work, including another sellout event at the Lincoln Centre in New York, where the CNN news channel covered their attendance (August 2005). They began selling their merchandise in selected *Hot Topic* stores around the US in September 2005 and were commissioned to make the US zero-hour launch video for *Xbox360* in November 2005. *Rooster Teeth* had solved the distribution problem both by creating demand for their products and taking the products directly to their audiences, including on- and offline.

And as if this was not enough, alongside their continuing productions of *RVB* (which had already reached 60 episodes) and *Strangerhood* (seven episodes), they had also been commissioned to make two new mini-series. One series comprised six episodes for broadcast TV by *Independent Film Company* (*IFC*), based on the *Strangerhood*, called *Strangerhood Studios*, on which they collaborated with Marino. The second series comprised five episodes called P.A.N.I.C. that pre-promoted *Monolith Productions*' new game *F.E.A.R.*, which was to launch in mid-October 2005.

The *IFC Strangerhood Studios* mini-series was, in fact, the first commercially made machinima. This had come about during 2004 and was the result of networking with the machinima community. It was Marino (*AMAS*) that had been approached by the *IFC* (owned by *AMC Networks* which also owns *BBC America* and *SundanceTV*) to discuss the sponsorship of the 2005 New York *Machinima Film Festival,* alongside organizations such as *Nvidia,* and also the potential for producing a machinima series. Of the discussion, Marino commented:

> *IFC* felt machinima was fertile ground for development - videogame worlds, with a guerilla filmmaking approach. It was very much what *IFC* was about, so it fitted with their brand… There were several rounds of discussions and they chose to partner with *Rooster Teeth* on the production side... with the *SH* production itself, I think it was an informal thing - Matt, Burnie and I discussed working together and it just spun up from there... In the end, while the SH episodes were well-received, I believe the visual aesthetic of the *Sims* proved to be too 'corporate' for their audience (even as the series was a direct commentary on that) and didn't connect well as a result. It may have also been a bit too ahead of its time. Beyond that, *SH* had its following on *RT.com,* which resulted in additional episodes/seasons.
>
> Paul Marino (interview, 2020)

Rooster Teeth became an unstoppable force, no longer bound by the internet, they were buoyed by an exponentially growing fan base which on their website alone reached over 400K by early 2006, then 500K six months later.

Their appearances at events and coverage in the international mainstream press continued to build and their endorsement became an event marketers dream. They had striven not simply to reinforce inside-gamer jokes which meant their fans were both male and female, as well as military personnel including those serving in Iraq and Afghanistan, to whom they sent DVDs and corresponded by email, at one time receiving in return an American flag that been used on a mission aircraft (Konow, 2005). Military staff evidently appreciated the reflection on their daily routines and down time, analogized in *RVB* (Thompson, 2005).

In an article appearing in *Tom's Hardware Guide* (Konow, 2005), *Rooster Teeth* were described as a cult and two of the team became immortalized as a cartoon in the game culture web comic, *Penny Arcade* (Krahulik and Holkins, 2005). They took a further step along the celebrity road when audiences began organizing their own *Rooster Teeth* content-focussed events, the first taking place in Toronto (*RvBTO*) in July 2005 and the second in February 2006 in South Carolina, called *RvBSC.* The *Rooster Teeth* team attended various events, for example in March 2006, Hullum appeared alongside Will Wright, creator of *The Sims,* at an event organized by Georgia Institute of Technology.

In the *Sundance Film Festival*'s official write-up of their appearance, which is the biggest film festival in the US, machinima had been described as organic (rather than commercial) and a crucial application of emergent technologies for indie filmmakers, reflecting comments made by *Intel*'s technology researcher, Joe English, whose view was that "*technology seems to find a way of finding its own applications*" (in Smith, 2005). Thus, *Rooster Teeth* inspired others to creatively express their opinion, as well as create machinima works.

Among the thousands of fan art and machinima pieces they inspired, one notable series to emerge was *Sponsors vs Freeloaders* (*Sevenar Productions,* 2004-2006). This comprised an activist group of *RVB Sponsors* who ran a forum thread on the *RVB* website and decided to make machinima about their experiences. Their aim was to both provide a means to connect *Sponsors* as well as deal with complaints by those who refused to pay for early access to *RVB* episodes despite apparently being able to afford to do so. *Sevenar*'s machinima series featured *Sponsors* as well as freeloaders (what they referred to as whiners and moaners). The plot was generally thin and series releases ad hoc, focussing on poking fun, but it nonetheless ran for two years and generated over 100 pages of forum discussion and tens of thousands of content views (initially on the *RVB* website and later on their own website, *SponsorsvsFreeloaders.com*). In fact, the idea for *Sponsors vs Freeloaders* had emanated from the forum, as Reece Watkins, *Sevenar*'s co-founder, commented:

> When I joined the *RVB* forums, I found a group that had been talking about doing a series to pay homage to *RVB's* creators, but there was no real organization behind it. Every fan wanted to be a part of *RVB,* but the creators couldn't let everyone have a part for obvious reasons. *SvF* was a way for everyone to be part of at least something related to the show, in theory. Nobody had a script, a production plan, or even just a vague idea of what *SvF* should be... once the forum fans saw we had actually managed to DO something instead of just talk about it, interest grew pretty quickly... That we managed to do it all before the creation of *YouTube* still amazes me. We were even recognized at the 2005 Machinima Awards, even though we weren't nominated for anything... it would have been nice to make some money, but I don't think I could have bought the experience itself for anything.
>
> Reece Watkins (interview, 2020)

The series evolved in direct response to arguments between fans. Laird MacLean, who had also created his own *Halo* films was a co-producer with Watkins, highlighted the passion in the community and their commitment to it, both in terms of rewards and also costs:

> … a bunch of people were complaining about having to pay for content on the internet. I know it's a crazy reason to start a parody web series over but that's the case. We figured 'if these guys can do it, why can't we?' so a group of us on the old *RVB V0.5* forums got together and learned the hard way how to create content and machinima. None of us had any experience in voice acting, or sound design, video editing, and many other things. It was all on the fly but we did it for the love of the show *Rooster Teeth* created… the love of having our own show that had grown in a modicum of popularity outside just the *Rooster Teeth* community. I mean somehow we got nominated for a *Machinima Arts and Sciences* award (I even won one myself a few years after *SVF* ended, that's crazy)… we were a bunch of friends goofing around on the internet and it entertained people and that was enough for a while. We (or at least I) lost money on [the *SVF*] project 100%. We had the actor George Lowe as our voice for Space Ghost; that cost a lot, our web servers were all paid for by us, our domain names, software, and licenses. The benefits for me eventually were the network I built from going to conventions, participating in this machinima series, the friends I made, and eventually my career in the industry, which eventually paid.
>
> Laird MacLean (interview, 2020)

Furthermore, the strength of the community also extended into other areas of activity, such as participating and coordinating community-led events to support the community. For example, the *RVBCanWest* (Vancouver) convention had begun in 2006, founded by Laird MacLean, as an event centred on *Rooster Teeth*'s local community but this inspired many others from different online communities to participate, leading to direct involvement with *Bungie Studios, 343 Industries, Xbox,* and others, as well as *Rooster Teeth.*

Ultimately, fan-coordinated events became charity fund raising in focus, donating proceeds from ticket sales to organizations such as *Child's Play,* the game industry charity that had been set up originally by *Penny Arcade,* in the US and *Special Effects* in the UK. This focus as an outcome has also been an interesting strategy, helping to legitimize the community and enhance its general public persona:

> The sentiment comes from a counter to the public's perception of gamers because the stereotype of the twatty nerd down in a basement playing video games, with no friends and all that – no, we're a very social bunch of people and playing video games doesn't rot our brain, it doesn't make us aggressive, it's not all these negative things that people perceive it to be, so it was counter to that image... It became the rallying cry that the community is doing something for a good cause, something we all have a connection to, and gives everyone a purpose.
>
> Jason Boomer (interview, 2020)

Their collective effort had been endorsed by *Rooster Teeth*, where other riffs on *RVB* content had apparently been killed off quickly – this was no doubt because, in true *RVB* style, the series effectively shamed those who did not contribute directly (or indirectly) to financially supporting their creative effort.

This form of fan activism had not previously been observed on the internet or in machinima communities. Their role is another major factor which contributed to the success of *Rooster Teeth*'s emergent business model which extended beyond machinima, knitting together creative content, IP owner brand endorsement, active audience engagement and generally embracing the celebrity status that was bestowed upon them.

4.6 Distribution disruption

A further contributing factor to *Rooster Teeth*'s success is their use of emerging distribution channels. Already known as advocates of new technologies associated with games and machinima filmmaking, their use of emerging technologies included those incorporated into their website, some of which sat behind their paywall. For example, their use of *Adobe Flash* enabled viewing content on the web possible, rather than downloading content (Shivakumar, 2016). Their attitude towards and use of social media platforms was, however, quite different. They were ambivalent towards the use of *YouTube* as a distribution channel at first. This was because they saw it as a direct competitor to their own channels which it clearly was, as outlined in our previous chapter, with considerable other machinima creators using it as a means to distribute and reach audiences since its launch in 2005. Instead, *Rooster Teeth* preferred to drive their audience interactions to their own production websites (Johnson, 2014a). Over time however, this approach changed, not least because *YouTube* became its own market-derived force, ultimately pushed by the weight of *Google* (from September 2006). Burns stated:

> … we've had to stay adaptive. I think the biggest place we've had to adapt, we've always believed we have to have our own corner on the web, that we don't try to build our own company on *Facebook*, or on *MySpace* back in the day or even on *Twitter* or *Snapchat*. We try to have *RoosterTeeth.com* be our destination. That being said, over time we've had to embrace things like *YouTube*, because *YouTube* is undeniable in that it grew to the point where it was… *YouTube* became a verb that meant to watch video online… and some of our other shows with *YouTube* specifically, it's helped take us to the next level.
>
> Burnie Burns (in Brouwer, 2016).

What is interesting is that *Rooster Teeth* rejected the methods of monetizing content that many had taken on *YouTube* with pre-roll advertisements, even after they began using the site. Burns had witnessed the dissatisfaction that had begun to rumble around the machinima community as *Machinima Inc.* influenced distribution methods and decided to do their own thing. In his view, *Machinima Inc.* had confused the market although *Rooster Teeth* was committed to using machinima as a production method (Kafka, 2017). Burns also commented that he had witnessed the disruption of new technologies in changing the ways audiences had interacted with content in both music and print (media) industries. The same impact was imminently anticipated in the video sector, and in order to capitalize on the move from TV, Burns wanted to be sure their organization was ready. For a short period of time, they collaborated with *Machinima Inc.* in an advertising partnership. Burns explains:

> … we actually ended up partnering with [*Machinima Inc.*] for ad sales, because the relationship was such that we had so much brand confusion, and it didn't seem to be going away, and it was better to try and figure out a way to have that benefit us in some way. So we had some ad partnerships with *Machinima* for a short period of time… initially our evaluation of all these platforms was to see them as competitors … [but] to their credit they were enormously progressive for creating [the network channel partner] model. But for a long period of time they didn't have it… We didn't get on *YouTube* until 2008 or 2009, and we ended up having to play catch-up. But it just reached a point as a brand where *YouTube*, you had to be part of the conversation. If you wanted to be in online video… However, for a really, really long period of time, and I don't know that we're beyond it yet, people who were on *YouTube* didn't leave *YouTube*. They didn't click away to go to anything else.
>
> Burnie Burns (in Kafka, 2017)

The online presence and momentum *Rooster Teeth* had achieved with its audiences as a machinima production studio, however, set them apart from all other machinima creators at the time. Burns' comment in *The Sydney Morning Herald* reflected his view:

> We get a lot of email from young filmmakers who have really been turned on by the possibilities of machinima. Machinima gives them the opportunity to hone their craft at an early stage… More artists are going to have to break away from making too many in-jokes. Not everyone plays video games!
>
> Burnie Burns (in Hill, 2006)

Their diverse approach to commercializing their proposition as well as their stance as a creative media studio attracted not only the attention of games developers and publishers but also commentators on the disruptive potential of new media and platforms (Johnson, 2014b) and potential investors. For example, *Electronic Art*'s *Madden NFL 2007* game reported record sales of more than $100M in its first week of release in no small part due to *Rooster Teeth*'s machinima broadcast commercials (Forbes, 2006). Furthermore, it was *Rooster Teeth*'s *RVB* series that laid the groundwork for the future of web streaming, which was first claimed by *YouTube* and subsequently others such as *Twitch* and *Steam*. At the 2006 *SXSW* festival (March), Burns presented a keynote speech in which he discussed the potential applications of machinima and by June, *Computer Gaming World magazine* asked the pointed question of whether amateur creators should quit their day jobs (Gladstone, 2006). The *Rooster Teeth* team already had.

Over the following years, the team produced new machinima works, including seventeen seasons of *RVB* with a series of different story arcs. Its *Blood Gulch Chronicles* series ended after its fifth season with episode 100, released with three different versions on 28 June 2007 (all answering the question *Why were we here?!*). Other machinima productions included the 2006 *1-800-Magic*, a four-episode series using the *Shadowrun* game (*FASA Studio*), the 2008 *Supreme Surrender*, made in *Supreme Commander* (by *Gas Powered Games*), and 2008 *Stroyent*, a four-episode *Quake Wars* series. They also branched away from machinima and dabbled with 2D in 2006 with a web comic series that satirized the daily lives of the *Rooster Teeth* production team. The web comic ran until 20 August 2011. The team then notably moved to computer-generated animation in season ten of *RVB* (2009). This was ostensibly because the team, under the guidance of self-taught animation expert Monty Oum, felt a need for greater flexibility in production approaches. This new approach was first presented at *PAX East* in August 2010. Thereafter, its CG animation series *RWBY*, also produced by Monty Oum, was described as a machinima-like production but was not actually based within or upon a specific game. Other CG animated productions included the 2010 *Drunk Tank Animated Adventures* (which in 2011 became *Rooster Teeth Animated Adventures*). This was a series that depicted stories first told on their *Podcast* (which had begun in December 2008). In 2016 they released *CampCamp* and in 2017 they released *gen:LOCK*. All these variously built upon their unique approach to observational humour with animated game-inspired characters.

Similarly, extrapolating their expertise in live performance for machinima creation that had often been showcased at events, *Rooster Teeth* developed a series of game player/viewer network channels. Their *Achievement Hunter* channel, formed in 2008, evolved from the use of an achievement mechanic found in *Microsoft*'s *Xbox360*, primarily by Ramsey. The channel began showcasing game play videos that illustrated how game achievements and *Easter Eggs* had been reached (*Easter Egg* is a term used to describe hidden objects, features, messages or images in a game). In 2012, the channel spawned a *Let's Play* sub-series which focussed on *Minecraft* (see Figure 4.1) and *Grand Theft Auto* games, the former of which had rapidly become the internet's hottest game-based property (Johnson, 2014c). This channel now includes numerous shows, such as *Game Night* which was first live-streamed in 2014. These game performance-based channels and shows have since become the staple of *Rooster Teeth*'s production and screening proposition, each channel with millions of viewers and tens of thousands of subscribers – it had already reached its 1Bth content view by April 2012 (Rigney, 2012).

Figure 4.1: *Rooster Teeth Achievement Hunter* let's play *Minecraft* team.

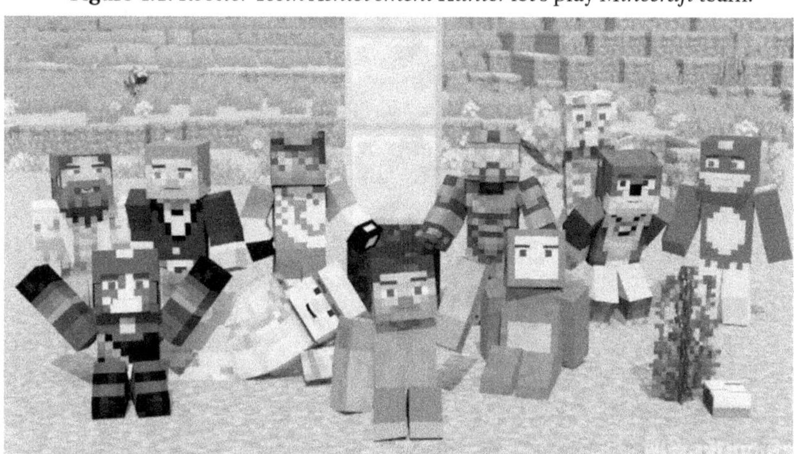

Back (l-r) Jeremy Dooley, Ryan Haywood, Jack Patillo, Geoff Ramsey, Gavin Free, Michael Jones, Lindsay Jones and front (l-r) Matt Bragg, Trevor Collins, Alfredo Diaz, Fiona Nova. Image used with permission, source: Okay Donuts 2020 ©

Their evolution from live performance also extended into game-inspired live-action entertainment that began with *Captain Dynamic* in February 2009, promoting the online game *City of Heroes* (*Cryptic Studios*) which starred *Barenaked Ladies*' Robertson. Following its success, *Rooster Teeth* produced its *Shorts* series (2010), a sketch comedy based on the web comic jaunts of the production teams' office life and in which later episodes they collaborated with the production team behind *Mega64*, a comedic video game centred TV series (2003-4). In 2013 they also produced a *Vine*-based series of *Shorts* (6 seconds long short videos). In 2010 they released *Immersion*, a live-action series that tested key concepts presented in video games, such as heckling (online harassment often seen in multi-player online games), driving from a third-person perspective and safe room doors such as seen in *Left 4 Dead*, with various members of the growing *Rooster Teeth* team becoming 'test subjects' (Sorrel, 2010). Subsequent series have explored various aspects of gameplay-related content from pure-play to story-based action in live settings, often displaying their brand of humour in the process, including *Million Dollars, But...* (2015), a scenario-based re-enactment series, *Day 5* (2016), a post-apocalypse style short series, a game show *On the Spot* (2015) and a feature-length sci-fi action comedy film, *Lazer Team* (2016).

Many of their creative efforts directly involved the *Rooster Teeth* fan base, with trailers and teasers often being showcased at events they attended and subsequently their annual exposition, the *RTX* convention which was first held in Austin, Texas, on 27 May 2011. This was not only a means through which to gauge audience reaction but also an opportunity to include the audience as participants in the creative processes *Rooster Teeth* employed. For example, their live-action June 2011 episode of *Immersion* included 400 fans filmed at their first *RTX* (over 500 had attended the event) and *Day 5* included 1,800 fans as extras who had attended the 2012 event. This homage to fans was undoubtedly instrumental in the success of the 2014 crowdfunding campaign for their proposed live-action comedy film *Lazer Team* and its board game version of *Million Dollars, But...* in 2016. For *Lazer Team* it raised $2.5M, having reached its original target of $650K in just eleven hours. The film received an award as the most crowdfunded film campaign on the *Indiegogo* platform (Busch, 2014), with a number of highest donors receiving credits as executive and co-producers as a benefit. In total 37,497 fans funded the film; the final push had taken place at the 2014 *RTX* event, where over 32,000 fans attended (Busch, 2014). Furthermore, on the film's release in January 2016, it achieved over $1M in box office ticket pre-sales (Hurst, 2016a). For the *Million Dollar, But...* game, *Rooster Teeth* raised over $1.3M from 30,546 funders, with an initial target of $10,000 having been reached within just five minutes of the crowdfunding campaign's release on *Kickstarter* (Hurst, 2016b and 2016c).

Unsurprisingly, community groups have now spawned in many US cities as well as countries around the world but only two have been formally recognized with local representation and presence. The first was in Australia, emanating from its '*Roo Teeth*' community which grew to be the biggest fan community outside the official website. The presence was managed by partner *Hanabee Entertainment*, a local firm which coordinated *RTOZ* events (the first was in 2011) and community activities, then sold and distributed merchandise as well as the *RTX Sydney* convention (first held in January 2016). *Hanabee* was headed Eric Cherry, who then also took on a role as head of global business development for Rooster Teeth. Already present with its *RTX London* convention (launched in 2017 with 15,000 fans in attendance), the second base for *Rooster Teeth* was subsequently planned for opening in the UK in 2020, headed by Cherry, through which its aim was to develop regional programming, licensing, consumer products and live events (Clarke, 2018; Sam, 2019). For various unreported reasons, however, the UK plans were subsequently dropped.

4.7 Boom

What is also notable in their journey is the way in which *Rooster Teeth* recruited staff, many of whom had demonstrated their chops originally as part of the community of followers and fans, often beginning their association as part of the *RVB* cast. Each member of the growing team brought new skills, enabling the portfolio of projects to expand significantly as they were inculcated with the *Rooster Teeth* family values.

Monty Oum (recruited in August 2009) had, for example, created a *Halo* pre-rendered film (*Haloid*) that attracted attention in 2007. Released on the *GameTrailers* website, the film received over 4M views and became the most-watched user-generated film on the site. It was during the production of his subsequent series, *Dead Fantasy* (which combined two different games), that he first met Burns whilst on a panel at the *San Diego Comic Convention* in 2009. Oum's specific contribution was extensive and detailed character design as well as animating complex combat sequences, the like of which had not previously been included in any *RVB* series. It is also his skillset that formed the basis of the CG animated *RWBY* series.

Jack Pattillo (recruited in December 2009) worked on live-action projects, including the *Achievement Hunter* channel as its co-founder (originally as a contractor) and became head of *Rooster Teeth*'s charitable arm. Chris Demarais (recruited in November 2010) was a writer for the *RT Shorts* and other live-action series, having begun as a bit part freelancer in *RVB* Season 9. Gray Haddock (recruited in August 2011) was a digital compositor on *RVB* and *RWBY* having joined *Rooster Teeth* also with acting and anime credits. He subsequently wrote and directed the 2018 series of *gen:LOCK* and then became head of the *RT Animation* department.

Between mid-2007 and December 2011, *Rooster Teeth* staff reached 20 permanent members from its original core of six and over the next three years (to the end of 2014), *Rooster Teeth Productions* released twelve new series, comprising machinima, CG, 2D, comics, board games, music video and live-action content.

In February 2013 they made their first acquisition with *The Slow Mo Guys*, a popular web series that used high-speed cameras to record pranks and stunts, often with a pseudo-scientific aesthetic. The series had been co-founded in 2008 based on an ambitious plan by one of its directors to acquire a work permit for the US by creating a viral series in order to work on *RVB* Season 7. The series was released on *Rooster Teeth*'s website as well as continuing to run on its own *YouTube* channel from 2013.

In November 2014, *Rooster Teeth* along with another studio, *ScrewAttack*, was acquired by *Fullscreen*, which itself had recently been majority bought by *Otter*

Media (a joint venture between *Chernin Group* and *AT&T*), as the media sector undertook a period of consolidation (Cheredar, 2014). For example, at a similar time, *Disney* acquired *MakerStudios, Rooster Teeth* and *Machinima Inc.*'s competitor; *Dreamworks* acquired *AwesomenessTV* (Fixmer, 2014); *Amazon* bought streaming service *Twitch* for $1B; *Microsoft* bought the *Minecraft* game and its developer, *Mojang*, for a reported $2.5B (Booton, 2014; Yarrow, 2014) and *Machinima Inc.* was in the midst of two rounds of investment headed by *Warner Bros.* (see Chapter 3). At this point, *Rooster Teeth* had reached 30 staff members (Eng, 2019). In November 2015 this was added to as *ScrewAttack* became its subsidiary and others joined the team working on new series-based content and formats, reaching 220 by July 2016 (Shivakumar, 2016), several of whom were contractors.

In sum, *Rooster Teeth*'s success was a wheel of fortune, where everything they touched boomed – see Figure 4.2.

Figure 4.2: *Rooster Teeth*'s journey.

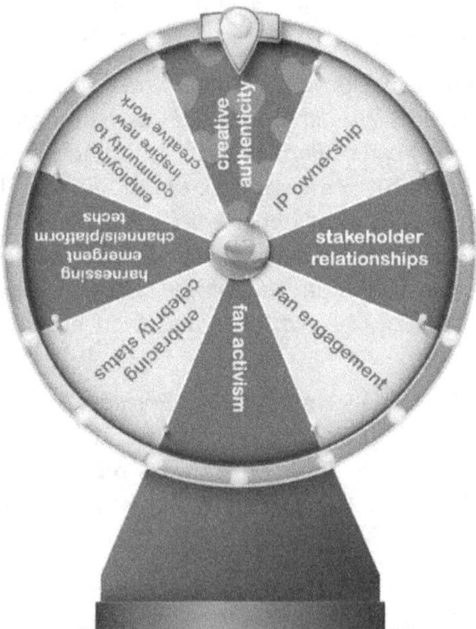

A wheel of fortune.
Source: authors.

4.8 Feeling the Corporate Burn

The amount paid by *Fullscreen* for *Rooster Teeth* was not made public, but its strategy as a multi-channel network was clear. At the time, it had around 70,000 creators alongside its distribution service which had 600M subscribers and 5B monthly video views (Business Wire, 2015). In addition to web series, Michael Goldfine, *Fullscreen*'s chief content officer commented in reference to *Rooster Teeth*'s feature-length film, *Lazer Team,* and two other similar projects in their media stable:

> [These projects] signify our commitment to produce movies at the highest quality bar. These movies allow talent who typically work in six-second or three-minute formats to tell more immersive stories, and build stronger relationships with their communities.
>
> Michael Goldfine (in Abbruzzese, 2015)

This reflected the race to the top of the media streaming heap being played out across the sector, as also discussed in the previous chapter. Specifically, it reflected *Fullscreen*'s move to a pay-to-view subscription-based streaming model (minus advertising) on *YouTube* as well as big-screen theatre releases as a means to capitalize on the strength of audience engagement that *Rooster Teeth* had achieved with the brand (Fingus, 2015). Indeed, when *YouTube Red* launched on 10 February 2016, *Lazer Team* featured alongside the internet's all-time highest viewed content producer, Felix Arvid Ulf Kjellberg's (known as *PewDiePie*) latest show, *Scare PewDiePie* (*Skybound Entertainment/MakerStudios*), who at the time had over 41M subscribers (Lardinois, 2016).

Such *YouTube* streamers, or *YouTubers* as they became known, were by now more popular with audiences than mainstream Hollywood celebrities. As *YouTube*'s global head of creative insights Vanessa Pappas commented:

> The biggest changes [on *YouTube*] are the massive growth in terms of numbers in our creator community. And with that, the breadth and depth of content – there's literally an audience for everything… This isn't just vloggers in their bedroom. Our creators are running full-fledged production companies and businesses where they're franchising into books, TV shows, movies and products [for example, *Rooster Teeth*]. And what's great to see is the audience has really come along for the ride… the authenticity of the content is still one of the main distinguishing factors on why *YouTube* creators resonate so deeply with audiences. That, and the fact that consistency of programming works... Ultimately we have witnessed over the last five years that the distance that mainstream media manufactured between a celebrity and fan has all but eroded online, community and the fostering of a direct connection is now everything.
>
> Vanessa Pappas (in Walk, 2016)

To compete in the channel stakes race, *Rooster Teeth* acquired and created more game inspired subsidiaries (e.g., *Funhaus* and *Cow Chop*) and began a partnering strategy that formalized relationships with *The Creatures* and *Kinda Funny* producers in Spring 2016 and *Sugar Pine 7* in May 2017, building content for its growing *Achievement Hunter*-based *Let's Play* channels. This focus has since grown further with new production teams joining, as well as a few departures.

By 2016 they were producing around 100 hours of content per month (Spangler, 2016a) and their business model included subscriptions, advertising, merchandising, content licensing and royalties, and live events, each roughly generating similar levels of income (Patel, 2016). They had 25M subscribers to their *YouTube* channels, 3M monthly visitors to their *RoosterTeeth.com* website and 1.8M registered community members (Spangler, 2016a).

Whilst central to their strategy from the outset, their subscription model now needed a revamp: they developed a tiered approach. Its core membership scheme had 135,000 members paying $5 per month for advert-free and exclusive content as well as early releases of popular series, merchandise offers and access to pre-sales tickets for events, contests and giveaways. This strategy had always been seen as insurance against the varying advertising and merchandise rates that can undermine a revenue model which is solely reliant on such components (Patel, 2016). Burns commented:

> You can't tell people how to [financially] support you. You make as many opportunities to support as possible. Give them tiers, give them the option to watch ads, give them the ability to buy a tee-shirt. If you are loyal to your audience, and give them ways to support you, they'll be loyal to you.
>
> Burnie Burns (in McAlone, 2017)

Thus, *Rooster Teeth* extrapolated the strategy to target its most passionate audience, taking their advocacy to the next levels of support for the business. *Rooster Teeth* announced a name change of the scheme from *Sponsors* to *FIRST* on 1 July 2016 at their sixth annual *RTX* convention in Austin at which more than 60,000 fans attended (Shivakumar, 2016). At the event, *Rooster Teeth* also launched its new premium tier of membership: *Double Gold* members who would pay $35 per month and receive a subscription box of merchandise.

To reflect the significant price differential of the new tier, *Rooster Teeth* also advised that new forms of content and formats which would provide for appropriate levels of perceived value would be released. This had potential also for attracting new top tier subscribers beyond its core fan base. It launched apps for game consoles, set-top boxes and mobile devices – stating *Rooster*

Teeth audiences preferred to watch streamed long-form content from the couch rather than the gaming chair (Spangler, 2016b).

In late July 2016, *Rooster Teeth* announced the addition of three new team members who would focus on the expanded subscription model: Luis Medina joined as co-manager of the *Let's Play* family, having previously been vice president of partnerships at *Disney*'s *Maker Studios*; Evan Bregman joined as director of programming, coming from *Portal A* studio as its head of original content; and Ryan Hall took on the role of director of development, having previously been in a similar role at *Roenberg Entertainment* where he worked alongside the directing teams for *Netflix*'s *Marco Polo* and *Disney*'s *Pirates of the Caribbean 5* film projects (Spangler, 2016c). These were the first of a number of appointments over the next couple of years that would move *Rooster Teeth* towards a corporate approach to digital media business management.

In the meantime, *Fullscreen*, its owner, was busy attempting to transfer the knowledge *Rooster Teeth* had on developing that intimate connection with its audiences for which it has become renowned, back into the *Fullscreen* platform-based proposition. Alan Beard, *Fullscreen*'s chief marketing officer, commented:

> I've spent a lot of time thinking about how we create fandoms [for example Rooster Teeth]. This audience is changing fast. The technology changes fast. So in some ways we're trying to take the best practices of traditional media companies and layer on top of that behavioral data and new technology approaches to having a different relationship, so that *Fullscreen* develops fandoms and not just fans.
>
> Alan Beard (in Jarvey, 2016)

By March 2017, *Rooster Teeth*'s subscriber base on *YouTube* had reached 35M subscribers and 5M unique monthly views to their 40+ channels (McAlone, 2017a) and a streaming app with 200,000 paying members (Patel, 2017).

With a view to leveraging its fan base further, *Rooster Teeth* launched a game publishing division, bringing in experienced game and entertainment executive, Michael Hadwin to lead the initiative (Takahashi, 2017). Six months later, it added former *Gearbox Software* vice president of business development and licensing David Eddings as division head. Their aim being to bridge the gap between indie developers and the avid community of gamer fans. Eddings also brought to *Rooster Teeth* considerable experience from his time at *Gathering of Developers*, whose ethos had been to empower indie game developers (McAlone, 2017b). He commented:

> *Rooster Teeth* has been killing it. They've had amazing growth, and they're like the *Desilu Productions* of internet content. *Desilu* created *I*

> *Love Lucy* and *Green Acres* and *Beverly Hillbillies* and also *Star Trek.* Every new medium has to have a breakout studio with the content that changes that medium. They just need somebody to publish games... the access to that network is like having a cheat code for game publishing.
>
> David Eddings (in Takahashi, 2017)

Whilst Burns emphasized *Rooster Teeth*'s creative business focus on fans rather than personalities was a means to build and sustain fandoms, *Fullscreen*'s CEO and founder, George Strompolos, was at pains to emphasize that its business model extended beyond being a multi-channel network (MCN). This had been the premise on which *Machinima Inc.* had originally developed but ultimately failed to deliver – whereby its model of acquiring content was ultimately flawed and investment strategy in new content, unsustainable. As Strompolos stated:

> The MCN is not our entire business. It's how we identify, develop, grow, partner with and monetize creative talent. How we apply that is where it gets interesting.
>
> George Strompolos (in Patel, 2017)

This comparison of business models is useful in understanding how online media organizations have evolved – on the one hand, content is king, and the growing professionalization with which it is made is a distinct trajectory for studios such as *Rooster Teeth.* On the other, the platforms and distribution channels must facilitate the formation of fandoms – most platforms are simply channels. What *Rooster Teeth* has achieved is a fandom built around game play and machinima creative values which has become channel-agnostic and is simultaneously everywhere for everyone. This is further evidenced in its 2017 launch of a podcast network which attempts to monetize its model in a new way by providing a space for creatives and advertisers to connect, called *The Roost,* and its 2018 launch of a $2.5M development fund for creators (Patel, 2018). Of the podcast, another of the original *Rooster Teeth* team, Sorola, commented:

> If we had stuck with the dominant platform at the time, we would have invested everything in our *Myspace* page. Platforms come and go. The big thing of the moment may not be the big thing down the road. Some days you have to decide if you're going to wear your creator hat or your business person hat – *Rooster Teeth,* or another business, can jump in and help alleviate that pressure for creators... [We can connect advertisers with] 30 to 50 really excellent shows with established audiences.
>
> Gus Sorola (in Main, 2017)

On the demise of *Machinima Inc.*, which had been blamed on a lack of investment in original content and a focus on often time-delimited personality-based channels (see Chapter 3), media organizations have also attempted to drop the MCN business model in favour of *Rooster Teeth*'s pioneering subscription-based model (Patel, 2017). *Rooster Teeth* has, however, continued to push boundaries, creatively summarized by the team in a documentary celebrating its 15 years history and creative ethos: *Why We're Here* (*Roosterteeth.com*), released on 20 April 2018 to its *FIRST* subscribers.

Earlier in the year, Ezra Cooperstein, the president of *Fullscreen* (and previously the founder and CEO of *MakerStudios* which he left in 2011) became *Rooster Teeth*'s president, at which point it reported 45M subscribers and 250,000 paying members (Baumgarten, 2018). Around them, *Fullscreen*'s ownership was changing along with consolidation in the media industry sector. In August 2018, *Otter Media*'s owner, *AT&T*, bought out the *Chenin Group* stake of the business for a reputed $1B (Spangler, 2018). This was then merged with its *WarnerMedia* division, which in turn owned *Machinima Inc.* – the division had been created when *AT&T* completed its acquisition of *Time Warner* earlier in the year (June).

In its stable at the time, *Otter Media* had two main strands of business activity: *Fullscreen*, which owned *Rooster Teeth* and a couple of other content creators, and *Ellation* which owned anime streamer *Crunchyroll* and its platform subscription service called *Vrv*. The merger reflected *AT&T*'s desire to focus on feeding the passion of online audiences by augmenting their portfolio of digital content and building on their engagement strategies for audience entertainment globally (Ha, 2018). Notably, it did this by taking *Rooster Teeth*'s anime series, *RWBY*, into the lucrative Japanese market, the first Western-made anime to do so, and then in 2019 teaming with *Warner*'s *DC Comics* on both its *RWBY* and *gen:LOCK* series (McMillan, 2019).

Thereafter, *Otter Media* sought to reorganize its portfolio in order to consolidate its advertising and partnering business activities, in the process laying off 10% of its staff ie., around 200 people (Chmielewski, 2018). *Rooster Teeth, Crunchyroll* and *Vrv* were repositioned under its *Ellation* division focussing on content creation and distribution ('direct to consumer'), while *Machinima Inc.* was subsumed by the *Fullscreen* division of the business, which would focus on creator services. The following January (2019), *Machinima Inc.* removed all its content from *YouTube* with some streamers being transferred to *Fullscreen* (Makedonski, 2019) and then it ceased altogether on 1 February. In a *Twitch* clip, one of its former content producers, who made the jump to join *Rooster Teeth* under the *Ellation* umbrella as part of the reorganization with his long-running *Inside Gaming* series, commented:

> *[Machinima Inc.]* at this point, cannot verify the copyrights to all videos in *Machinima*'s network, and there are a ton of videos. It'd cost a lot of money to do it, and this is on videos that aren't getting any views. So, they cut it loose. That's that. It's a business. That's how it goes, man.
>
> Lawrence Sonntag (in Knoop, 2019)

Otter Media's CEO, Tony Goncalves, described the absorption of *Machinima Inc.*'s key productions as reinforcement of *Rooster Teeth*'s appeal to its gaming fans (Spangler, 2019a), expanding its team to around 450 by summer 2019 (Shanley, 2019).

Its rapid growth is evident but such a comment also hints at potential challenges in the management of such prolific yet diverse creative forces. Difficulties emerged in June 2019 when anonymous posts were made about the treatment of *Rooster Teeth* employees summarized in an article on *Popdust.com*'s site (Kahan, 2019) which completely contradicted its long-portrayed values – as one fan stated on the *Reddit* platform community thread: *'People have got to stop thinking it's still the 6 dudes in a spare bedroom'* (WillTroll, 2019). With the senior team depicted as an 'extreme bro/friends club', a crunch culture is described, typified in the game industry sector where creators' passion for their work is exploited by managers with unrealistic production deadlines, zero overtime pay, oppressive work conditions and unkept promises for improvement.

4.9 Fallout

The fallout from the problems rumbled across multiple fora including its own website culminating in Hullum, as CEO of *Rooster Teeth*, commenting on changes that were being made to address the issues highlighted. Haddock was moved from his position as head of animation to a creative role (and shortly after resigned). The head of *Ellation*, Margaret Dean, was appointed as a consultant to advise on developing *Rooster Teeth*'s workflow, pipeline and production structure as well as bringing in a new head (Aguilar, 2019).

By September 2019, *Rooster Teeth*'s plight had deepened and Hullum announced redundancies of 50 of its team, around 13% of the staff (Blake, 2019) – the biggest staff cuts it had made in its sixteen years history. Two weeks later, it was announced that the original driving team behind *Rooster Teeth* would be stepping away from their management roles into creative positions. Burns moved from chief creative officer into an executive producer role focussing on new projects, Hullum moved from CEO into a chief content officer position whilst Ramsey took over Burn's previous executive creative director role, among other senior manager moves.

At the same time, a new CEO for *Rooster Teeth* was announced: Jordan Levin. Levin had been one of the formative voices in the early days of the *WB Television*

Network (now *CW*) which developed *Buffy the Vampire Slayer* and *Dawson's Creek* for teen audiences, then as president of programming becoming the youngest CEO in broadcast television history. He had also been the *NFL*'s first chief content officer, general manager of *Xbox Entertainment* and CEO of *AwesomenessTV*.

Of the changes announced, Burns and Hullum commented briefly on their journey and their passion for a creative future focus:

> After spending time with my newly-expanded family and reflecting on the path of my career, I have decided to step down as the Chief Creative Officer of *Rooster Teeth* and the day-to-day productions of the company. Tomorrow, I transition into a producer role in the newly formed *Rooster Teeth Studios* division, reporting to Ryan Hall. Building *Rooster Teeth* from a small start-up in a spare bedroom to the media empire it is today has been the proudest accomplishment of my career. We have truly built a company unlike any other and I want to thank every person who has helped make that journey possible. Now, I plan to focus on the passionate reason I began the company all those years ago — to work on my own projects telling captivating stories to the world.
>
> Burnie Burns (*Roosterteeth.com*, 2019)

> Leading *Rooster Teeth* has been one of the greatest privileges of my life. Despite an ever-changing industry and an ongoing series of acquisitions and integrations, we managed to grow the company to more than ten times the size it was when I began as CEO just over 7 years ago. It's been an incredible ride, and now I'm beyond excited to be returning to the creative work that inspired me to want to co-found Rooster Teeth in the first place.
>
> Matt Hullum (in Whittaker, 2019)

Ramsey's comments reflected on the impact of the changes on fans and his renewed focus on creators:

> This is not me taking a step back from *Rooster Teeth*, if anything, it's the opposite. I'll basically be doing for the rest of the company what I've been doing for gaming content, and I couldn't be more excited... *Rooster Teeth* has been an all-consuming part of my life since the day Burnie, Gus and I filmed episode one of *Red Vs Blue*. That won't change. Will this affect my on-screen time? Invariably. [I'll be] spending most of my energy doing the absolute best I can for *RT* and our future as a company, in the best way I know how. A lot of that is imparting my experience on the next generation, while continuing to drive the vision and identity of this company going forward.
>
> Geoff Ramsey (*Roosterteeth.com*, 2019)

With each remaining visible at a creative level within the business, fans appeared to take the decision by *Rooster Teeth*'s founders supportively and positively, not least because there remains considerable nostalgia for the early shows, core values espoused and represented throughout the fandom. Furthermore, each of the remaining team members having remained active in the community at different levels. As one fan replied to Burn's post:

> I still remember when the first episode of the podcast was released, I was in the 7th grade and was over the moon lol. Your personality on screen is so energizing and you bring so much to the shows you're a part of. While I'm sure we're all sad to see you stepping away from the cameras, I'm excited to see what you're up to next.
>
> Handy (*Roosterteeth.com*, 2019)

Furthermore, many of the shows now produced had their own casts, beyond the founders – as was the original intention with the formation of *Rooster Teeth* back in 2003. The single greatest challenge for each show, however, is visibility above the noise of the now very crowded internet space, much of which is not about quality but generating hits for instant reward of advertising revenue – a challenge that the *Rooster Teeth* model for creative support was attempting to actively address.

At the same time, there is a significant level of criticism towards the apparent corporate takeover. This was exacerbated with the release of *Rooster Teeth*'s major new endeavour *gen:LOCK* (Season 2) on *WarnerMedia*'s new *HBO Max* platform on 27 May 2020, with an exclusive 90 days run on the service before it would be made available to the *FIRST* paying subscriber community and fan base. Moreover, it indicated possible further consolidation of the media sector and synergies across the business which would result in further rationalizations to facilitate 'profitable growth' (Spangler, 2019b). This was compounded in the announcement of the closure of the Australian store, due to a breakdown of the partnership between *Rooster Teeth* and *Hanabee Entertainment*. Cherry, its president, announced in December 2019:

> It became clear over the last year that *Rooster Teeth*'s global growth would lead to a crossroads. Their merchandise team is world-class, and they started pumping out a range of products as fast as Zara. Even *Amazon* struggles to keep up with those logistical demands. Although we fought like hell, ultimately, the Australian store couldn't keep up. So the hard decision was made, and we started the process of untying *Hanabee* and *Rooster Teeth*'s long-standing relationship. That lead to a restructure; the original staff since moved on to a variety of new challenges. I know what they're capable of, and I am certain they will all do amazing things. *Hanabee* survived. There are some bruises and scars,

> but also wisdom and maturity. The company is more sustainable, and at the end of 2019, we have a clear agenda [for 2020].
>
> Eric Cherry (in Sam, 2019)

Rooster Teeth reported staff changes in December 2019 with the promotion of three of the creative team who worked on the most popular shows into leadership roles: Joe Clary and Sean Hinz became joint heads of animation and Doreen Copeland overall head of production (Spanger, 2019c) and the departure of another long-standing member of the team, Ian Kedward, lead animator on core shows (Baculi, 2020).

As a consequence of COVID-19 pandemic impacts on tourism and travel with access restrictions to events and infrastructure, their 2020 *RTX* convention was pushed back to later in the year, then cancelled (Whittaker, 2020a) and finally reformatted to an online podcast version, badged *RTX at Home* and held in September 2020 (Whittaker, 2020b). It was the first opportunity the new leadership had to engage with anticipated 70,000 fans face-to-face. Whilst its online format fell a little flat among hardcore fans who clearly preferred a physical event, for others its accessibility opened new doors for interacting with community members through online channels. There follows, however, a long lead for reflecting on how the community is valued by the corporate machine which now has its hands on the reins of *Rooster Teeth*'s fandom. Notwithstanding this, one of the first major announcements to emanate from the restructure is a new season of the machinima series, *RVB* (Season 18) teased in January and subsequently launched on 19 October 2020 as *RVB: Zero*, available to its *FIRST* subscribers. Thus, it seemed *Rooster Teeth*'s creators were returning to their machinima routes.

Various institutional problems remained, however. Around 1 June 2020, Heyman had been pushed from the organization over a reported social media faux pas. His departure was not announced and much speculated on by followers. An extensive social media thread (4 and 5 June 2020) on comments by Mica Burton, the former editor and head of streaming for *Achievement Hunter* at *Rooster Teeth*, aired her reasons for leaving. As a woman of colour in the gaming sector, the thread stated it was the lack of leadership in addressing issues of equality rather than community-instigated abuse, which had been something she had been subjected to during her time at the organization. On her Twitter post and a subsequent personal exchange with Burton, Burns reflected:

> ... 'Helping' people have platforms isn't enough. I need to be better in my continual support of them... [Burton] made an excellent point about the power of my voice in the brand that I started and my lack of backbone in using that voice to affect change. Very powerful words that I should have been saying to myself.
>
> Burnie Burns (Twitter, 2020a)

Hours later, an emotional podcast with an extensive apology was aired on *Rooster Teeth*'s *Achievement Hunter* channel, hosted by Ramsey.

A week later on 11 June 2020, apparently unrelated to the fallout, Burns stepped away from *Rooster Teeth* in one of the most anticipated changes in management in the organization since September 2019. On his new personal website, Burns commented on his updated status:

> … my time walking the halls here at *Rooster Teeth* has come to an end. As some of you have predicted over the past year, my steady move away from a public life was in preparation for this change. So I hope this will not come as too much of a surprise. A few months ago, I enjoyed returning to the spotlight for a short podcast run with my old friends, and I would like to be able to continue to explore my creative passions. To that end, *Rooster Teeth* and I are currently working on a first-look agreement, which will enable me to incubate my own projects and then present them to the company for possible development… Starting this company and growing it in the early years were some of the hardest but greatest moments of my life. The constant camaraderie of Gus, Geoff, and Matt always made the impossible seem achievable; I could not have asked for better companions on this journey… Thank you to every person who has walked through these doors as a collaborator or tuned in to one of our videos as a viewer or made the choice to become a member of our community…
>
> Burnie Burns (Burnie.com, 2020b)

Undoubtedly the end of an era, of his departure Jordan Levin *Rooster Teeth*'s general manager commented:

> Burnie is a visionary and we look forward to his new ideas continuing to energize this unique company that he and his founding partners built. We are thankful for his continued passion and enthusiasm for *Rooster Teeth.*
>
> Jordan Levin (in Whittaker, 2020)

What is perhaps interesting is the manner in which the news emerged with no announcement direct to the community by the remaining *Rooster Teeth* founders who were attempting to reconfigure the brand and its focus on community. This undoubtedly presents a new challenge, leaving many speculating on how long it may be before they also depart.

4.10 Impact and Influence of Rooster Teeth's machinima productions

Rooster Teeth has achieved what other machinima creators only dreamed of doing in the early days; moreover they are now part of what has become one of the top ten global media entertainment companies, *AT&T* (Seth, 2019). As Jason Boomer, founder and leader of the *Rooster Teeth* UK community group since 2003 reflected:

> *[RVB]* marks a change in the way that machinima was created and consumed. Before it felt very experimental and felt like people were doing something they were passionate about but didn't necessarily have a plan for, at least not in a grand sense, whereas *RT* really captured an audience in a way that no other machinima ever has, and probably at this stage, ever will... *RVB* has been their flagship title since day one, I think that's the thing that people will never be able to surpass. It will go down in history as one of the most important machinima pieces ever to exist, not only because of its longevity but because of the way it was there in the relatively early days and how it is still there today.
>
> Jason Boomer (interview, 2020)

The convergence of game and film in media production industries, whilst a growing specialism within the filmmaking sector, has so far remained a limited form of media entertainment. For *Rooster Teeth,* it is their creative ethos that has stretched the medium, rather than their machinima production specialism that has enabled their central proposition to grow into the organization it now is. Boomer again:

> It used to be that everyone plays *Halo,* whether you found *RVB* first or you found it through *Bungie* forums and things like that, but now with *RWBY* and *CampCamp* and these other animated shows and the growing emphasis on podcasts there are people that are joining the community that have no connection to *Halo, Griffball* or *RVB*... the podcast was the game-changer for all of this. Up until that point it had been about the show, the content they're producing, that's the part that the fans were obsessively consuming but once the podcast started it suddenly became about the people and the personalities.
>
> Jason Boomer (interview, 2020)

Rooster Teeth has created a phenomenal ecosystem of fandoms based on creative story arcs that draw heavily on their game-based ethos of having fun, creating content they want to see, and actively engaging with audiences and communities but that move continually with contemporary socio-cultural, political and technological advancements. It is this evolutionary spirit that reaches and sustains audiences over time that Burns attributes to *Rooster Teeth's* longevity. As he commented in his Vlog in 2017:

> You have to be able to continue to grow your voice and not just exist in some space where people can fondly remember you. Who wants to have

> a career that's that? At *Rooster Teeth* we walk that line every day – we started a company that began with one person in a spare bedroom, then grew to five or six people and then over the course of fourteen years now have almost 300 people. We have to take a company photo with a drone at this point! When I started, I wanted to make videos that made my friends laugh… I approach everything in that way. I think if I do that, keep that same spirit, then the thing that made *Rooster Teeth* what it is will continue… it is a perpetual journey of figuring things out!
>
> Burnie Burns (Vlog, 2017)

That authenticity of voice is what resonates so well with other creators. Marino reflects on his first meeting with the *RVB* team at the 2003 panel held at Lincoln Centre in New York:

> I remember thinking how similar they were to me – creatives who also loved games. They were really easy to speak to and we had a common language through a love of games and filmmaking.
>
> Paul Marino (interview, 2020)

Other machinima creators were similarly inspired. Chris Burke, who now works in *LittleBigPlanet* with Tamara Yadao (aka *foci + loci*) and scores grindhouse horror films (currently *Mandible Judy*), is a performing musician and machinima producer of long-running *Halo* series *This Spartan Life* which ran between 2004 and 2015, reflected on *Rooster Teeth*'s influence on his work:

> I performed music at the opening night of the *New York Video Festival* in 2003. It was curated by Katie Salen, a talented game designer, educator and animator and I was asked to perform one piece and I decided to do a cover version of the original theme from Zelda. It turned out the show also featured folks from *ILL Clan*, Corey Archangel, Ze Frank and they screened the first episode of *Rooster Teeth*'s *Red vs Blue*, which premiered earlier that year… We launched our first episode on June 28 2005 and a string of blog posts led to tons of traffic within a month – first *Create Digital Music* and then *Boing Boing*. Our ISP shut us down, throwing a huge bill for bandwidth at us (in the thousands) and Claude Errera stepped in to host us for free on Halo.bungie.org; bless him. We had something like 1.5 million downloads in the first year before getting on *YouTube*… I interviewed Burnie [Burns] in-game for Episode 4 of *This Spartan Life* and we shared the bill at live events here and there, notably at the *Australian Centre for the Moving Image* in 2007. I remember Burnie telling Jack, his 5 year old,'This is Chris. He's the only other guy in the world that does exactly what I do for work'… *RT* and *TSL* have always had a super friendly relationship though. We had Geoff [Ramsey]

and Jack [Patillo] on the show as well in 2012 and we saw some of them in Austin whenever we were in town. Burnie helped us out by suggesting *TSL* as content for 343's *Halo Waypoint* channel, which we did for about a year. They are tireless and endlessly creative media makers.

Chris Burke (interview, 2020)

Alexander Winn, founder of *Edgeworks Entertainment* and of another popular dramatic *Halo* series that launched in 2005, *The Codex*, commented:

> I'd never seen anyone making original movies out of a video game before, and it opened a huge world of possibility. After that we went off and did our own thing with it but *The Codex* definitely wouldn't exist without *RvB* establishing the precedent of what could be done. *Rooster Teeth* holds a strange place in my heart: simultaneously the shining example of what's possible, but also the passionate rival. *The Codex* was the #2 machinima series in the world, but we could only ever be #2 because *Rooster Teeth* had been given a license from Bungie and we were repeatedly refused.... We actually met the *RT* guys a few times, at various conventions and such. Burnie Burns was very kind, and even hung out with us for a while outside of a party that we (as high school kids) couldn't get into. They've done incredible things, and in many ways they're doing what I hope to do with *Edgeworks Entertainment:* producing multiple projects, owning studio space, working in film/TV, etc. They got there first, but we're catching up!

Alexander Winn (interview, 2020)

Edgeworks Entertainment now makes computer video games from its Los Angeles studio, their latest venture being *TerraGenesis*, a game which has at July 2020 been downloaded 18M times (Winn, 2020).

Whilst for Laird MacLean, co-producer of *Sponsors vs Freeloaders* and founder of the *RVBCanWest* fan event, commented on how the experience of being part of a community impacted his career development:

> *[Rooster Teeth* influenced] my future career path and relationships within the larger Halo community and gaming industry. Over time with working alongside *RT* on their first prototype *Rooster Teeth* events for *RVBCanWest* I moved on over to the games industry working on various titles including eventually a *Halo* title.

Laird MacLean (interview, 2020)

In 2006, Burns had reflected on his experience with the machinima community at large and his contribution to it. His comments highlight his deep respect for the community and its stakeholders that has continued to resonate with audiences as the creative work of *Rooster Teeth* has evolved. Importantly, this includes the ways in which games developers and publishers are treated in the process:

> I always keep in mind that while we did not invent machinima, we have certainly forged some new paths in the genre. We always try to conduct ourselves in a manner that would make people in the future point to us as an example of why machinima is a good thing. I would hate to think that some young filmmaker wouldn't get the necessary permission to work on his machinima video because we did something that left a bad taste in the industry's mouth.
>
> Burnie Burns (in Frankie, 2006)

At the same time, Burns also recognized the path to future recognition of the genre of creative practice, at least at a commercial level, was far from straight forward:

> Machinima is just going to grow and grow. Real-time animation still has a long way to match the quality of pre-rendering. But, that gap is closing at an amazing rate. Look at the difference in visual fidelity between *Marathon* (1995) and *Halo 2* (2004). Then look at two pre-rendered movies from that same time frame: *Toy Story* (1995) and *The Incredibles* (2004). Sure, both sets had improvements in technical quality, but the real-time achievements gained a ton more ground. They haven't caught up yet, and I don't know that they ever will, but the differences will soon be insignificant.
>
> Burnie Burns (in Frankie, 2006)

Rooster Teeth, and particularly *RVB*, was both an influencer in the machinima community and was also inspired by the work of others. Burns again:

> There's a ton of great work out there. Randall Glass was an inspiration for some of our first *RVB* vids, and his work never fails to impress me. Overall, my favorite piece is one called *My Trip To Liberty City*, which is a piece made using *Grand Theft Auto*. The author did a fantastic job of capturing the spirit of machinima. It shows him playing *GTA* and talking about the game, then he goes on to say how he doesn't really want to beat people to death with baseball bats, so he re-skins his character with a Canadian tourist texture and starts wandering the city taking pictures of architecture and prostitutes. To me, that's the essence of machinima in a nutshell, wandering around in a virtual space and exploring it in a unique way...
>
> Burnie Burns (in Frankie, 2006)

Significantly, the team inspired many machinima creators, with works that reflected different aspects of games, film and creator personalities. Importantly, however, it is their approach to delivering creative works, that Burns described as being similar to the *Saturday Night Live* (*SNL*) US variety show which parodies contemporary culture and politics, and distribution methods that have become a model of practice beyond the machinima community. As Burns commented in 2017:

> [When] we started in 2003, we thought we were late to this. It turns out we were about eight years early. And I give a lot of credit to *Netflix* when they converted from a mail-DVDs-to-your-house service to subscription digital. That was, I think, the moment when everybody suddenly was… so that inevitability was imminent. So we wanted to be able to compete in the world of *Netflix, Hulu, Amazon* video. We wanted to be able to make that kind of content and compete on that level, and that's why our relationship with a company like *Fullscreen* just made sense… but my life didn't change because I was already doing what I wanted to do. It was my passion… *Rooster Teeth* is one of those rare online entities where we now have multiple generations of talent that our audience loves. Kind of like an 'SNL' model that we follow. And developing some of those people into huge personalities, that's a huge goal for me.
>
> Burnie Burns (in Kafka, 2017)

As Boomer and Burke commented though, it has moved beyond machinima into other creative genres now:

> It's the shift to let's play content that has cemented their position, but also in a way the shift of people consuming that content away from machinima to let's plays means that there's no longer an appetite for that content in the same way.
>
> Jason Boomer (interview, 2020)

> It's interesting to see how *[Rooster Teeth's]* work changed from the *Why Are We Here [Episode 1]* in 2003. I think, once you find you have a huge audience, you aren't satisfied with doing the more oddball stuff. That first episode made me think of *Waiting For Godot. TSL,* similarly started with an emphasis on the art side of things and moved slowly to being a talk show about the games industry… *RVB* and *TSL* both slowly became more about the characters, game-related jokes and entertainment than anything really subversive or arty, which worked for us both for a while. But *RVB* especially spawned a ton of knock-off series, with wise-cracking characters and over the top acting… *RT* are clearly the big success story to come from the first generation of machinima makers.

> Burnie et al. were very smart about how they maneuvered around the usual pitfalls for a growing media company. They should be remembered for their ability to make truly inventive and funny content while appealing to a huge audience.
>
> Chris Burke (interview, 2020)

Indeed, a number of key points in the evolution of their creative work and distribution methods have been identified as impactful turning points for *Rooster Teeth* from a community perspective: firstly, the appeal of *RWBY*, their anime show, to a younger female audience helped move their programming into a new and more diverse realm; secondly, the shift from series-based narrative work to let's play; and thirdly, their use of new streaming platforms changed the ways they were able to engage and interact with their community. Boomer commented:

> *RWBY* was a major milestone because up until that point it was very adolescent male-dominated community. With the introduction of *RWBY* it shifted and has now become 50/50 male/female split and it actually dropped the average age fairly significantly. Successive shows have done the same – they've brought in their own audiences... [and] when *Achievement Hunter* was formed, that is where a lot of the focus for gaming content went. It became very let's play driven and a lot of it is also personality driven... The other thing that had a major influence, and in my opinion for the worse, was when a lot of the content was hosted on *YouTube*... comments are notoriously toxic and it's got no community spirit there. It's a platform that is a hub but has no forum that you can really use. When they put a lot of their content out on *YouTube* there were people that were used to that environment finding the content and then joining the community itself and it was bringing with it a hostile and negative perspectives which didn't gel as well with the community.
>
> Jason Boomer (interview, 2020)

Thus, community remains central to their proposition. As Mary McDowell, *Rooster Teeth*'s head guardian for its *RTX Austin* community events since 2010, reflected:

> With the rise of social media, the community has more outlets to create and celebrate their love of the content. I've made life-long friends being part of this community. I've been to weddings, I've travelled to States and countries for community events, I've lived with this community, and I have worked alongside this community. Since *Rooster Teeth* began making more than just *RVB*, the community has grown exponentially. With every site change, program shift, new hire, or talent exit brings a shift in

> community. However, the energy and the positivity of the community feels constant and I appreciate that. Many of us have seen our community friends get hired by *Rooster Teeth* and so we really sink our teeth into that emotional attachment – I want this to be successful because it will make my friends successful! ... Like any other community, there will be issues to work through and solutions to discover. Having Community Managers who are attentive, invested, and validating really keeps this train moving. Our Community Managers are actually from the community! That right there is super important because our CMs understand the culture they are supporting. They come directly from the community and get to amplify it and/or change it for the better.
>
> Mary McDowell (interview, 2020)

For many, however, machinima and the underpinning creative processes developed through the evolution of *RVB* remain the heart of *Rooster Teeth*'s proposition. As McDowell explained:

> As an older fan, *RVB* will always be my first *Rooster Teeth* love. With more content being created, there comes a huge shift in content relevance. I feel like *RWBY* was the game changer for *Rooster Teeth* in that regard. *RVB* is not as prominent on the content line-up as it used to be. I don't know if that's a good thing or a bad thing. I miss the days when *RVB* was THE prime content of the site, but *Rooster Teeth* has developed some truly terrific content outside of Halo-themed comedy. This is like *Disney* creating content without *Mickey Mouse*: awesome stories without the need of the company's original figurehead to be involved...
>
> *RVB* is an absolute triumph. In its humble beginnings, it was a group of gamers animating within a game using console controllers. Now, the show has several dedicated production teams that make up a very large animation department. Look at how far we've come! From head nodding in time with dialogue to Monty Oum mo-capped fight sequences to creating worlds outside of an Xbox universe – *RVB* machinima paved the way for *RWBY* and *gen:LOCK* to be so worldly successful. The machinima skills of *RVB* opened the door to all sorts of animation advancements in the company. *Rooster Teeth* was able to take chances that larger and more established studios are too afraid to try for fear that they will create a losing product. Machinima made *Rooster Teeth* brave to try new things and look at what we have now!
>
> Mary McDowell (interview, 2020)

It is therefore with some hesitation that the community awaits the next phase of *Rooster Teeth*'s development under the guiding hand of *AT&T* and beyond the influence of its originating driving force at the creative helm, Burns et al. As Boomer observed:

> The shift to having these bigger companies behind *RT* is reflective of their desire to produce bigger or more diverse content, and to support a larger staff that allows them to do all these various productions – I think people are just scared that that might be a sign of things to come, with big media. But I don't think the content has reflected that in any way.
>
> Jason Boomer (interview, 2020)

Thus, the *Rooster Teeth* story continues.

4.11 Vignettes

Vignette 4.11.1 Halo | Halo 2

Figure 4.3: *This Spartan Life* (*Halo*).

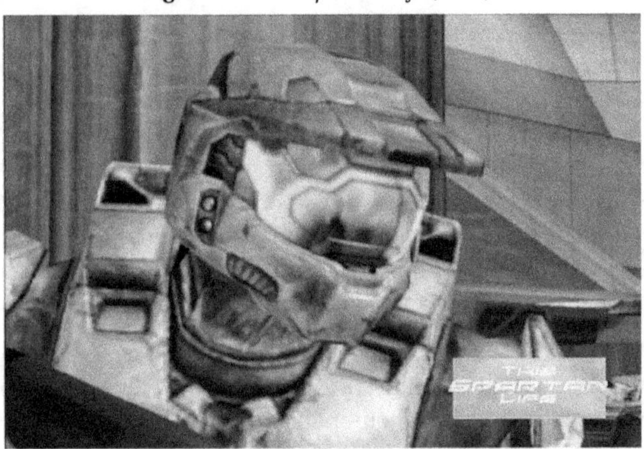

Source: Burke, 2020.

Halo was released on 15 November 2001 for Xbox and 30 September 2003 for PC.

Halo is what made the *Xbox* special for eager buyers of the console. It also attracted an interesting following of movie makers. Movies made within *Halo* were made possible because the *Xbox* was connected to a video capture card and could be edited with a video editor. *Halo 2* was released on 9 November 2004.

As well as the *RVB* series, which by the release of *Halo 2*, had completed 3 seasons, several other series were released. The most notable were a dramatic series entitled *The Codex*, one of the first Halo machinima dramas, and *This Spartan Life*, a long-running series.

Chapter 5

The French Democracy in Action

> Hearing some police siren all the night or SWAT helicopter at night made me feel as if I was living in a movie or on another planet.
>
> Alex Chan (in Totilo, 2005)

5.1 Introduction

This chapter outlines the impact of a small and, some argue, poorly made machinima film, but one which ultimately had a unique impact on the genre and society more generally. The film was made by a disaffected young man living in the suburbs of Paris, France who witnessed the pains of a country and its peoples dealing with civil unrest as it attempted to resolve political differences. The story Alex Chan told through his film was simultaneously harrowing in its portrayal of unfolding events, authentic in its voice and democratizing in its outcome. The media storm this film created, and the resulting many machinima films and trajectory of creative works it subsequently stimulated, makes Chan's work a worthy contribution in our review of pioneers, highlighting the socio-cultural impacts of machinima.

In this chapter, we describe the back story to the film, the story itself and its impacts, with reflections on Chan's work in its thematic content by those whose attention was piqued as a consequence of his breakthrough film.

5.2 Back Story

Alex Chan was a 22 years old graphic designer, living in the Parisian banlieues, the working-class suburbs that circle the city, where his parents had moved several years earlier from Hong Kong. They had moved for work, he was born and grew up there. His experience of living in the suburbs alongside that of his friends from local neighbourhoods is what inspired him to make *The French Democracy*.

Chan lived in the Seine-Saint-Denis department of one of the most populous regions of the Ile-de-France region, colloquially known as the *quatre-vingt treize* or *neuf trois* (administrative number 93) region. This is a poor area of the city, and indeed has become known as the poorest part of mainland France, often reported as a 'breeding ground for hooliganism, drug trafficking and radical Islam' (Harding, 2019), with many of the young leaving school with no qualifications (Chrisafis, 2015). It is also known for inspiring break-out talent in sport, notably football, as well as music and culture, such as R&B artist, Aya Nakamura.

Growing up, Chan had experienced the challenges of living in the region first hand. He was once attacked by local gang members who had tried to steal his mobile phone, putting him in hospital. He also knew of the many difficulties faced by local citizens as they tried to deal with crime and racial tension. He had been the victim of discrimination when he had been denied an apartment along with his girlfriend, apparently because of race. Many of these issues had been reported by the local press, often portraying the area as a 'no go zone' (Harbin, 2019) with one major incident that was captured on film by a reporter just three months before Chan made *The French Democracy.*

In 2005, the 93 Region erupted into riots, although they did not actually take place in the area where Chan lived. Nonetheless, as events unfolded around him, Chan heard the police responders in their various vehicles – reflected in our opening quote. The riots were a consequence of the perceived unjustified stigmatization and discrimination that the suburban youth were facing, many of whom became increasingly angry and disenfranchised from the policies of the day and the attitudes of others. They were jobless and marginalized because of ethnic origin and the choices their parents had made (Chrisafis, 2015). The discord led police to retract neighbourhood services and instead periodically use elite force (Chrisafis, 2012). Stop and search was commonly used on non-white citizens, leading to a culture of fear and intimidation. One day, three youths who had been to a football match during the half-term school holiday, crossed paths with a police van (Henley, 2005). They ran and the police chased. They hid in a power sub-station; two were electrocuted and died (Chrisafis, 2012). The third survived with severe burns (Chrisafis, 2015). With the deaths of two of their number which occurred as they attempted to escape brutal policing, social tension exploded into the streets, resulting in weeks of running battles between the youth and police during which citizens threw Molotov cocktails. Ultimately, this rioting led to the death of another citizen. Thousands of arrests were made for civil disobedience including the burning of over 9,000 vehicles that had been parked around the focal area of the 93 region, Clichy-sous-Bois, and dozens of public buildings.

The Rebellion, as it is often referred to by locals, had apparently been misread by the media, which stated it had been an attempt by the young to say 'we've had enough, we want to be heard' (Bonheur in Harding, 2019). Years later, despite continued investment, the regions remain challenging environments resulting in calls for high-level political intervention. The events have influenced each and every subsequent government in France since the riots took place. France, for example, is recognized as having one of the developed world's most unequal school systems which, together with a lack of social integration, poor quality housing and breakdown of trust between police and youth, has continued to contribute to ghettoization in the banlieues regions.

The socio-cultural crisis is what inspired Chan to comment, making the film within a week of the cessation of civil disobedience. He was not a filmmaker, had never before created a machinima and knew nothing of the community of machinima film creators that had developed over the preceding years – furthermore, his command of the English language was poor. As an industrial designer, he experimented with new software and was one of the first to use *The Movies* following its launch in Europe – but acquiring the game with his limited means had meant he had had to sell another of his technology possessions.

The Movies studio filmmaking simulation game was released on 11 November 2005, with an official creators' website that had been released in August 2005. By November its community website contained a number of example movies, managed by its developers *Lionhead Studios*. Chan realized the game would be a tool through which he could express his views about recent events in his locale. He uploaded his film to the community site on 22 November, having spent a couple of days making *The French Democracy*. The film quickly attracted attention and became one of *The Movies* community site's highest-rated and most discussed machinima films. Its message was reported in the media around the world.

The film was technically weak and grammatically poor in its use of English subtitles, but its authenticity was evident and its impact was profound. Of its immediate influence, Marino (*AMAS*) stated:

> Machinima, in this context, allows for an 'on-the-ground and in-the-moment' visual product - an easy analogy can be to blogging, though in visual form, a self-published and widely distributed visual narrative of these events as seen through the creator's eyes.
>
> Paul Marino (in Totilo, 2005).

This was also reflected in Chan's comments about the film:

> Through these tools you can get some more spontaneous reaction or reflection, not from mass media but from a simple citizen like me… by making this movie I really think that I did something good for my country.
>
> Alex Chan (in Totilo, 2005).

Of course, it was not the first creative work to have used cultural means to comment on a political issue but it was a breakout machinima that attracted significant attention, not least in the media, but also from politicians and other artists. Following its success, Chan went on to make another film, *Seeds of Terrorism*, released in June 2006, and then created a politically-inspired series released by and co-produced with *Eyeka*, a French broadcaster that distributed the series through the web channel *20minutes.fr* and TV channel *NT1* in 2007, called *World of Electors.* This series provided insight from Chan's perspective into the campaigns led by various French politicians in the run-up to the 2007 presidential election (*20minutes.fr*, 2007; Perrier, 2007).

5.3 About the Film

The French Democracy presents a fictionalized version of events that led to the Paris riots taking place in the streets of Clichy-sous-Bois in October 2005. The specific incident which sparked events reportedly took place on 27 October. The film shows local police and a group of African teenagers close to a power station. During a chase, two of the teenagers broke into the station to hide and were accidentally electrocuted in the process. They were 15 years old Bouna Traore and 17 years old Zyed Benna in real life – immigrants who had travelled to the city with their parents.

Figure 5.1: Screencap *The French Democracy.*

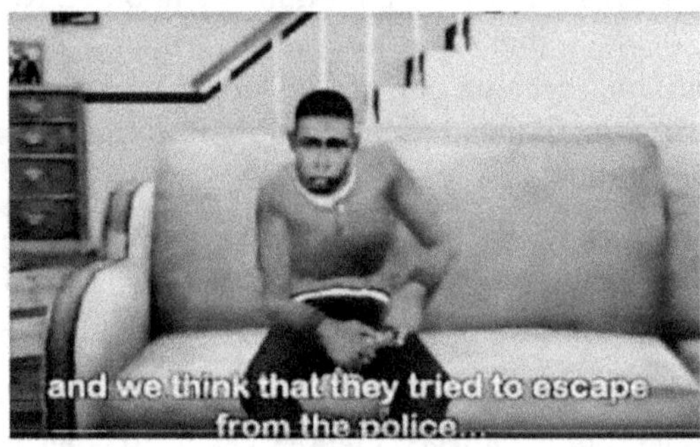

Source: Chan, 2005.

In the film, Chan presents a series of fictional events told through the experiences of the youths who each follow different paths. Other characters represent the then Interior Minister, Nicolas Sarkozy, as he sought tighter control over the rioters, and others who represented right-wing political candidates calling for foreigners to be removed from France (CTV News, 2005). The interconnected stories demonstrate what Chan described as racially motivated discrimination: refusal to rent apartments to people of Asian, Arabic and African decent or offer them jobs; a scene where citizens are attempting to defend themselves against malicious police behaviour, etc. These experiences and events collectively create a tinderbox within the community portrayed in the story which is then sparked by the deaths of the teenagers. With reporters covering events on TV news channels (Figure 5.1), the film then illustrates how the violence between police and citizens quickly descends into destructive chaos, resulting in a nuanced reflection on Government policy and the national

French constitutional motto: *Liberty Equality Fraternity*, based on the United Nations' *Universal Declaration of Human Rights* which states that every human is born free and is equal in dignity and rights (UN, 2020).

The film used overlaid English subtitles to describe the scenes and conversation between characters. The text represents the voices of the characters as they experience and witness the events unfolding around them. Chan used the standard character set within *The Movies*, including American city locations to portray events with a music score, also from the game, which made it reminiscent of a detective movie. The final film is 13:09 minutes long.

5.4 Re:Action

Within hours of the film's release to *The Movies* creator community site, Marino (*AMAS*) was contacted by Xavier Lardy, the French machinima community coordinator and founder of the *Machinima.fr* website, who brought the film to his attention. As Marino commented of the machinima work:

> Up until now, most machinima has been comedy-based, with a number of dramatic works surfacing over the last couple of years. *The French Democracy* shows that machinima can be politically driven.
>
> Paul Marino (in Totilo, 2005)

At the time, Lardy commented *"There has never been a machinima with such a clear and prominent political message"* (in CTV News, 2005) and subsequently expanded on his thoughts:

> The French machinima community was not that large at that time, and it certainly wasn't homogenous. I think there was some kind of 'soft divide' between the people seeing themselves primarily as gamers making machinimas with their favourite games and people seeing themselves as directors making machinimas with games that featured dedicated filmmaking tools (a rare thing at that time). It's important because *The French Democracy* was primarily a sensation both in the national and international press for what it represented – both a unique and personal testimony and a cultural landmark with historical weight; but at the same time it came as a surprise within the machinima community, a kind of UFO, and at first was appreciated, discussed, praised and criticized for different aspects... [it was a] significant film made by a person actually living at La Courneuve - a 'suburb youth'* - during the events, in a time and place where no camera can go, a film whose first purpose was to correct how the foreign media depicted what was happening. (*'suburb youth' is a poor translation of 'jeune de banlieue', it has been and still is negatively connotated in France). All of

> this happened before we had social media and streams of live events, and we could imagine that Alex – and virtually any people living at La Courneuve – would have been able to film what happened from the inside and comment on it.
>
> Xavier Lardy (interview, 2020)

This is interesting not least because the film highlights what Marino, Hancock and others in the machinima community had said all along: that machinima democratizes filmmaking by reducing barriers to entry for filmmakers, without the necessity of high technology investment to create effects, sets and live-action budgets, and skillsets in animation or coding. Indeed, that had been the ambition of *The Movies'* creator and founder of *Lionhead Studios'* Peter Molyneux whose ultimate idea was to facilitate the best films created to become live-action entertainment:

> One of the dreams for the game was that as you play, you realize you could direct a movie of your own.
>
> Peter Molyneux (in Musgrove, 2005)

Moreover, the speed at which this film was made, sharp on the heels of events that had inspired it, means it is as much an example of creative journalism as it is of documentary filmmaking. Marino wrote on his blog on 25 November, a couple of days after the film's release:

> It's a simple yet effective piece - a straight forward recount of the how/why behind the recent civil unrest in that country... The film itself is almost documentarian in its structure, and we're left with nearly a Gus Van Sant-experience of interpreting the unfolded events... Blogging has clearly given voice to the numerous masses, but the message behind this film says more than anything I've read about the riots to date. While I'm not sure Machinima can or will propagate political rights activism across borders or cultures, the medium does provide the power to do so. And where else is that more appropriate but in the hands of people who need to have their message seen?
>
> Paul Marino (*Machinima.org*, 2005)

Within days of its posting on *The Movies* website, the machinima community rallied around Chan to help him address some of the more disruptive technical mistakes he had made, enabling him to upload a slightly refined version of the film a few days later.

Before this, however, a number of others had become aware of the film. Clive Thompson, an author and technology journalist who writes for *New York Times Magazine* and *Wired*, wrote the day after its release:

> This flick is hardly going to win the *Palme d'Or* at Cannes. But it's easily one of the most impressive and emotionally affective pieces of machinima I've ever seen. When I was writing my feature this summer for the *New York Times Magazine* about machinima, I saw a lot of stuff that made me laff, but very little that made me *think*. This one accomplishes that, not merely because of its unexpectedly heart-warming political message, but because its cinematography has such a weirdly mongrel flavor: It borrows as often from the visual conventions of games as from film... There are plenty of other aesthetically nifty things about this movie, not least of which that the creator decided not to use voice-overs; the characters' speech appears as slightly-mangled English along the bottom of the screen. This creates the odd effect of a movie that feels both incredibly new – it's created using a video game – and incredibly old: it uses speech-frames straight out of silent movies. Better yet, the guy clearly didn't do this to be self-consciously, super-ironically retro. He just doesn't speak English very well and couldn't afford voice actors who did. The raw DIY feel of this project is more punk rock than anything anyone's done with music in about 20 years.
>
> Clive Thompson (*Collisiondetection.net*, 2005)

Similarly, Gonzalo Frasca, co-editor of the *Water Cooler Games* forum which already included a series of articles on the development and use of videogames for purposes of activism, commented:

> While some details are questionable (cops don't ask for passports but for I.D.'s) the film is a quite powerful example of the potential of *The Movies*. When *The Sims* was launched, some players started creating social commentary photo albums in order to tell stories of abuse. Technically, the quality of these videos is impressive.
>
> Gonzalo Frasco (*Water Cooler Games*, 2005)

What Chan had attempted to do with his film was not simply tell the story of recent events but shine a light on youth culture more generally, both within his own country but also the US. His selection of English as a text meant that his message might have a broader reach. His film was not an attempt to activate people but an attempt to call for greater tolerance among young people by using a game, rather than traditional media (CTV News, 2005). In an interview, he stated:

> Many French people still don't know or don't want to really understand what happened in their neighbourhood. That's why I chose this ironic title of *The French Democracy* in order to refer to the fact that the youth prefer to use Molotov cocktails than ballot papers to get heard by the government. In this way in my movie, I try to bring people to think or to

> understand – not to necessarily forgive – what can push a young person or teenager to act like this.
>
> Alex Chan (in Totilo, 2005)

Of its impact, Marino commented:

> There have been a few politically aware machinima works, but none that had the same impact/attention as *The French Democracy.*
>
> Paul Marino (in Totilo, 2005)

Chan's story was not, however, picked up in the French media immediately – in fact, it was actively ignored. Isabelle Arvers, a French machinima curator and researcher, recalls:

> I remember the first reaction [in France] was quite negative until the point that it started to be hyped… In the US, the media totally understood that it was another voice, another type of message regarding the events and they got interested in it. In France it was more that it's not very well done… they didn't care about the duration, conditions of productions, nothing. And then when they realized that in the US media were interested, they started to think 'ah yes, maybe we should interview him'.
>
> Isabelle Arvers (interview, 2020)

Reported in the centre-left French newspaper, *Liberation*, one of France's most popular newspapers, Chan's film was criticized in France for its over-simplification of events which portrayed the social context as clichéd and inaccurate: "*The poor people of color against the bad police … Pfff*" (in Lechner, 2005). Chan defended this criticism, stating:

> Some have even found that Hollywood decors bring a universalist note and that foreigners could thus better identify with this story… [The game] is not suitable for depicting the real, because (…) the real is far too nuanced… We must consider this film rather as an educational fiction… the software does not really offer the possibility of making a real documentary. It is obvious that the reasons which pushed these young people to act thus go far beyond what is shown in the film… [but the] events more or less really took place. The police blunder refers to the France 2 video filmed at La Courneuve. I used the words of our Minister of the Interior, I also quoted Philippe de Villiers.
>
> Alex Chan (in Lechner, 2005).

What his words and the film reflect is that machinima could reach different target audiences, and that it was capable of reflecting a political opinion in ways that other more traditional media formats could not. Chan again:

> They grew up with this mode of representation that is video games. Machinimas, by adopting a mode of communication that is familiar to them, can reach them differently from the usual media. In addition, they are free, easily downloadable and generally have no economic or directly political interest (unlike newspapers for example). This brings a whole other credibility, admittedly subjective, but which can come from any citizen.
>
> Alex Chan (in Lechner, 2005)

It is not therefore surprising that the film inspired others to create similar types of work. Notable examples are Australian, Thugen Nguyen, who created *An Unfair War* (*Sims 2*, 2006). This is a machinima film about an Iraqi civilian caught up in war. It also similarly inspired Joshua Garrison, who used *Halo 3* to recreate events of the April 2007 Virginia Tech school massacre, highlighting what he saw as the failings that had enabled the killer to succeed in his aim (Gish, 2008). Of *The French Democracy*, Peter Molyneux stated:

> People are beginning to find uses for [*The Movies*] that we didn't even think about when we designed the game. What is also incredible is that there's a lot of movies that are coming online that have been inspired by *The French Democracy* that are actually commentaries about society in America, society in the UK... It's almost as if this has opened a floodgate.
>
> Peter Molyneux (in CTV News, 2005)

Chan reflected on his influence at the time:

> I was completely unaware of this milieu when I bought the software to make my film. I have had emails and seen a lot of blog postings from people who say that my film has inspired them to express themselves. I am very pleased if my little animation helps young people become more engaged in society.
>
> Alex Chan (in AFP, 2005)

His message, which attracted significant attention in the media around the world, caused him some concern as reporters interpreted the youth characters in the film as Muslim men. Media had mistakenly made a connection between the riots and terrorism, situating the blame with the community. His concerns led the *Washington Post* and *MTV* to correct their reports, deleting references to Islam. As Chan commented, however, the discrimination represented in the film was something different: "*In France, racism is often hidden and subtle. It is not just racial, it is cultural too*" (Chan in AFP, 2005).

His point had been well made, bringing the potential of machinima to the attention of others who might use its cultural aesthetic to promote key messages. Chan was asked to produce a fifteen-episode politically inspired series by *Eyeka,* a French broadcaster who distributed the series through the web channel *20minutes.fr* and TV channel *NT1.* For this series, called *World of Electors,* Chan presented a local perspective on key political issues in the run-up to the 2007 French presidential election. These were interviews undertaken on the street, capturing the voice of citizens on key issues of the day and influential issues for the upcoming election. On the new series, Arvers commented:

> What he did was, between two sessions in the presidential elections, he went into the streets during the day and interviewed people on different subjects, such as national identity, if kids could vote, these kinds of subjects, and that night he was transforming these interviews and making avatars talk... he used *The Movies* as well. He was interviewing during the day and doing the machinima at night, and the day after he was publishing it – it was like a daily publication to the website, which was a daily free newspaper, *20Minutes,* also it went out on *NT1* and I showed it at festivals after, particularly 'if the kids could vote' because it's a lot of fun.
>
> Isabelle Arvers (interview 2020)

What is also interesting is the impact of one particular episode of the *World of Electors* machinima series which focussed on national identity. This became a thread in a political central tenet of the presidential campaign by notoriously hard-line conservative minister at the time, Nicolas Sarkozy. Sarkozy's approach to the ethnic and racially mixed-race suburbs was reminiscent of the National Front and his approach had been responsible for stoking tensions with policing that eventually erupted into the 2005 riots (Tshimanga, 2009). In the period before the 2007 election, however, Sarkozy's focus had also been on attempting to break with traditional French politics by embracing technological innovation and 'speaking the truth'. Sarkozy was, for example, noted for being the first in French politics to use email and online advertising in a debate, thus his use of Chan's machinima film as a unique voice against which to rally is not surprising. He became president on 6 May 2007, achieving one of the highest turnouts recorded for a French election. Albeit the result was dominated by older voters, it was also notable that his primary opposition (Socialist Party, led by Segalène Royal) won almost 60% of the under 25s vote in a hitherto unheard-of turnout for the French elections.

Perhaps surprisingly therefore, it is interesting to note that it was also Sarkozy who was responsible for reinvigorating the French honours system to include a global concept of culture. He created awards for people that have 'distinguished themselves in the domain of artistic or literary creation or for the contribution they have made to the spread of arts and letters in France and the world'. Peter Molyneux, the creator of *The Movies* in which Chan had made his machinima and numerous other games, was bestowed with the Chevaliers de l'Ordre des Arts et des Lettres (Knighthood of the Order of Arts and Letters) on 12 March 2007 (Foyler, 2007). He was the fourth game developer to be honoured in this way, with three being honoured the previous year. This reflects Isabelle Arvers' view that videogame culture before 2007 had been largely frowned upon in France, particularly as an educational tool. Arvers, as an independent machinima arts curator, for example, used it in her workshops from 2009 onwards. At the award ceremony, the minister of culture at the time, Renaud Donnedieu de Vabres, commented on Molyneux's award: *"I am particularly glad to salute today a veritable visionary, who shows for every creation of his own how video games have their place in this stateroom"* (Faylor, 2007), recognizing the contribution of games to French culture in general.

Chan's film had apparently generated a window of opportunity for a new way to communicate political opinion; rather than extending the use of *The Movies*, they had instead gravitated towards *Linden Labs' Second Life* virtual world simulation game. Each of the political parties created a presence for the 2007 French election inside *Second Life*. Initially, this was instigated by Le Pen's far-right Front Nationale party, who created a virtual headquarters (Burkeman, 2007). Others soon followed, as Christine Webster, a 3D sound engineer, digital artist and one of the Socialist Party representatives who had worked on their *Second Life* simulation, commented:

> They [other election candidate parties] were afraid that *Front Nationale* would have an advantage and so this motivated the *Socialist Party* to create *Comité 748* and we were followed by *Moderne*, the centre party, and then Sarkozy's party came in last.
>
> Christine Webster (interview, 2020)

Comité 748 was an offshoot of a think tank created by Segolène Royal's Socialist Party, focussed on 'desires for the future' ('Désirs d'Avenir', Eschwege, 2007). It was mandated to run the simulation inside *Second Life* and invite participants to its events to discuss key issues, regularly engaging with thousands of avatars. As an 'open to all' simulation environment, this led to unprecedented exchanges between different ideological perspectives, resulting in some virtual attacks on avatars. On the other hand, *Sarkozy Island* had been exclusive to invited participants only, with the simulation campaign being focussed on 'opening the debate to a new kind of citizen', a generation inspired by game spaces (Ducrey, 2007). As Webster reflected:

> The rule was on *Comite 748* that we had no restrictions, we had to welcome everybody… We were directly in front of avatars from the Left Wing, *Front Nationale*, the *Moderne* centre party and the *Union for a*

> *Popular Movement.* All these people came to gather to discuss the semis, and this gave a surrealistic discussion... the confrontation between different ideologies was exhausting... We were in fact the only simulation who had total acceptance of everyone, which was also interesting and exhausting because we had to face attacks. We had to face assaults, digital assaults, with 3D weapons so people came with an arsenal of weapons, the language of their ideology and the use of scripts – people could install objects and I remember I was trapped in objects that the *Front Nationale* created. It was very interesting, every day a fight... *[Island Sarkozy]* was bugged. They installed also scripts and if we wanted to go to Island Sarkozy, we were banned automatically because of the scripts.
>
> Christine Webster (interview, 2020)

Apparently unaware of *The French Democracy,* Caroline Piras, a French film producer who was at the time experimenting with *Second Life* as a filmmaking environment, had approached the political parties to film the series of virtual debates that were taking place and streamed inside *Second Life.* She had been fascinated by their use of the environment and wanted to capture events – they all agreed, some inviting her to their physical offices in Paris to record interviews that would then be streamed in the world including, for example, a debate involving one of Royal's sons.

The parties' use of the filmmaker to produce content was clearly an attempt to reach a younger audience: by harnessing the game-like environment, politicians attempted to communicate through a novel cultural medium, albeit the core community of users of this environment were typically older than those targeted by Chan's work, made in *The Movies.* This therefore presented an interesting dimensionality of how games may be used to present contemporary cultural perspectives on ideological positions. To increase reach, the machinima films that Piras created were also streamed on *YouTube* and other social media platforms, comprising interviews alongside key industry supporters' advertising messages.

Some months later, Piras was approached to create machinima for one of the advertisers she had worked with on the political machinima. It was only at that point she realized that Chan's work had been an inspiration for their willingness to participate in *Second Life.* She comments:

> It was only when the advertising company hired me for this campaign for [the client] that they said they had seen Chan's machinima. It was their reference. So they came to me and said they wanted the same. This was the first time I'd seen his film... they used Chan's film as a reference and for the election it was the same, it was because at that time people (youth) no longer used newspapers. They [political parties] were using

> games a lot and using machinima as that was a way to reach them and for saying to them, 'we are talking the same language as you'.
>
> Caroline Piras (interview, 2020)

5.5 Reflections

The Movies Online, the game's content sharing website, ran for three years between 2005 and 2008, closing on 5 December. During its life, it had received a year's worth in time of movies posted to it and had more than 2M visitors. As it closed, it summarized its impact, highlighting *The French Democracy* as its only movie that had made headlines and mainstream media. Mark Webley, *Lionhead*'s development director, who had led *The Movies* team commented on the closure:

> *The Movies Online* has shown how much creativity and originality there is amongst games players. The Movies helped create movies like The French Democracy which attracted world-wide media attention. But three years on, would-be film makers now have many more outlets for their creativity which also attract a wider audience.
>
> Mark Webley (*Lionhead.com*, 2008)

If Chan had made the film today it would likely have been much more difficult for it to be found. When *The Movies* website had launched, and indeed when Chan uploaded his film, *YouTube* and similar platforms had only just started. Of course, social networking platforms became a major competing force in the subsequent years for those wishing to reach an audience beyond the immediate community of creators, as explained in our preceding chapters. Ironically, it was *Machinima Inc.* that partnered with *Activision* (publisher of *Lionhead Studios*' games) using *Machinima.com* as its main promotional platform in 2005 – *Machinima Inc.*'s first game channel – which provided tutorials for filmmaking as well as a means to promote content beyond *The Movies* game's own website.

Furthermore, following the break-through of Chan's work, machinima quickly became known as a means through which videogame narratives were crafted into social commentaries for cultural criticism. This was reflected in articles by Jones (2011) and Brown and Holtmeier (2013) who discussed the confluence of media, language and cinema in the context of machinima as a democratizing medium. It is still true today, as Lardy comments:

> If we consider the cinematographic qualities of [Chan]'s film as a written, shot and edited artwork, all by a single individual, then we could say that machinima still holds some power, because of its nature: if it is difficult for you to film the reality you're in with your smartphone, then

> you can still use fictional universes from popular video games to create a film that metaphorically speaks about the reality you're in and you want to share with the world.
>
> Xavier Lardy (interview, 2020)

Even film directors such as Spike Lee used machinima as a cultural reference, based on *Rockstar Games' Grand Theft Auto,* for glamorizing gang culture and videogame use in his crime film *Inside Man* (2006). This popularization of video games is an aspect that particularly captured attention in games and film industries. Habib Zargarpour, who was a senior art director at *Electronic Arts* at the time, highlighted that it was both the look and feel of the content as well as the speed with which it could be created that contributed to its use as a means for social commentary:

> The video game narrative is defining its own genre partially because of its look but also because real-time graphics engines allow people to work faster and get ideas but. That development really puts animated storytelling tools in the hands of almost anybody who has a computer, and that opens doors to thousands of new voices.
>
> Habib Zargarpour (in Crabtree, 2006)

Similarly, John Gaeta, best known as the visual effects supervisor of *The Matrix* film trilogy, argued the use of machinima as a means for creating personal stories that reflect societal critique was the next logical step in the evolution of cinema and gaming:

> We'll see a movie that preserves the singular vision of the creator that also allows the viewer-player to observe it, to play it and go into a hybrid exploratory mode. That's the most exciting format I can possibly think of. That idea is the most powerful new idea. You can't call it filmmaking, you can't call it games.
>
> John Gaeta (in Crabtree, 2006)

Extrapolating this point, Lardy stated how the film influenced others both within and without the community:

> The press coverage of *The French Democracy* gave many machinimakers reasons to believe that machinima was (finally) recognized as a legit way to make real films and be considered as real filmmakers – which is, in hindsight, probably a little bit delusional. I don't think people started to make different things, but they certainly started to see themselves differently. Most of all, I think that *French Democracy* had a more significant impact outside of the machinima community, by showing many people that if they had something to say, they could grab a virtual

> camera and make their own movie. Now cultural centres have machinima workshops to teach people how to make their own movies using their own games – and it's a good thing.
>
> Xavier Lardy (interview, 2020)

Arvers, digital arts and machinima curator, was inspired by *The French Democracy* to create her workshop concept for suburban, displaced and migrant young people. Since 2009, her workshops have involved over 10,000 participants around the world, and is a project she continues with today. As she comments:

> Thanks to that movie, I created my workshop for teenagers in the suburbs and the camps. The first time I presented the project to get some funding it was 2006 but when I succeeded to organize the first workshop it was 2009... The concept of the thinking is that perhaps you are from the ferry, you are not very good at school or school is not for you, but then you can play games, are a very good gamer and you are able to express yourself in the game... then you can change the narrative. The main impact of *The French Democracy* is this. After that, in each of my workshops I always show it... I have now done thousands of workshops... each time I have 10-15 people attend.
>
> Isabelle Arvers (interview, 2020)

Figure 5.2: Screencap *Son-in-Law.*

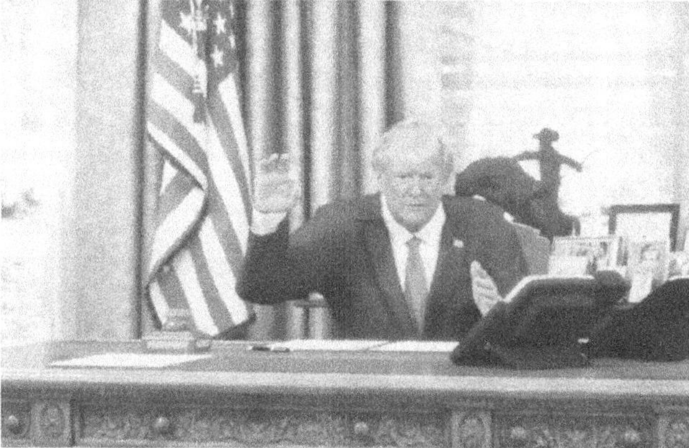

Source: Shearer, 2020.

However, Allen Varney, author and game designer, believed the impact of machinima films on politics and political awareness was small primarily because these communities rarely if at all overlapped. Whilst that may have been true in 2005, with the benefit of a generation of born-digital citizens growing up with computer games and streamed content as a main form of entertainment, that overlap is now much more significant, albeit perhaps expressed more commonly through let's play and other live-streamed formats. There are, however, still examples of political commentary through machinima. For example, Trump's presidency (US) has generated much criticism and was the subject of a recent machinima produced by *The Simpsons*' Harry Shearer (Clifton, 2020), working with Australian-based Mod Studios (figure 5.2).

As Clive Thompson, the blogger/author and reporter who had broken the original news story about Chan's work explained:

> … before *The French Democracy* I had seen a lot of machinima and often it was very witty and enchanting but as far as I can recall there hadn't really been people doing ambitious stuff that was trying to grapple with everyday serious political issues, something that was dealing with the hot button issues that were in the real world at the time… [but] what are we really talking about when we talk about machinima? … it's something that's a subset of a larger thing done by people who regard things that happen in games as worthy cultural aesthetic and spiritual moments that ought to be shared, in the same way that a movie is someone saying that things that physically happen that have been captured through a camera are cultural moments that ought to be shared… maybe machinima is just everywhere now, in a way that we haven't recognized.
>
> Clive Thompson (interview, 2020)

Varney (2007) also argued that the copyright issues (as we highlighted in Chapter 3) were likely to result in restrictive distribution of content, specifically where games owners were unhappy with the creative output or message, which in turn led them to issue 'take-down' notices. Marino agreed, arguing that a controversial film, such as *The French Democracy*, could prompt a game developer to enforce copyright but also suggested that the game is merely a facilitator of creative expression, particularly when it enables machinima making explicitly (or even implicitly) by building into its engine machinima-making tools. Marino stated:

> Will a machinima surface that forces a game developer to issue a damage-control press release stating they have nothing to do with the work? ... [A]s a supplier of technology, do they get to dictate the how, what and why tech is used? ... I believe it is in the interest of the developers to handle the 'how' specifically and not become mired in the 'what' or 'why'. The developers, and technology, are enablers.
>
> Paul Marino (in Varney, 2007)

Far from the case, the reach of *The French Democracy*, particularly given its relation to *The Movies* where the game was all about creating a machinima film and sharing the work, could only have benefitted the developer by giving it exposure and free marketing. Since its release, the film has been downloaded over 1M times and, on the various blogs, posts and platforms that it was released to by numerous community and non-community members, academics and fan followers, there have been thousands of comments both good and bad about the work. Such breadth and quantity of discourse also makes removing the work and restricting distribution over the internet significantly more problematic, if not impossible to achieve. Of its reach, Lardy said:

> The media were part of the *French Democracy* phenomenon… [Chan]'s film was featured in one key newspaper, and then it spread all around the world like fire. As a funny anecdote, one of his aunt's living in Asia phoned him because she read in her local newspaper news about her nephew and was worried.
>
> Xavier Lardy (interview, 2020)

Furthermore, the nature of discourse about the film alongside that of other similar works, demonstrates the ways in which games may be used to comment on societal issues, which led some to argue that its impact legitimizes research into the more general relationship between citizenship and videogaming (Sotamaa, 2007). For others, this discourse stimulated debate about the roles of new digital media forms in politics, for example, by giving a voice to youth and games-based culture (Lowood, 2008; Harsin, 2014). Howlett (2020) makes the point that political machinima is not so much a form of activism, which is how Chan's work has tended to be viewed through the academic literature, i.e., where the creator uses the media form to express a politicized viewpoint, but is more about antagonism. He comments:

> Chan's *French Democracy* engages deeply with a political situation, yet this does not provide the framework for political dialogue. This is instead achieved through his aesthetic decisions. Chan's methodology of antagonistic digital strategies resulted in a techno-stice: An inbetweenness made possible only through intermediality, digital software, oppositionality, user-generated content, and the resulting dissensual states generated by the wider public. It is at the intersection of antagonistic digital strategies that political machinima can become a more sophisticated and poetic conduit of politics. Without this techno-stice, Chan's situation would not have achieved dissensus, and his antagonistic wishes for his reality to become my reality would have been reduced to mere noise.
>
> Chris Howlett (correspondence with authors, 2020)

This perspective, therefore, reveals more about the receiver of or commentator on the work, reminiscent of a view that machinima converges context with culture, resulting in an intervention which can be read in multiple ways but is fundamentally co-created and time-dependent (Harwood, 2011). Chan's work was of its time, reflecting the conflicting political viewpoints of different generations in both the US and France. Hindsight is a wonderful thing!

This is also reflected in comments made by another machinima creator, Thuyen Nguyen, whose film *An Unfair War* (released early 2006) attracted attention after Chan's because it followed a similar trajectory of storyline and social context, also using text subtitles (see Figure 5.3). The film was made in *Sims 2* and was uploaded to the *Sims* community site as well as *Machinima.com.* Nguyen's parents had travelled to Australia as Vietnamese boat people and he had grown up with stories of his family's displacement from their farm as communists overtook local communities during the Vietnam War in the 1970s. He had been shocked by the stories emanating from those caught up in the Iraq war and which were spread across his mediatized world in 2005. His film was intended to be a representation of the horror of facing displacement because of war, yet be independent of locale. Nonetheless, he received threatening feedback from viewers who saw it as anti-American propaganda, in much the same way that Chan's film had been seen by media as a critical reflection of their social context. Nguyen comments:

> I wanted to make *[An Unfair War]* generic. I didn't want to attach an accent to the character which would make it an obviously Middle Eastern person – it was intention not to have a voice-over. He is a guy that has the barest access to the internet, he's using an old computer, he's barely got a connection and he's just typing away on his blog or some sort of public forum and just trying to get out as much as possible because the sound [of bombing] is coming closer and closer. His family has left and in his mind he just wants to write as much as he can whilst he can before he has to leave the house and chase after his family, wherever they've gone, and he has to catch up to them. Before it's too late…
>
> Thuyen Nguyen (interview, 2020)

That said, he feels the film created an opportunity to highlight the potential of games in general:

> Anything that draws attention to games as a medium – I'm a big gamer, always have been – it's an entertainment medium that's on a par with books and music... Games are not just men in a basement, they are worthwhile from entertainment and artistic points of view. Sometimes you have to have these kind of crafted projects [such as *French Democracy* and *An Unfair War*] that take some flak because of it just to show games are worthwhile things to have in this world.
>
> Thuyen Nguyen (interview, 2020)

Figure 5.3: Screencap *An Unfair War.*

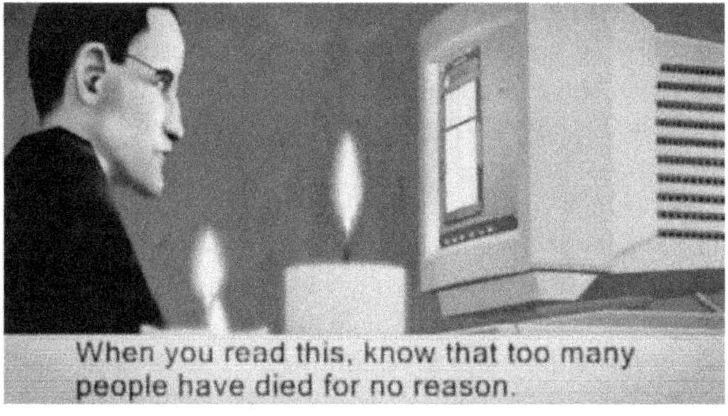

Source: Nguyen, 2006.

As a medium for amateur filmmakers using it for socio-political commentary, however, it is probable that machinima has lost its footing. For Arvers and Lardy, there are few examples on which to draw and a key reason that Lardy ceased the *Machinima.fr* community site in 2010 was because of the increased focus among its newest community members in becoming famous online rather than creating quality work or artefacts through which to engage in critical debate. This tension is something that has been evident since the early days of machinima but is perhaps more nuanced than simply a distribution platform versus creator tussle. In Chapter 3 we highlighted how machinima has become professionalized within the film industry but, alongside this, with the improved graphics quality and computer processing capacity, so too have games become considerably more complex to play and therefore to use as filmmaking tools. Nguyen argues this has simultaneously significantly increased audience expectations of the quality of any creative work produced. He comments:

> From the early days, machinima was a little bit clunky and I don't think there's a viewer for that any more… people had to accept the kind of amateurish nature of what machinima used to be but now I think people expect too much, which is a bit of a shame. Games nowadays are so breath-taking at times… both from viewers' and a filmmakers' points of view. The games are so complicated – they're really difficult to use, you've got to learn so much more about the game and the tools, so it's time-consuming to get started. Plus, people expect to see perfect models and perfect lip sync and all that kind of stuff which they would easily ignore before. So the expectation, and to create machinima now as an amateur, it's just not there.
>
> Thuyen Nguyen (interview, 2020)

Thus, political machinima is now more the domain of those who are eloquent at positioning their argument by embodying their message within a game context, by employing gamer values and by distributing their work through channels that reach their target audience – and, by artists with game coding skills. For example, DAISH (Al-Dawlah Al-Islamiyah fe Al-Iraq wa Al-Sham or Islamic State) terrorist group uses *Grand Theft Auto* machinima as an online recruitment tool whilst artist Joseph DeLappe protests against government policy using *America's Army* game (*Dead-in-Iraq*, 2006-2011) online and in art galleries. DeLappe's work among others, for example, is now recognized as contemporary activist art (e.g., Howatt, 2020) rather than machinima per se. In such cases, machinima best describes both the creative process and the final artistic output as a state of encounter or performance. For further information about this work and perspective, see DeLappe's description of his artwork, *Dead in Iraq* in Ng (2013).

The use of machinima by politicians themselves seems to have been a passing fad: with parties and political groups from Japan, the UK, Egypt and the US experimenting with virtual presence inside *Second Life* (see Hogg, 2007; Crikey, 2007; BBC News, 2009; RogueShadowAngel, 2011; Messinger and Ge, 2011), records of game-based virtual events (in the form of machinima films) have been few. Although it has been argued there is a legitimate application for political experiences in virtual environments, justified because of the representation in games of business brands in general, most commentators have considered this to be a gimmick rather than a serious endeavour. Indeed, numerous games have thematically employed politics in their story arcs. Evidence of presence and activity by the French political parties within *Second Life* was removed within six months of the French election in 2007 and there has been no repeat performance in subsequent elections. This is also likely to be a consequence of greater insight now provided on the use, reach and impact of virtual environments for social action and the longevity of machinima as cultural assets. Indeed, many of those who participated in creating virtual simulations for the political parties have remained active as digital artists. For example, Webster's experience led her to specialize in 3D virtual sound engineering in *Second Life* and the digital arts focussed open sim, *FrancoGrid*.

Unreal Engine and *Unity3D* game engines are now commonplace in the development of virtual reality experiences, which together with motion and volumetric image capture techniques provide new opportunities for politicians to demonstrate their technological empathic tendencies to contemporary youth (Gajsek, 2020). It perhaps takes a global crisis for virtual environments to be revisited as a serious tool for citizen engagement, where physical presence is restricted or desirable (e.g., Bailenson, 2017).

5.6 Vignettes

Vignette 5.6.1 The Movies

Created by prolific game developer Peter Molyneux, this sandbox game specifically targeted machinima movie makers and was first promoted on the gaming website, *Gamespot*, on 11 March 2003. Six months later, its website was opened to the public (27 September 2003) and the first promotional video of the game was circulated the following year (28 April 2004). The game was finally released in November 2005 and showcased at the *Sundance Film Festival* in January 2006 with a 'stunts and effects' expansion pack launched in June that year. *The Movies* was produced by *Lionhead Studios*, and their online forum (movies.lionhead.com) became a popular place for *The Movies* machinima. The most notable machinima created was Alex Chan's French Democracy.

The Movies uses a formula with 200 factors that enable the player to rate a movie, using such mechanisms as the number of costume changes, how well the actors like each other, the genre of movie it is, etc.

Molyneux later described *The Movies* as a distraction (they were attempting to scale the business in the process of becoming publicly listed) and ultimately a disaster due to the lack of playtesting prior to release (Stanton, 2016).

Chapter 6

Stolen Life Lives On

> Seeing the animation with the music was like experiencing the film for the first time all over again. The glass wall between you and the story is broken and you walk in.
>
> Peter Rasmussen on *Stolen Life* (in Sluganski, 2007)

6.1 Introduction

Stolen Life is an award-winning feature-length film released in 2007 and written by established Australian filmmaker Peter Rasmussen and directed by Jackie Turnure. It is the first Australian feature-length machinima, a product of Rasmussen's experimentation with the science fiction genre, inspired by Scott's *Blade Runner*, Tarkovsky's *Solaris* and literary works by such as Asimov and Bradbury that illustrated various aspects of sentient robots, artificial intelligence and outer space exploration. In fact, Rasmussen had written and released two previous machinima films, *Rendevous* (2001) and *Killer Robot* (2003), both of which play with concepts in content, form and creative process that led him to develop *Stolen Life* as a feature film. It was considered by many in the machinima community at the time of its release to be the best piece ever made in the format.

Whilst a comparatively small repertoire of machinima work, Rasmussen's contribution to filmmaking and the genre was significant, both during his life and after he passed away in 2008. He was active in the earliest days of the *Machinima.com* community, particularly in relation to sharing knowledge of filmmaking from his professional industry perspective to others. For example, he contributed to Brown's documentary on machinima in 2003, see Chapter 3 (and figure 6.1). He was one of the first to note that machinima as a filmmaking process requires little in the way of expertise in industry-based filmmaking, low/no budget (just one of the benefits we have highlighted throughout) and others he noted, including the ability to create and re-use assets and resources, and the ability to automate some aspects of the filmmaking process by embedding common routines in code. Notably, however it is the ability to use the game engine as a means to view and review some creative piece from multiple perspectives that made his choice of machinima an appropriate one: it meant he could continue to tweak it until such time as he was happy with the creative output, editing content in such ways that his human actors were promoted through the process in the ways he intended. Rasmussen coined this malleability of machinima as a form of digital 'clay' and this, alongside other creative methods he used in his filmmaking practice, is why he became known as a pioneer in the Australian film industry.

Figure 6.1: Peter Rasmussen.

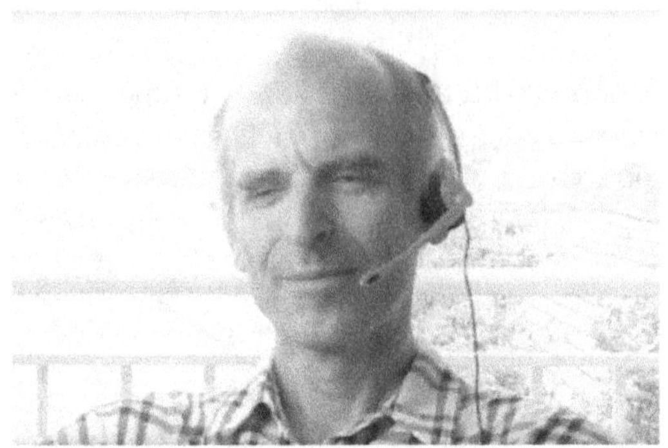

Recording for AMAS' Machinima Film Festival, 2003.
Image used with permission, source: AMAS ©

Tragically, however, Rasmussen did not live long enough to make more films and machinima. His legacy was recognized in an Australian film festival award, the *Peter Rasmussen Innovation Award,* managed by his former friends and colleagues in the industry. The award was given to similarly pioneering filmmakers between 2009-2012 at the *Sydney Film Festival.*

In this chapter, we outline the back story to *Stolen Life* and Rasmussen's contribution to machinima through his work and its impact on the creative industries beyond.

6.2 Back Story

Rasmussen was a Danish-born Australian filmmaker, best known in the Australian film sector as the co-writer of the 1998 feature film, *In the Winter Dark* (co-written and directed by James Bogle, starring actors Brenda Blethyn, Ray Barrett and Richard Roxburgh). His work was considered to be predominantly non-commercial and included Australia's first no-budget grunge classic feature film, *Mad Bomber in Love* (1992, directed by James Bogle) as well as award-winning shorts, *The Picture Woman* (1998) and machinima films, *Rendevous* (2001, see Figure 6.2) and *Killer Robot* (2003, see Figure 6.3). His production company, *Nanoflix Productions,* was established in 2003.

As an artist, Rasmussen's films were independently generated and passionate creations made through any means necessary. They were often described as being 'made on the smell of an oily rag' in the film industry (*Inside Film*, 2010). He was also an enthusiastic gamer. The lack of investment and minimal budget used in his art was not something that held Rasmussen back: it is because of the low budget potential offered by machinima that he worked with the genre. In an early interview about machinima, he commented:

> I was playing a game called *Marathon*, made for Mac by the same people that made *Halo*. It occurred to me that here was a living environment that you could move a camera through and use it as a sound stage and actually make a film in it. I took this idea and pitched it at the people who I made The Picture Woman with and said let's do something. I actually got *Quake II* and did extensive story boards within it and we were going to do a demo for an idea within that... One of the things about [machinima] is it is a very tiny cost to set up to do. I found personally that I'm able to sort of, in the same way as with writing, I can often tinker an idea into existence. I'll pick at this idea, and that idea, and on the computer you can do that. You can say I'll build a room and I'll put a camera in it, and move the character round and see what I've got. That's the way the first animation took place. I started playing with the stuff. And then Tim Quarry [visual effects, *The Core* 2003, *X-Men Origins: Wolverine* 2009] pointed me to Game Studio which is what both *Rendevous* and *Killer Robot* are made in – it's ideal for that kind of experimentation...
>
> Peter Rasmussen (interview, *Machinima Film Festival* DVD, 2003)

The first two of his machinima works were really 'digital doodles' and prototypes both of form and process using *Quake* models in *TrueSpace* (see Figure 6.4). The next two of his machinima works were nominated for *Machinima Film Festival Awards*, respectively in 2002 for *Rendevous* and in 2005 for *Killer Robot*. These shorts (*Rendevous*, 8:00 mins and *Killer Robot*, total of 70:00 mins) both conceptually informed and ultimately led to the development of Rasmussen's ground-breaking machinima film *Stolen Life* (2007, 80:00 mins, directed and co-produced by Jackie Turnure), the first Australian feature-length film in machinima. *Rendevous* was a film about a chance meeting of sentient robots in outer space, one imploring the other to 'misbehave'. *Killer Robot* was released as a weekly series of nine chapters, influenced in part by films such as popular science fiction as well as classic 1940s detective noir stories and adventure games. His decision to release in chapters was pragmatic – file sizes were large and streaming services were non-existent!

Figure 6.2: Screencap *Rendevous.*

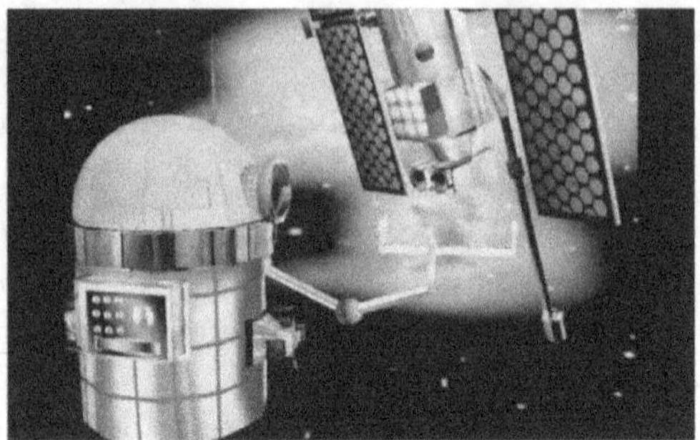

Source: Rasmussen, 2000.

Figure 6.3: Screencap *Killer Robot.*

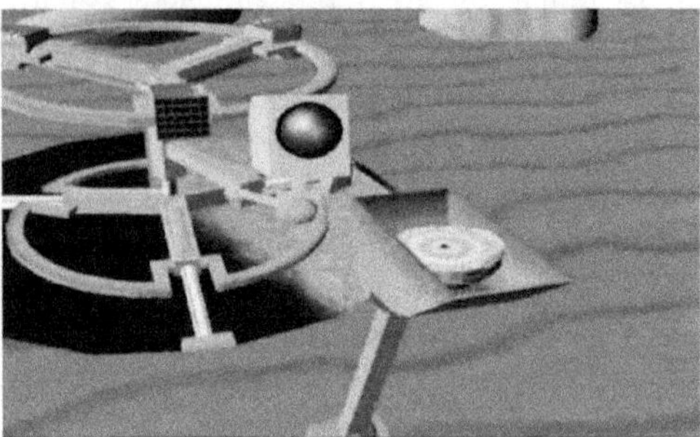

Source: Rasmussen, 2003.

Work on *Stolen Life* had begun during the making of *Killer Robot.* This was a film about a construction robot on Mars, using synthetic voices for characters and an animation system that formed the basis of the more ambitious *Stolen Life* film. Whereas *Killer Robot* had been a solo project, *Stolen Life* was considerably more complex with multiple characters. Writing the first draft of the script was completed by the end of filming *Killer Robot,* which Rasmussen said helped take the pressure off the new project. He had also worked on the *Killer Robot* script with Jackie Turnure, a filmmaker who specialized in creating game scripts, whom he then approached to collaborate with on *Stolen Life,* bringing her in as director and co-producer. Turnure became a sounding board for character and plot developments, whereas the animation system for production was more Rasmussen's special interest, using his approach and wider experience to frame shots.

Figure 6.4: Screencaps *Red Igloo* (2000) | *Joy* (2000).

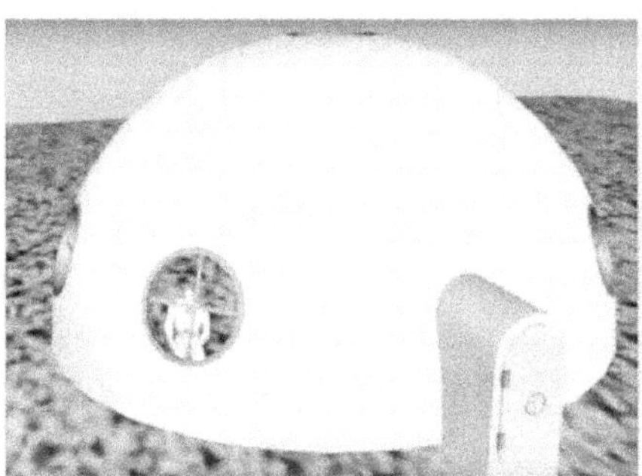
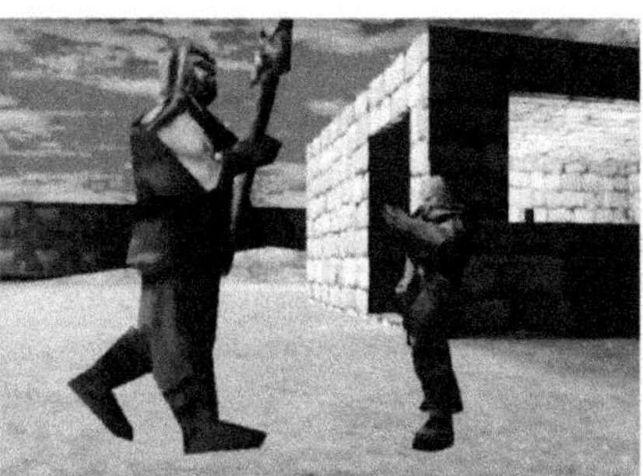

Source: Rasmussen (2000).

On completion of *Killer Robot,* he had been discussing potential references for the DVD sleeve with *Machinima.com*'s co-founder Hancock. He identified Chris Jones, the creator of the highly innovative *Tex Murphy* adventure game series (1989-2014) as someone whose opinion in his film he would greatly value. Rasmussen felt there was synergy in his approach to filmmaking and Jones' early (eg., 1989) use of novel technologies for games, including DVD (rather than CD) and particularly his use of one of the first computer-generated sound programmes, called *RealSound* (developed by Steve Witzel of *Access Software, Tex Murphy* series developer/publisher), although this subsequently became obsolete with the standardization of soundcards in computers. As Rasmussen approached Jones, he realized he would also be an excellent lead for his *Stolen Life* male character. Jones had considerable game-based voice acting experience as the *Tex Murphy* character, a similar detective hack to the sci-fi character Rasmussen had created for the film. He had also worked on a preliminary script with Steven Spielberg for his film, *A.I. Artificial Intelligence.* After Rasmussen sent Jones the draft script, he duly agreed. Commenting at the time of the release of *Stolen Life,* Jones said:

> The prep work for the character, I was helped out because I had worked on a project with Steven Spielberg, *A.I.* There were a lot of preliminary discussions in terms of how do we deal with artificial intelligence, when does artificial intelligence discern that it has become an entity and when does that entity become what we would consider to be 'human'. Through that experience there was a lot of rich background that I got to deal with… here I thought the character was better developed.
>
> Chris Jones (interview, *Nanoflix Productions,* 2007)

And years later, Jones reflected:

> I was happy to do voice acting for Stolen Life, but it was kind of hard for me to believe they really wanted me to do it. I really don't think of myself as an 'actor'!
>
> Chris Jones (in Ivey, 2012)

As he turned his attention to Jones' opposite character, having been inspired by Claudia Black's character representation in the cult sci-fi series *Farscape*, Rasmussen approached her agent with information about both the script and the machinima filmmaking method. Black also supported the project on the basis of its originality as a screenplay, having been aware of Rasmussen's previous work, notably *The Picture Woman*, a film that had opened the *Sydney Film Festival* in 1998, as well as the technology used to create the piece. Whilst participating in a fan convention *Farscape* panel at *DragonCon* (2009 in Atlanta, US), Black commented on her role and machinima:

> When I read [the *Stolen Life* script], it was this really lovely story about these robots who had been posted out on a station and they'd been forgotten about. It was this whole idea of artificial intelligence and whether these beings actually have a soul and feelings and what their real objective is. Turns out these robots on this station do all have their own agenda, so it's a detective noir... The interesting thing about that piece was that he had embraced a technology and a form of animation called machinima, which uses platforms from games to make animation and then making your own software, so he made what you would refer to as a crude animation film using this platform...
>
> Claudia Black (in *Claudia Black Unofficial*, 2013)

For *Killer Robot* he used a 3D game authoring package as an animation tool called *TrueSpace* (Kelland, 2011) and for *Stolen Life* he used *Maya* and *3D Game Studio*. To help him produce his scenes, Rasmussen created code to automate and run routines in the game engines which enabled him to replay scenes and rapidly review the work, once describing his use of these tools for machinima as being "*video editing software except that you can go into the picture and look at it from anywhere*" (Rasmussen in Sluganski, 2007). Rasmussen's view was that it is the ability to review output quickly and from multiple perspectives that makes machinima such a promising creative process:

> It's this that is at the heart of what makes machinima so powerful. I have my hands directly on the 'clay' of the scene. I can tweak and look tweak and look until it's right.
>
> Peter Rasmussen (in Sluganski, 2007)

Following an invitation to participate in a *Farscape* panel with Claudia Black, *Stolen Life* was introduced with a preliminary trailer at *DragonCon* (September 2006, Atlanta, US). Thereafter, a trailer comprising a seven-minute mix of *Stolen Life* was entered into the 2006 New York *Machinima Film Festival* (*AMAS* November), where it was nominated in six categories receiving the Best Original Music award. The film was first screened in full at the *Metro Theatre* in Sydney on 11 June 2007 (Kolan, 2007). Subsequently, it was shown at the *Sydney Film Festival* (June 2007) by invitation and then entered into the *European Machinima Film Festival*, an event jointly sponsored by De Montfort University's Institute of Creative Technologies (directed by co-author, Tracy Harwood) and *AMAS*, taking place in October 2007 in Leicester (UK). The film was awarded the festival's Best Picture as well as Best Direction, Best Story and Best Visual Design awards. Never once was Rasmussen's serious eyesight condition mentioned; the film competed with that of others on its own creative merit in the machinima festivals – machinima was evidently the perfect democratic medium which emphasized his filmmaking, screenwriting and creative talent, and is also testimony to the collaborative power of the internet. As Turnure commented:

> [Working on *Stolen Life*] I felt like that was the first time that I really understood that niche communities when you are online become really great global forces. Peter had a direct relationship with the machinima community... it made me realize that the support of like-minded people, you don't have to just find them in your own back garden. He would not have made *Stolen Life* without that community. He was inspired by them. He was galvanized by them... I think that grassroots community was pivotal to the work. *Stolen Life* wasn't just our film, it was that community's film, because they were right there with him.
>
> Jackie Turnure (interview, 2020)

The following year, at *AMAS'* New York *Machinima Film Festival* in October 2008, an annual honorary award was named in recognition of Rasmussen's memory and his contribution to the world of machinima filmmaking. A few weeks later, the first *Machinima Expo*, an event which took place wholly online inside *Linden Labs' Second Life* virtual environment, hosted a memorial exhibition of his work. This was attended by many international machinima community members participating as avatars, including Turnure.

Rasmussen's creative trajectory had led to his becoming known as a pioneering and, ironically, visionary filmmaker in new media, also inspiring the *Sydney Film Festival* to offer an award in his memory. The *Peter Rasmussen Innovation Award* was launched in 2009, having been developed by a group of his former friends and collaborators. The award was managed by a board of trustees (see Table 1) from the filmmaking sector who raised an annual amount of $5,000 as a prize for filmmakers who worked in either film, machinima or new media and that reflected Rasmussen's visionary spirit and creative determination to create work under difficult conditions, such as severe financial or other constraints. A candidate's work may be described as 'fringe, maverick, or innovative', could push boundaries none others had previously done and incorporate new technologies and tools in making work for any or all types of screen-based format.

Table 6.1: *Peter Rasmussen Innovation Award* board of trustees (2008).

Mark Abicht (actor, production assistant)
Rosemary Blight (producer, *In the Winter Dark*)
James Bogle (director, co-writer)
Lucas Bone (editor, sound mixer, *Stolen Life*)
Martin Brown (director, writer, producer including *Moulin Rouge! Strictly Ballroom, Mad Bomber in Love*)
David Caesar (director, writer, actor, *Strictly Ballroom*)
Robert (Rob) Connolly (director, producer, screenwriter, *Three Dollars* 2005 and *The Bank* 2001, special mention *Stolen Life*)
Liz Doran (film editor, *The Picture Woman*)
Victor Gentile (producer, *The Picture Woman*)
Susan Gibbeson (Paramatta City Council, Attractive City Manager, Sydney)
Peter Giles (Australian Film Television and Radio School, Head of Digital Media)
Ben Grant (sound editor, *Farscape*)
Chris Hilton (producer, director, writer, actor, *A Traveler's Guide to the Planets* 2010)
Phillip Johnston (composer, *Stolen Life*)
Lech Mackiewicz (voice actor, *Stolen Life*)
Leon Marvell (writer, *Mad Bomber in Love*)
George Mannix (co-writer, *Mad Bomber in Love*)
Shilo McClean (producer, *The Beat Manifesto* 1995)
Marty Murphy (voice actor, *Rendevous* and *Stolen Life*)
Mary O'Malley (producer)
Daniel Nettheim (director, *The Beat Manifesto* 1995, *The Hunter* 2011)
Linda Tizard (NWS production crew, *Bright Star* 2009)
Jackie Turnure (co-producer and director, *Stolen Life*, triple Emmy Award-winning producer)
Mark Ward (sound and effects editor, e.g., *Bartleby* 2000, *The Quiet American* 2002)
Greg Woodland (director, writer, script editor, *The Bet* 2006)

Various sources, IMDb and Sydney Film Festival, collated by authors.

6.3 About Stolen Life

Written in the tradition of film noir, with *Pi* (Jones) in the leading role as the detective, and *Kieru* (Black), as the supporting role as the femme fatale. Both characters are robots, however, and the film is set on a far-flung asteroid within our solar system some-time in the future. Shot on location on the asteroid, *Stolen Life* tells the story of sentient robot characters – the two leads plus a host of supporting robots.

Figure 6.5: Screencap *Stolen Life.*

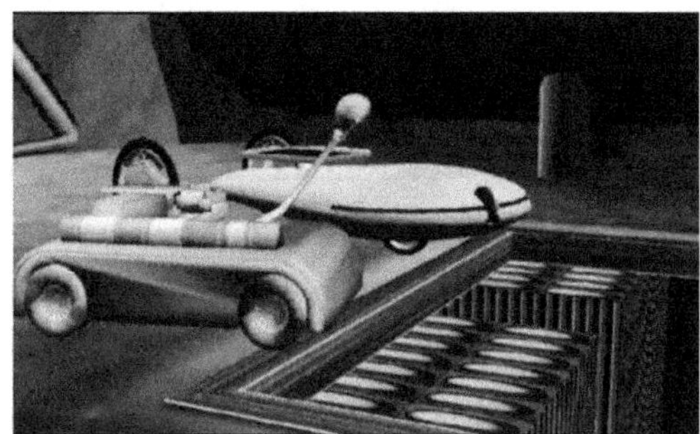

Source: Peter Rasmussen and Jackie Turnure, 2007.

A solitary spacecraft makes a landing on a seemingly barren asteroid. The traveller is himself a machine, a private investigator. He pries open an old hatchway to go below. Under the ice, tunnels descend deeper and deeper into the dark. It's a refuelling station, a halfway point for missions to the outer reaches of the solar system. It was, until they shut it down. What happened here? *Pi* (the investigator) finds an inactive robot. He revives her. This is *Kieru,* the facility manager. Why did the company take so long to send an investigator? It takes a bit of work to get it out of him, but *Pi* admits there is trouble in other facilities.

Pi is investigating the disappearance of thousands of dollars in company property and the mysterious demise of one of the workers who goes by the name of *Faraday.* What is the project *Kieru* is so desperate to conceal? And what really happened to *Faraday*? *Pi* investigates this eccentric crew who had cut out an existence for themselves in the rocks and ice of the asteroid, always under the shadow of the Company.

Doc and his crazy projects. *Daisy,* skittish and nervy. What is she so nervous about? *Grip* is like a pair of disembodied arms joined at the shoulder, a good-natured beast. *Cutter* says little and works away cutting tunnels deeper and deeper into the ice. They all seem innocent enough but how safe is *Pi* alone with this motley crew under the fractured and creaking ice of this far-flung asteroid?

As the story unfolds, we learn of an intentional ploy to lure the investigator and a lot about the back stories of the characters, their motivations, inner conflicts, desires and obstacles. The robots are sentient and technology aware – they are even capable of exploiting virtual reality for their own purposes. The plot uncovers the uniqueness of the asteroid and how creative the robots have been in order to mine it for valuable resources. But there is a secret to which they are all party: time is of the essence! The surface structure of the asteroid influences their behaviour in multiple different ways, and they must each weigh their roles against the others.

The style of the storytelling is humanistic: although the robots are clearly industrial in application, there is banter and even sexual tension evident in the plot. In many ways, the quality of the play is driven by the voice acting and the machinima is a clever juxtaposing reference against which to make sense of the artificial alien life forms and animation style.

Of the respective performances of Black and Jones, Rasmussen commented:

> [Black] came with a fully formed idea of what her character and the scene needed but energetically applied herself to alternative ways of working the script. With some actors if you ask them for an adjustment to what they did on the first take they will go to the other extreme. With Claudia she hits the mark exactly... Jackie was impressed to discover Chris [Jones] has never had formal training as an actor. He's a natural. In my opinion he's got more discipline and pure talent than many actors who have had a long career in the business. Being a creator in his own right he has a nuanced understanding for what a scene needs in the context of the overarching story...
>
> No matter how many times I had to play the scenes through over the months I never got tired of hearing those performances. Claudia got things out of a scene I didn't realise were there. Chris has a great sense of humour. He can put a witty twist on a line without losing any of the drama or tension. I remember accidentally starting up one of Chris's lines for an upcoming scene. The way he delivered the line was so playfully smug I laughed out loud. Even before I had checked I knew that would be the take I would use.
>
> Peter Rasmussen (in Sluganski, 2007)

and on his blog, he commented:

> It continually amazes me that even though Chris Jones and Claudia Black have never met, their chemistry is excellent. I can only put it down to how sophisticated their understanding of the story and the characters is. Even though it's essentially a drama you get some surprisingly delicious humour between the characters.
>
> Peter Rasmussen (blog, 2007a)

In her directorial statement about the film, Turnure commented:

> For me, the appeal of the script lies with the clever juxtaposition of a well-worn genre and all its attendant conventions, with an entirely new world. In considering the direction, I aim to find a balance between honouring the conventions of the film noir genre and play with and against these conventions in both the performance and the stylistic look and feel... Ultimately what Machinima allows Peter and I to do is to make an animated feature film based on a compelling story, with strong characters who engage, entertain and move us, for a very low budget. In terms of professional benefits, *Stolen Life* pushes us into an exciting new medium that hones our existing skills and challenges us to discover and develop new ones. I am very excited about working on *Stolen Life* and see it as a quantum leap in my work as an animation director.
>
> Jackie Turnure (directorial statement, *Vimeo*, 2007)

It is the sound track that Rasmussen considered to have pulled the project together, where each frame is connected to the actor's delivery of the scene. Rasmussen described the music as another character in the film ("*Like a good performance it can bring things out of a scene you didn't know were there*" blog, 2007b). The sound design (by George Turnure) was created in just three weeks in the studio, a considerable feat given the level of detail. The music score was designed to evoke both a film noir and sci-fi feel to the movie, originally intended to reflect a 1940s B-movie. Music was composed by Philip Johnston, of whose creative work Rasmussen commented:

> [Johnston] uses a magnificently haunting piece at an important point late in the film. I was so captivated by this piece I asked if a variation could be used to open and close the film. The opening music in the trailer was what was originally intended. The version now at the end of the film is a very sparse 'dance' of two saxophones. Philip explained that the piece has no musical centre. The way I understand that is that the silences become so rich because you are kept anticipating the next note. I can't resist comparing it to a binary star system where two suns revolve around each other... Seeing the animation with the music was like experiencing the film for the first time all over again. The glass wall between you and the story is broken and you walk in.
>
> Peter Rasmussen (in Sluganski, 2007)

They did not make a 'making of' film or take photographs of the production phase of *Stolen Life* which became aspects of its unique production process that were in demand post-production. Much of the preparation for voice recording involved making the scenes without voices, an animation process that took approximately ten months to complete. Turnure directed and recorded the voice acting mostly 'by correspondence' over the internet because of both time and financial constraints with the back-pocket production – despite Rasmussen's approach to the Australian funding council, the project was 'too unusual' for their more conventional film taste and was funded by Rasmussen and Turnure to the amount of Aus$25,000, also using contracts with performers that would allocate income from future sales. Recording was undertaken in a local sound studio in Sydney with Black and others but Jones was recorded at his home in Salt Lake City (US). The total production process took three years.

6.4 Impact of Rasmussen and his work

On the release of *Stolen Life*, Rasmussen had been so embedded in the creative processes involved in making the film that he found he had little time to consider how the machinima medium was evolving. He was, however, particularly aware of the development of new machinima filmmaking tools that were close to his own filmmaking process, such as UK-based *Short Fuse Limited*'s forthcoming *Moviestorm* (released in October 2007). To catch up with the state of the art, he attended and participated in the Melbourne *Machinima Film Festival* held at *Australian Centre for Moving Image* (*ACMI*, February 2007) in order to explore. This was the second machinima festival that took place in Australia (Shea, 2007), and involved *AMAS*' Paul Marino and Friedrich Kirschner (see Chapter 3) as well as the *Rooster Teeth* team, showcasing the latest season of *Red vs Blue* (see Chapter 4). Rasmussen presented a workshop on making machinima alongside Kirschner and the *FRAPS* moving image screen capture software developer, Rod Maher of *Beepa*. Rasmussen's thoughts at the time were of a medium that allowed for considerable experimentation, including avant-garde, arts and political commentaries. In an interview for *IGN* that took place during the *Sydney Film Festival* later in the year (June 2007), he commented:

> They've [work of other machinima filmmakers] been inspirational, not so much in 'I want to be doing what they're doing'; more in that it's fascinating to see what they've been doing with this form. Some of it is very experimental, very out there, but a lot of it has a great sense of humour in what is being done.
>
> Peter Rasmussen (in Kolan, 2007)

Over the years since it opened to the public, machinima and its multiple different creative applications have been incorporated into teaching and learning resources, reaching hundreds of students through courses made available at *ACMI* in Australia (see e.g., Trundle, 2014). Indeed, machinima in general has become a widely used teaching and learning medium globally, reflecting the broad influence it has had discussed in previous chapters.

Introducing *Stolen Life* on Rasmussen's production company *Nanoflix Productions'* website, Claudia Black, the actress who played voice character *Kieru* in the film, commented:

> What I loved about machinima ... to be involved in a new technology, this piqued my interest enormously, to be part of something that may end up really growing and developing and giving the big boys like Pixar a run for their money one day.
>
> Claudia Black (interview, *Nanoflix Productions*, 2007)

Turnure also reflected on this in her directorial statement:

> In terms of the style and design of the characters and location the use of Machinima poses particular challenges. Whilst the images will not have the high resolution of animated feature films such as those being produced by *Pixar* (*Toy Story, Monsters Inc, Nemo*), the graphic quality and attention to camera angle, movement, editing and soundscape will more than compensate for any reduction in visual detail. Lighting and design will follow the film noir style and the use of music and sound design will be employed to create a rich and ambient sound track. As demonstrated in *Killer Robot,* a strong script more than makes up for low production values.
>
> Jackie Turnure (directorial statement, *Vimeo*, 2007)

In April 2007, Rasmussen had written an extensive article on his blog about the significance and potential of machinima as a creative medium. He argued that it is not simply a new form of traditional filmmaking but a completely different approach, where the messiness of creative processes associated with traditional filmmaking does not need to interrupt the practice of developing a creative project. He said:

> Machinima is not a branch of an earlier kind of film making like video from celluloid. Machinima is a completely independent eruption. It is not just a new image recording medium. What used to be a video game add on is now a new approach to storytelling that has its own community and culture. It's a movement that is currently free of most of the intrinsic encumbrances of conventional filmmaking... The feedback loop between trying something out and seeing the result is so much shorter... There is much less of a gap between having an idea and seeing how it actually looks on the screen. And straight away you can see if it works for the audience. It's not just the speed of production. It's very much about the attitude people making machinima bring to what they do...
>
> It's like Machinima is in the first few microseconds after its big bang. The particles are basic but very powerful. I expect that over the next few

> years we will see more long form productions as serious machinima makers settle in for the long haul… There is an opportunity to, refine is the wrong word, to bring this new medium to a state where it can be produced for a return of revenue that allows the machinima makers to continue to deliver to their audience something fresh and original in a sustainable way without outside interference in the creative process.
>
> Peter Rasmussen (Blog, 2007c)

These comments reflect the trajectory of the medium as it has been adopted by producers such as Favreau (see Chapter 3). Furthermore, within Rasmussen's own circle of filmmaker colleagues, Rob Connolly, Australian film director, noted years later how such innovation would influence the filmmaking process:

> I know that I can go into my post house and they can build 3D models and I can see all the stuff I'm doing, animate stuff and move the camera around, storyboard, etc. The stuff I can do now with technology was really what Peter was doing in the game engines fifteen years ago [except] Peter would not have been dealing with high end computing.
>
> Rob Connolly (interview, 2020)

Rasmussen's strategy of seeking out commercializable actors would also help him portray a richness in the sound quality that the animation quality was less able to achieve, being machinima. Their credibility beyond the machinima community as characters in other media formats helped him to generate an audience for the work which was shown some time after its release not only at film festivals in Australia but also internationally, such as the machinima festivals in New York and Leicester, and fan conventions such as *DragonCon* (Atlanta, US). Of its showcase at *Dragon Con*, machinima panel organizer Tina Crawford (aka Romily Machinima) commented:

> *Stolen Life* showed you can do a lot with minimal visuals… I remember that *Stolen Life* was well received… I personally still find it an excellent and entertaining piece. It shows how with fantastic voice talent, writing, music, sound, etc. even fairly simple visuals can be intensely engaging and tell a terrific story.
>
> Tina Crawford (interview, 2020)

On its internet introduction, Randy Sluganski, editor of the game review website *Just Adventure,* provided an overview of machinima. He had also orchestrated the introduction between Rasmussen and Jones, who is best known as the designer of the *Tex Murphy* computer game series (1989, first developed and published by *Access Software* and from 2014 *Big Finish Games* and *Atlus* respectively). Sluganski commented:

> ... at that time I didn't have a clue as to what a machinima movie was and I was just secretly hoping that I had not led some lunatic to Chris' doorstep! Machinima movies are a new form of filmmaking that utilize computer technology – most commonly first-person shooter engines – to shoot films in the virtual reality of a game engine. These films are produced using the tools – camera angles, level editors, etc. and resources – backgrounds, characters, skins, etc. – available in a game. In many ways, machinima movies could be compared to independently developed adventure games – they are made on a limited budget with a small, but talented and devoted, staff. They are also a glimpse into the future of filmmaking.
>
> Randy Sluganski (*Just Adventure*, 2007)

To the machinima filmmaking process, however, Rasmussen had brought new insight for others. His comments in 2003 reflect how the traditional filmmaking process had been turned on its head:

> The thing about making conventional films, even if you are making films for no money, you have to convince people to participate. With filmmaking the actual work is about 10% and the other 90% is convincing people either to give you money or arrive on set on time, for nothing! So about the business of turning to animation, I've always loved animation, but it hadn't occurred to me that I could actually be an animator myself. With machinima you can because, even with having no previous experience, I could try things immediately. And if it's wrong, I could make it slower or faster or move the camera. It's very akin to script editing because it's very plastic in the same way.
>
> Peter Rasmussen (*Machinima Film Festival DVD*, 2003)

From the machinima community perspective, Phil Rice, founder of *Zarathustra Studios*, part of the *Machiniplex* community team, machinima podcast *The Overcast* and subsequently one of the founders of the *Machinima Expo*, commented:

> Peter brought a sense of authenticity to machinima that few others could have done. He had a pedigree, a background in real filmmaking working with real / accomplished filmmakers, and that showed in the level of polish he brought in particular to *Stolen Life* – a feature-length work that still holds up extremely well today. He also elevated the art form with his intelligent subject matter and dialogue. There were no jokes for gamers only, no toilet humor... I told Peter once that his work reminded me of Isaac Asimov, which he took as the high compliment I very much intended.
>
> Phil Rice (interview, 2020)

On release, fans of the *Stolen Life*'s leading actors, Rasmussen and sci-fi in general reviewed the film. Few had previous experience of the machinima medium. As Turnure reflected:

> It didn't do that well on the big screen. That big, it was not super hi-res. But it was very affecting and people in the audience really enjoyed it. What was interesting is that it looked experimental but sounded very familiar because it's a detective noir genre and so the fact they're robots on an asteroid doesn't really matter – you just know that there is a team and they're hiding something, and there's a detective and he knows something is going on, so it feels both familiar and unfamiliar at the same time… Some of the journalists who reviewed it, they were initially like most people with machinima kind of 'what is this' and then 'actually this is amazing' as they got totally stuck into the story. It was one of those things where you had to get past the first five minutes and then you've gotten used to how it looked. It is quite crude animation.
>
> Jackie Turnure (interview, 2020)

Others, such as Sam Sloan, managing editor of the popular *Slice of SciFi* podcast, whilst supportive of the film was less enthusiastic about the creative medium (Sloan, 2007). Mat Van Rhoon, Australian graphics artist who became lead visual effects artist on the *Tesla Effect* title in the *Tex Murphy* game series, had a different view. Posting on the *Tex Murphy Unofficial* fan community site, he said:

> One thing I noticed towards the end of the film was that, despite the fact that I was sceptical of the whole idea of machinima, the formula seemed to work. It may not have had stellar imagery (compared to computer animated films lik*e Final Fantasy: The Spirits Within)* but it has its own unique presence; a presence which I certainly hope becomes recognised in the industry... *Stolen Life* is a first step for the *Nanoflix* folks towards getting their formula into the bigger market. Of course, this market would not exist without fanboys and sci-fi nuts like us, so we gotta band together! There is a lot of room for development in machinima and for the Nanoflix crew, so expect to see more from these guys in the future. Of course, exposure is the most important thing at the moment. I believe there is a place in the market for films like *Stolen Life.* It might not be Hollywood, but to the thousands upon thousands (even millions) of sci-fi fans out there tired of having their favourite shows either cancelled or shunned into graveyard time-slots, there are those who will be supportive and appreciative of this kind of film, to no end! I give *Stolen* Life thumbs up, and eagerly await further developments with

Nanoflix and machinima in the future; and if you too want to see the genre flourish, make yourself heard, and start by seeing *Stolen Life!*"

Mat Van Rhoon (in *Tex Murphy Unofficial* website, 2007)

Similarly, Steven Rainmaker, reviewer for *Robots.net*, commented:

> The animation can be very distracting at first. Eventually you learn to ignore it. One solution is simple to tune out the visual experience and listen. My wife compared the experience to listening to an old-style radio play where you have sound but no picture. To me it brought to mind the experience of watching the animatics or storyboard run through during the pre-production stage of a film. At other times it felt like watching someone else play a videogame. I wanted to reach for the controls to steer a robot away from a precipice before it fell in. After a while, though, I began to stop noticing the form and pay more attention to the content; the story, the voice characterizations, and the music.

Steven Rainmaker (in *Robots.net*, 2007)

In many ways, this is a highly perceptive observation of Rasmussen and Turnure's focus the quality of the script, but it was also a reflection of the way in which quality of animation, whether in games or on film were evolving. As Turnure says:

> We realized that, and it was one of the things we argued about quite a lot, was fidelity [of *Stolen Life*]. We were at the time when the Pixar films were massive and the quality of the video games had really hit a new high. The lo-fi nature of it [*Stolen Life*] felt really like a hard barrier… [but] it was a shock that people couldn't get past some of the crudeness and look of it.

Jackie Turnure (interview, 2020)

Rice reflected on why it worked so well as a feature film:

> The dialogue is superbly written and is amplified by some spectacular voice performances. The story is a mystery which unfolds as the detective interviews various suspects, who have secrets and motives, they lie, they scheme, they mislead, they CARE (these are robots we're talking about, remember) – it's just delicious. And there are a number of moments where story is revealed with no dialogue happening whatsoever. Peter did an extraordinary job of conveying actions and emotions using characters with fairly primitive-looking robot body types. The fact that he was legally blind for the entirety of the production makes that all the more amazing.

Phil Rice (interview 2020)

It was not simply for his creative work that Rasmussen was known. On the release of *Stolen Life*, Rasmussen focussed on its distribution, attempting to overcome some of the issues numerous other machinima creators had found over the years in reaching target audiences. As well as DVDs, the most popular independent distribution method at the time, he found streaming services that enabled him to reach a target audience. Notably, *Si-Mi* was a *YouTube Red*-like service that enabled him to generate income from downloads. The film however never managed to cover the costs of its original investment (Turnure, 2020). He and Turnure refused to use a distributor or sales agent and took control of sending out the DVD from home to customers all over the world. He discussed both his approach and the challenges they faced in a review he completed for Sluganski's post and on his blog:

> So now we are in uncharted territory. We have to find the right distributor and the right deal. Once we have that we can promote it over what is now called the 'long tail'. The old [distribution] model uses a big splash cinema release to draw as much attention to the film as possible in one big blast. The success of the movie is measured by how sharp or gradual the drop off in interest is after the first week. This approach requires truckloads of money and if you get it wrong there are no second chances. Now with the Internet once a title is available to buy online you can keep pushing the project as long as you have energy for it with viral campaigns and word of mouth and blogs and forums and whatever else you can think of. It's all about the right kind of energy applied in the right way. Bring it on.
>
> Peter Rasmussen (in Sluganski, 2007)

> We have been offering the *Stolen Life* DVD as prizes in robot contests around the world like robot soccer and robot Sumo. There are even some dance contests. And of course search and rescue. I'm really enjoying the responses from the robotics groups. They are very much used to the idea of robots as heroes.
>
> Peter Rasmussen (Blog, 2007d)

The direct-to-consumer distribution method is really only viable when there is a long tail of community members willing to engage with the work and finding these individuals online was always a challenge. As highlighted in our previous chapters, this is easier as an established platform and streaming content distributor but considerably harder as an independent filmmaker. As only the second machinima movie on IMDb (submitted 23 July 2007), however, Rasmussen noted the film had been easier to distribute using DVDs and content sharing platforms but considerably harder to list on the official movie database. Rasmussen commented that his success with this was "*a good sign for machinima*" (Blog, 2007b). That said, Rasmussen's work was never intended for mass-market consumption. Rice reflects:

> Peter's work had a seriousness and intelligence and credibility that put him in a fairly exclusive club. His stuff wasn't designed for mass market consumption, it wasn't constructed to capitalize on a trend or a popular meme. He wanted to tell interesting stories, with interesting characters. Machinima as his medium, for Peter that came a distant second to story. It just happened to be the method he could use which granted him independence in his work. But I truly believe if he'd been able to tell compelling stories using piles of colored sand or a group of highly trained desert insects, he'd have done that instead. Machinima for him truly was just a tool to get a job done, that job being STORY. And that informed every aspect of his approach to machinima.
>
> Phil Rice (interview, 2020)

This is also reflected in Connolly's comments about Rasmussen's work:

> *[Stolen Life]* was at a time when feature films were an impossible narrative to achieve and that he was able to do it on his own – that was ambition. I had a sense that this was the infancy of technology and the infancy of storytelling as well, and how you would tell a story over that duration. He constantly surprised me whenever I talked to him about it. This technology was allowing him to realize his creative ambition. I had a sense of him being ahead of the curve, you could feel something coming.
>
> Rob Connolly (interview, 2020)

Having acknowledged the comments on his film, Rasmussen became more active in the machinima community, developing new projects with a number of its members including Ricky Grove, actor and director of the *Machinima Expo* (2009 onwards), and Rice. With a feature on *The Overcast* dedicated to Rasmussen and *Stolen Life*, Rice, commented:

> Rasmussen is one of the genre's most respected and prolific directors and advocates. He is proof positive that one can make machinima, be taken seriously while doing so, and end up owning what he creates. His story in this field is a personal inspiration.
>
> Phil Rice (*The Overcast*, 2008)

What makes Rasmussen's work so poignant, however, is that shortly after completing *Stolen Life* he committed suicide, on 8 March 2008. In the period before this, Rasmussen had been diagnosed with congenital macular degenerative eye disease, a serious condition that rarely affects such young people and which left him with only peripheral vision. The condition had forced him to re-evaluate his career as a cinematographer some twenty years previously to one of screenwriter. In order to write, he invented and adapted various optical apparatus to enable him to 'see' computer screens. His early career as a scientific instrument maker had enabled him to devise and build a monocle lens, similar to a director's lens, which he strapped to his head. He worked with this just a few centimetres from the screen (Stephens, 2008; Turnure, 2020). Rasmussen's use of synthetic voices in *Killer Robot* had been informed by his personal use of the tool, which had helped him to read web pages and emails he received. He was both frustrated and angered by his condition which gradually worsened, and he became more socially isolated from his local friends. With increasingly difficult financial circumstances, he would not ask for help and indeed was adamant that he did not want to be known as 'the blind filmmaker' (Turnure, 2020).

His death came as a shock and major blow to his colleagues and the machinima community – there had been no unusual sign of change in his behaviour towards his friends and colleagues. Jackie Turnure, director and co-producer of *Stolen Life*, commented in her blog:

> Making *Stolen Life* with Peter was honestly the best creative collaboration I have ever had. And it went beyond the film – Peter and I had so many long conversations where one of us was feeling down, losing faith or confidence and we would pep each other up… Peter had a degenerative eye disease and only had his peripheral vision. He was adamant that only a few people knew – he didn't want pity and his greatest fear was that he'd be known as some kind of freak: 'the blind filmmaker'. But he was seriously debilitated by it and our only real fights were when he felt I was patronizing him about his eyesight. But it was astonishing what he achieved in spite of it. He taught himself a complex 3D animation software, *Maya*, and modelled and animated a feature film on his own. He was so determined – nothing was going to stop him.
>
> Jackie Turnure (blog, 2008)

In fact, Rasmussen had been an active contributor to the machinima community for many years, appearing in Brown's 2003 documentary on machinima, featuring numerous others who had been involved in its development such as Hancock, Dellario and Marino. What was apparent and surprising was the number of people in the machinima community Rasmussen had contact with on completion of *Stolen Life*. Many posted tributes and comments on blogs and websites with a connection to gaming, machinima, film and fan communities. Posted on the *Machiniplex* community site, Ricky Grove summarized thoughts of many in the machinima community:

> It's perverse that a man as talented and as smart as Peter could be whisked away into oblivion just like that. A man who had just released one of the best Machinima films ever made *(Stolen Life)*, won practically every award at the recent 2007 *European Machinima Festival*, had set up a monthly meeting (along with Phil Rice) of Machinima filmmakers and was starting research for his next film. A man who gave to a largely insular community his time, his care and his wisdom, in order to make Machinima better.
>
> Ricky Grove (blog, *Machiniplex*, 2008)

The development of an award for innovation in filmmaking in his name was an obvious response. This came to fruition with the *Sydney Film Festival*, orchestrated by Rob Connolly, Rosemary Albright and others who had been close friends of Rasmussen since his early days in the film industry. Trustees each recognized the huge challenge of taking pioneering work to an audience within the existing film industry structures, not least getting access to funding for work that 'fell between the cracks' of innovation and demand. At its launch, Peter Giles, the Head of Digital Media at the *Australian Film Television and Radio School* in 2008, commented on his creative work:

> Peter was a pioneer in the field of machinima with the imagination and determination to shape a new means of expression. The Scholarship will continue Peter's spirit and generosity with his knowledge and ideas.
>
> Peter Giles (in *Inside Film*, 2008)

Of its impact, Connolly commented:

> It encouraged emerging creators. My concern is that 9 out of 10 emerging creators who are ambitious in their career, tend to do work that doesn't fit the current dogma, like classic short films as a stepping stone, so we were trying to incentivize the people that are actually on the fringes, as we can see with Peter's case, who are pioneering and who can maybe then go on and contribute more.
>
> Rob Connolly (interview, 2020)

The award ran for four years during which trustees raised the funds between themselves, attracting numerous applications. Ultimately, this became unsustainable, ironically because the trustees struggled to find the funding themselves, and so the award was closed. Connolly commented:

> What we were trying to do was offer an award in his name that recognized people that had an innovative spirit like that – when [the award] ran it was high profile, but we just struggled to raise the funds. We had a couple of years where none of us had much money and every

> year we had to pass the hat around to get the money together. Like a lot of these things, its longevity was cut short sadly but it was a great initiative in his name – we all of us wanted to help others that might be working on the fringes and were not being recognized for their work.
>
> Rob Connolly (interview, 2020)

With technological advancements in streaming platform development, access to increased computing power, resources and tools for filmmaking, it has become much easier for creatives such as Rasmussen to create and place work in the public domain. The challenge is now one of attempting to cut through the noise and volume of content, generate an income from an audience, and overcome platform dominance to ensure a fair contribution for the quality of the work. As Connolly noted:

> I've tried to get some of my early films out there and you get offered $1,200 by *Amazon* to put it on *Amazon* globally for two years or something. I'm almost like 'let's do it for free', to just give it to the world for free because that's just insane. The promise of the long tail has really only been of value to the bigger platforms for games and content.
>
> Rob Connolly (interview, 2020)

Turnure, subsequently a triple Emmy award-winning producer for creative design in various film and storytelling related projects, attributed Rasmussen's pioneering attitude to her success:

> The big thing that I took away from [working with Rasmussen] was that you don't have to lose the art and craft, things that work well in traditional film and media, like a well-crafted story and multi-dimensional characters that are beautifully performed performances, that are compelling – they don't get chucked out when you're working with an experimental new form… I still lean on my understanding of story structure and how to engage and create a relationship with the audience through those materials. That was something that Peter and I really nailed… and the other thing is the work ethic around 'fuck it, I'm just going to do it, I'm not going to wait to get the funding'… we had this maxim of building a plane as we fly it, we weren't waiting until we had it all figured out, we just started making stuff and that informs the process and the project.
>
> Jackie Turnure (interview, 2020)

Connolly, also subsequently an award-winning filmmaker, commented on the impact of Rasmussen's work on his own creative ethos:

> The characters and how to tell their stories within the game engine, that's the thing that stands out for me. I could feel that he was pioneering something, and like a lot of pioneers, I knew he was going to struggle to be recognized because he was ahead of the curve... The adage that someone said early in my career 'everyone wants to be a first person to do something second' comes to mind. Peter was the first person to do something first... His work instilled in me this value for innovation and for thinking and doing things that are not necessarily the dogmatic, contemporary view. It's been a massive impact on me to try to be the first person to do something first, which has great value... I try to instill that value in my own children and my business collaborations; it's a great model for my creative endeavours... What machinima did was make it economically viable to do that. That's quite invigorating, that spirit of doing work that's liberated from the cost structures of doing film and television is really key.
>
> Rob Connolly (interview, 2020)

Each of the *Peter Rasmussen Innovation Award* recipients are ground-breaking digital artists and filmmakers working with a breadth of creative technologies, and becoming increasingly recognized for their innovative approaches to storytelling.

The inaugural winner (2009), Michela Ledwidge, had an extensive background in the world of innovative interactive storytelling. With a background in computer science graduating in 1993, she had created New South Wales' first web service as part of her degree. She then went on to work on pioneering platforms for Reuters and the BBC in the UK. She won the *Web 3D Award* for her short film, *Horses for Courses*, at *SIGGRAPH* in 2001. She also found machinima albeit from a more commercial perspective (see also Chapter 3) having briefly worked with Hancock among others in the gaming community, producing and chairing the first machinima panel at the *BAFTA Interactive Festival* (in February 2004). Other panellists at the *BAFTA* event included Peter Molyneux, creator of *The Movies* (see Chapter 5) who brought along an avatar from the game which was subsequently released in 2005, Marc Evans (director of *My Little Eye* – a kind of horror-themed version of *Big Brother*), Jason Kingsley (*Rebellion*, publisher of games such as *Sniper Elite* and *Alien vs Predator*) and Don Daglow (*Stormfront Studios*, developer of *Never Winter Nights*). She commented:

> By the time the Peter Rasmussen Award happened, I was ten years into my real-time filmmaking career and had had some investment but largely it was self-funded and small projects that stretched the budget.

> But five years before the *Rasmussen Award*, I had won a *NESTA* award for creating remixable film. That was partly inspired by knowing people like Hugh Hancock who coined the term machinima. I was part of that whole scene. Not so much as a content creator working with *Never Winter Nights* and the game engines but as someone who was working with commercial engines, either designed specifically for machinima like *Brilliant Digitals* or more as a software developer just trying things out. The funding was never there to do anything big but my whole shtick was trying to convert my career as a corporate systems architect.
>
> Michela Ledwidge (interview, 2020)

Her application for the award in 2009 was somewhat serendipitous. At a mentoring event in Sydney, she had connected with Rosemary Blight, one of the Board of Trustees of the *Peter Rasmussen Innovation Award*, who suggested she apply. She stated:

> It was one of those things – I didn't see any press about it, I hadn't heard of Peter Rasmussen until I won the award, and then I looked deeply into his story and it was really touching and I felt very honoured to have been the augural recipient… The *Peter Rasmussen Award* started my project *Sanctuary* [but] I still do what I do and the world didn't really change that much. I'm still on the outer of the film industry as much as ever here in Australia. We do most of our work with the US. The Australian industry barely understands games let alone machinima. I felt very honoured indeed.
>
> Michela Ledwidge (interview, 2020)

Sanctuary was a three-partite creative project once described in *Wired Magazine* as the first massively multi-player movie (Silverman, 2006). The *NESTA* award (of £150,000) had funded the creative component, a viewing system had been self-funded and the third part was supported by the Peter Rasmussen Innovation award. Ledwidge has since gone on to form *Studio Mod* (2010) in Sydney, produce the Emmy award-winning multi-platform series, *dirtgirlworld*, was Vice President of the *Australian Directors Guild* (2015-19), and is currently developing room-scale virtual reality and mixed reality experiences working with *Unreal Engine*.

Peter Morse, the 2010 recipient of the award, was another pioneering artist with 20 years plus experience working with considerably more sophisticated visualization techniques than game engines could handle at the time, for example, 4K plus visualizations of Earth science data. His content creation was based on complex scientific datasets, drawing on skills in 3D data visualization, volumetric rendering, stereoscopic immersive virtual and augmented reality systems and computer programming as well as video, photographic and film production, audio design and music. Morse exhibits digital media works around Australia and internationally including in USA, Germany, Britain, France, Finland and Holland. Nominated by Vicky Sowry, the director of the *Australian Network for Art and Technology* (*ANAT*), Morse was awarded for his development of innovative visualization techniques for new types of cinematic experience. Of his award, he commented:

> I worked on a project visualizing ocean data and data about Antarctica with the scientists from the *Australian Antarctic Division*. Some of this was rendered out for full dome, so this was all satellite-based scientific data and I also experimented with a few different platforms for doing things... The award was for developing innovative visualization techniques for new types of cinema that encompasses full dome, stereoscopic, VR, immersive content, primarily photographic-based but also bringing in the possibility of photogrammetric reconstruction and running things in games engines. Most of my work had been done on essentially zero budget because it doesn't fit into the film industry. I'd applied for grants but got feedback like, well you don't have 17 TV credits so sorry we can't fund you. Or if you go to the arts grants, they would say well you're not really about arts, its film. I was in this kind of no-man's land falling between film and media arts practice so it was difficult getting funding, which meant it ended up being self-funded or getting permissions from museums... I think that's the connection with Peter in the sense he was a bit of a maverick, not well financed and did something because he loved it. That's very much my motivation as well. You have a passion and an interest and if it doesn't fit in somewhere, well that doesn't stop you.
>
> Peter Morse (interview, 2020)

As another pioneer, Morse noted that the award helped him to connect with other mavericks and gave him a sense of community that his search for funding had lacked. The award has subsequently made him reconsider the potential of game engines for working with his datasets:

> What it led on for me, from a technical point of view, was to appreciate again the utility of game engines for creating stuff and virtual production, which is what I'm very interested in now. Things like *Unreal Engine* – I've got a big project now that's going to be running in *Unreal* or *Unity* where you can get much more photorealistic rendering in real-time in a game engine. That's now at a stage where its technically very approachable, its visually sophisticated and you can create immersive real-time experiences for museums or public display and also commercial release through the advent of the various publishing platforms, like the *App Store* or *Steam*.
>
> Peter Morse (interview, 2020)

Similarly, 2011 award winner Dario Russo is recognized as a pioneer in using social media for a retro webisode teaser of an imaginary recovered film reel from the 1960s, an 'Italian Spiderman'. The teaser reached an audience of millions that was then successfully converted to a broadcast platform. The project (*Danger 5*) was financed by *South Australian Film Corporation* and was then commissioned by *SBS* for a television series, airing in 2011. The 2012 winner was Justin Wight, a founder of *Monkeystack*, now also an internationally recognized producer with a multi-platform transmedia studio working on interactive storytelling through adventure games, animations and comics.

Thus, Rasmussen's legacy of both his own work and work ethic, as well as through the *Peter Rasmussen Innovation Award* managed by his former friends and colleagues who recognized the considerable struggles he faced to innovate through adversity, is a significant and noteworthy contribution to the socio-technical history of machinima.

What is different now to the environment in which Rasmussen and other early pioneers worked in, particularly the broader machinima community, is the accessibility of creative toolsets they may use which clearly recognizes the issues faced by indie pioneers. For example, *Epic*'s sophisticated 3D real-time environment *Unreal Engine, Unity, Blender, Valve*'s *Source Filmmaker* and *Nvidia*'s *Omniverse Machinima* toolset (announced in September 2020 and open beta launched on 15 December 2020) truly democratize access to powerful real-time rendering tools and virtual reality creative best practice that may be integrated into game development, film-making and transmedia projects. Such technological advancements have addressed some of the early issues highlighted by Rasmussen in the design and development of his workflow. Furthermore, there is now much wider recognition of the impact and value of interactive methodologies which produce experientially rich media products for a wide range of audiences. It is both ironic and poignant that Rasmussen's methodology and skillset are much sought-after today, as we highlight in our exploration of industry perspectives in the next chapter, Chapter 7.

Chapter 7

Begin Again?

> At times, it seems that every breathless technological advancement revealed today becomes an arcane relic within the lifecycle of most flowers. Many of these instantaneously primitive inventions pass away but a few of the primitive (i.e., original) ideas behind them keep evolving. Some of the most intriguing ideas deal with creative expression and the retelling of stories across generations.
>
> John Gaeta, foreword (in Marino, 2004)

7.1 Introduction

In this chapter, we explore some of the threads highlighted in previous chapters on the roles of key industry players in the emergence and impacts of machinima. Whilst we often observe that machinima was a bottom-up community-driven movement, demonstrated throughout this text in our various discussions, there was also a movement within the creative industries, notably film and game sectors, that sought to incorporate innovative practices into its established industries. Far from being vaguely interested observers in machinima and the community of creative practitioners, there was an active strategy by a number of organizations that sought to benefit from the pioneering work of machinima creators by following their lead and adapting their processes to position what has now become a common, albeit still innovative, digital workflow. John Gaeta's (eg., *The Matrix Trilogy*, Academy award-winning designer and part of the special effects team that invented the *Bullet Time* shot, volumetric cinematography and universal capture) foreword in Paul Marino's (*AMAS, ILL Clan*) seminal text on machinima intimates the groundswell.

Whilst the machinima community often referred to the processes they devised within other sectors they observed at a distance as opportunities to include new creative practices, machinima is now embedded and indeed has seeded an entire generation of creative industries. One might argue game and film innovations would have been successful without the machinima community but this is not the case. The machinima community was instrumental in its influence albeit most community members were not even aware of the sectoral developments taking place around them, particularly in filmmaking as highlighted in our Prologue interview with Kim Libreri, as the groundwork for the current mainstream digital workflows were beginning to take shape. The machinima community, being untrained in traditional industry practices, was excluded from the table in discussing the development trajectory of innovations it was pioneering; most did not really care.

Many of the workflows industry sought through the integration of technological advancements were to enhance the real-time nature of production through the use of 3D animation for cinematic story-based experiences. Experiences may be in film, game, or potentially numerous other possible applications such as theatrical performance, interactive advertising, etc. It is the storytelling aspect, enabled by technological advancements, that has been most challenged. As Sam Barlow, director and writer of interactive stories (e.g., *Her Story, Telling Lies*) points out, it is understanding what the role of the audience is that becomes a focal consideration when boundaries between genres dissolve (Stolz, 2020).

Thus, in this chapter, we examine the industry pioneers and key innovations that have emerged in game-based and film industry sectors, how they have connected with the machinima community and their influence beyond.

7.2 Small Beginnings

Within the game design and development sector, the influence of machinima has been profound, where the community was both directly and indirectly involved. We have identified few machinima creators who historically worked closely with games developers and publishers in developing games, ostensibly because creators were not primarily games developers. That said, some did actively contribute to the development of game and/or creative tools albeit most efforts were never incorporated into the games themselves but became standalone tools, such as Hancock's *Strange Company*'s series of tools (*StrangeUtil, StrangeSaver, Lippy, FreeCam* and production kit bundled with *Antics*). Notable exceptions were Girlich's *Little Movie Processing Centre* which was used within *id Software*'s *Doom* (from 1993) and a later spin-out initiative by one of *id Software*'s directors who founded *Fountainhead Entertainment* that went on to create the *Machinimation*™ tool (see Chapter 3). Other machinima creators by dint of their command over a game's target audience were able to leverage their presence into the development process. Notably, *Rooster Teeth* worked closely with *Bungie* on various tools and techniques to support its machinima filmmaking for its pioneering *Red vs Blue* series using *Halo* (see Chapter 4).

These examples are, however, few and far between when reflecting on the breadth of community creators. As machinima began to gain more traction with its focus on storytelling with game, there are more examples of game developers using machinima content within the game design itself. This was primarily used to enhance gameplay experiences through, for example, cut scene processes that added cinematic value to the player experience. Some of this was created by machinima community members, but much of it was adapted practices by game developers without direct reference to the machinima community. By the mid-2000s, as noted in Chapter 3, some of the original machinima community filmmakers were directly employed within the games sector because of their skillset. For example, Marino, Lucien-Bay and others became creative directors working on behemoth titles such as *Electronic Arts' Mass Effect.*

We have also discussed the range of games that have emerged which facilitate machinima filmmaking directly by providing creative environments as toolsets to be openly explored. Whilst the original goal of the developer may have been to create a game environment within which to while away a few hours in virtual fantasy as a social or creative experience, it is the virtual photography and machinima films that have preserved and archived the game for wider audiences. Machinima has been a natural byproduct for the many players and users who chose to record their adventures and creative endeavours in such virtual spaces. *Electronic Art*'s *Ultima Online* (1997), *Sims* (2000), *Linden Lab*'s *Second Life* (2003), *Sims 2* (2004), *Blizzard Entertainment*'s *World of Warcraft* (2004) and *Lionhead*'s *The Movies* (2005) were all designed as various forms of open role-play platforms (some known as massively multi-player online spaces, or MMOs) through which users could experience the environment and experiment with creative concepts including filmmaking by editing video-captured experiences into artistic and media formatted outputs. Other developers took machinima as a focal segue into the games sector. *Reallusion*'s *CrazyTalk* (2001) and *iClone* (2005), *Short Fuze*'s *Moviestorm* (2008) and, notably, *Epic*'s *Unreal Tournament 2003* (2002) were all positioned as creative 'sandbox' toolsets for machinima creators although the latter was also a game. Other sandbox tools positioned as modification toolkits: *Unity*, for example, mainly targeted the game developer sector in its early days following its launch in 2005 and is now also targeting film and TV studios. It was recently used in the production of *Disney Television Animation*'s *Baymax Dreams* shorts (2018). *Source Filmmaker* (*Valve*, released as an open beta in 2012) specifically targeted the machinima community and is another similar toolset that enables video editing, keyframing, motion capture editing and sound editing to produce film with reusable assets (e.g., Minor, 2015). A number of these developers actively promote community support and streaming platforms for content. For example, *Linden Lab's Linden Endowment for the Arts* promoted engaging virtual experiences working with the arts community; *Valve*'s annual *Saxxy Awards* recognizes the best machinima films produced using its *Source Filmmaker* toolset, a similar model to *AMAS*.

Thus, it is through the recognition of the demand for creative endeavour by game developers that machinima became the keystone practice. Its format is what informed the development and emergence of a platform industry sector dedicated to creators, including *YouTube*, *Steam* and *Twitch* alongside games' own community platforms, becoming a direct-to-consumer medium which effectively cuts out both the game and the cinema experience for audiences. Machinima works are accessible in a breadth of live-streamed, asynchronous and social media formats, perhaps now most often comprising follower game user-generated content emanating from such as *Mojang Studio*'s *Minecraft* (2009) and *Epic*'s *Fortnite Creative* (2018), where the emergence of community-created 'indie' cinematic projects receive tens of thousands of views online. This is, however, a film-like experience, where the audience is passive rather than active in its role. What game adds to film-like experiences is the interactive process but in early pioneering open form games, the approach to storytelling was emergent through its design.

Second Life is a notable pioneering development in game design. Its build began in 1999, simulating physical aspects of the world such as water and its movement, the sun/moon cycles, etc., and culminated in challenging other physical properties like gravity and movement through time and space (teleportation). Unlike many other game environments at the time, it was predicated on the concept that it was not necessary to simplify the virtual space because, eventually, computers would enable the creation of a whole new world, not identical to Earth but of potentially similar scale. The premise was to facilitate collective creativity across multiple computer servers: users would create everything inside the environment together. The original concept was not an easy sell and Philip Rosedale, the founder and CEO of *Linden Labs' Second Life* and now CEO of *High Fidelity* another company exploring similar concepts, was not in the business of its development purely for the money. His vision and life ambition have been to create something new and different. He commented:

> We could convince absolutely no one that what we were doing made any sense. People said the technology can't possibly be made to work smoothly because there are too many problems with building a simulation combined with broadband, combined with streaming, combined with rendering, talking to many computers at once, the whole idea is just completely impossible. The second thing they said was this is not for ordinary people. Even if it is compelling, there will only be a few crazy people that want to do it. Oh, and user-created content had never been a fundable idea. Now, everybody's doing it. But in the beginning the idea that random people were going to build a three-dimensional world was just impossible for people to understand...

> [Now] an enormous amount of intellectual energy is going to move into this world, and some of what we are doing in the real world will therefore be displaced. You can imagine New York City being kind of like a museum. Still an incredibly cool place to go, but with no one working in those towers because work, creative work, where you are engaging with other people face-to-face, you are going to do in a virtual world. It's going to leave these cities [gestures toward downtown San Francisco] and move into digital worlds. It is easier to do things there.
>
> Philip Rosedale (in Fitzgerald, 2007)

Naysayers were proven wrong as *Second Life* became a global phenomenon, with more than 2M registered users by 2007 (Terdiman, 2007). This was not about storytelling in the familiar way through creative writing or scripted film, but through interactive processes more akin to theatrical devising, where multiple videographic pathways could be developed through which a collective story may unfold. It was lucidly described as 'not a game' but more of a multi-sense multi-dimensional immersion (Byerley, 2019). Furthermore, unlike many contemporaries, any intellectual property emanating from content created by players and users was commuted to the creator, not owned by the developer. It is this stance which is largely responsible for the phenomenal diversity and depth of creative work produced as well as the digital trade practices that emerged as a consequence, leading some to describe *Second Life* as a black-market economy (e.g., Reilly, 2014).

Over time, the ways in which *Second Life* stories were shaped became increasingly industrious and traditional in filmmaking method and output, with many creators documenting their virtual travels and propositions using machinima. Whilst many early machinima pioneers dabbled with in-world experiences, some began using it as a creative space (see, for example, Boellstorff, 2008; Johnson, 2010; Ng, 2013). One such pioneering machinima production team already identified was the *ILL Clan*. Its 2007 award-winning *Grid Review* series was a popular humorous reportage on *Second Life* events. Markedly, *ILL Clan* had merged in 2006 with a 3D virtual world creative agency, *Electric Sheep Company*, which itself was launched in 2005 capturing a client base including the likes of *AOL, Reuters, Nissan, Sony, Starwood Hotels, NBC, Paramount, Universal, MTV, IBM* and numerous others, with a remit to create virtual brand experiences. In 2007, *Electric Sheep Company* produced machinima for the popular *CBS* TV series, *CSI:NY* (episodes 405 *Down the Rabbit Hole* and 415 *DOA for a Day*) where characters followed clues inside *Second Life* to solve a murder mystery, whereby creators were attempting to merge traditional and new media formats through which to interact with audiences. Generally, however, as also articulated in the political experiments previously described in Chapter 5, the attempts of most brands to recreate their physical properties as in-world experiences ultimately failed and *Second Life* began to evolve as an extended real-time life story experience. As Rosedale once said, if something is going to be exactly the same as a physical thing, why not just stick with the original? Residents, as they are called, now play out any fantasy they choose through avatar modifications to set experiences.

Whilst the significance of machinima to *Linden Lab*'s *Second Life* is perhaps limited in its output, the creative process intimated in Rosedale's quote above certainly offers new potential. Ebbe Altberg, its current CEO, sees machinima primarily as an output:

> It's an interesting use case that people can actually record and play back scenarios using *Second Life* as a creative environment. Since we are all about empowering creative people to create all these incredible experiences within *Second Life*, not only does it have to be real time and you can stay within *Second Life* but you can direct or basically make a production out of experiences within Second Life and have it played back outside the context of *Second Life*. So it's another possibility that the Second Life creative engine allows users to take advantage of. It also brings an interesting audience into *Second Life*, it actually has marketing value for people to do some incredible, many award-winning machinima productions that attracts more users to *Second Life* as well. It's a perfect fit for people to use machinima as a creative outlet. The fact is that it is not just a game, it's a storytelling platform to some degree. Whether those are real-time stories that are being created and experienced or thought through and produced stories, that's great.
>
> Ebbe Altberg (interview, 2014)

Rosedale's comment on its creative story potential has, however, never been fully explored or realized, despite the numerous texts illustrating thousands of examples of creative endeavours in the virtual environment. That said, a few notable producers of *Second Life* machinimas include Pooky Amsterdam (eg., *Time Travelers* series), Saskia Boddeke (eg., *Obedience*), Ricard Gras (eg., award-winning *Silver Bells*), Chantal Harvey (eg., *Scissores* series with Tony Dyson), Bryn Oh (eg., *Rusted Gears*), Bibbe Hansen (eg., *Car Bibbe* recreating the Fluxus *Happenings* artwork of her late father, Al Hansen), Tutsy Navarathna (eg., award-winning *Journey into the Metaverse*) and Douglas Gayeton (*Molotov Alva and His Search for the Creator*, a feature-length machinima distributed through *HBO*) among numerous others. Suffice to say, there continue to be important exhibitions of *Second Life* creative work presented in various events around the world eg., the *2010 Shanghai Expo*, the annual *Milan Film Festival* whilst one consequence of COVID lockdowns during 2020 has been a new impetus to the use of the virtual environment as a creative and social platform.

The sub-optimal use of *Second Life* is something that Peter Greenaway, BAFTA award-winning British film director (eg., *The Cook, The Thief, His Wife and Her Lover*) was keen to highlight whilst keynoting the 2010 *48 Hour Filmmaking Project's* machinima judges' panel, hosted by Dutch *Second Life* filmmaker and machinima festival organizer Chantal Harvey (figure 7.1). Greenaway (whose wife is Saskia Boddeke, an established and well-known *Second Life* machinima artist) stated that cinematic processes were now largely devoid of genuine creative practice. He argued that film aesthetic is dominated by a Hollywood format that produces no more than 'illustrated books', citing recent examples such as Jackson's *Lord of the Rings* and Rowling's *Harry Potter* series. Reflecting that machinima is the beginning of a digital image-based paradigm in an 8,000-year-old tradition of audio-visual entertainment, where film comprises the previous 115 years and TV the last 40 years, he argues that machinima is considered a promising new medium. He commented:

> [In the 12-14 years since machinima was first invented] maybe enough years have gone by now for us all to feel that we're into the beginnings of a new child media which I believe has enormous potential in future... I have repeatedly bored people by announcing certainly for the last 10 years that in the big change, the new visual digital vocabulary now at our fingertips is actually in a curious way relative to what I believe is the demise of cinema. To put it bluntly, I believe that cinema is now dead... We've seen 115 years of illustrated text – but to think in text is not to think in image... [yet] although we are not in the age of cinema any more, we are certainly in the age of screen, and the potentiality of the screen is eventually going to make things like *Star Wars* and *Avatar* and all those apparent benchmarks of contemporary cinematic activity look like late 17th-century lantern slide lectures...
>
> [In the history of audio-visual media] the phenomenology of machinima is of considerable importance, rising out of game shows and game reality and associated very much with all the excitement of *Second Life* and all it means, has created a new arena and playground through which we can express ourselves in the world... We should use machinima as the new embryonic breeding ground. As Umberto Eco says, the text masters have got to move over now and allow the image masters to come in, the people who can clear the ground of the clutter of text so we can begin to communicate very strongly our abilities to manipulate the notions of a new visual literacy... It's a medium about space and mutability and change – not cinema, not video, not animated painted image – let's not imitate the characteristics of the notions and technologies that have gone by. Primacy is of the image; the image has to control the image.
>
> Peter Greenaway (2010)

Figure 7.1: Peter Greenaway at *48 Hour Film Project.*

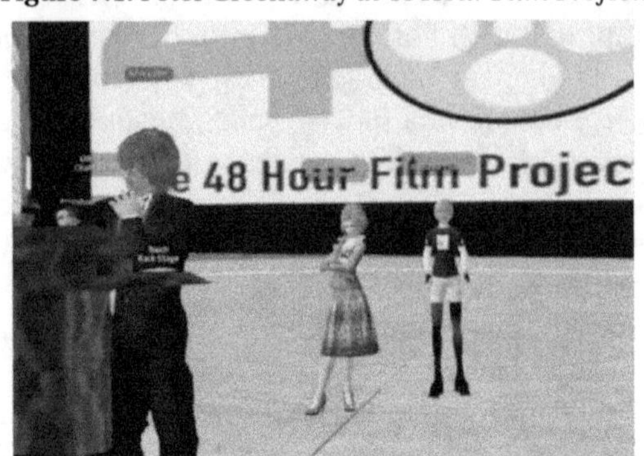

Source: Machinima Judges' Panel, *Second Life,* 2010.

Greenaway's comments, however, confounded the machinima community, most of whom had striven to become filmmakers using key literary texts and Hollywood classics as their golden threads. The community saw themselves as storytellers, where familiar tropes are retold, redacted, revised, reformatted and ultimately remixed. Creativity as a democratic process became the mantra, and games became toolsets as well as the inspiration for new stories. It is, however, the production process and the way in which multiple image-based pathways may be navigated (rather than narrated) that makes machinima a new and powerful language in contemporary creative practice. It is its performativity and malleability that actually inspired others from well beyond the sight of the machinima and game communities to explore machinima's potential in very different ways. In many ways, Rasmussen's methodology (Chapter 6) was a microcosmic reflection of what machinima could be.

7.3 Alternative Beginnings

It is therefore with some irony that tracing an alternative beginning to machinima takes us to Australia, rather than Hollywood or the European centres of filmmaking. This in itself is interesting because Australia has never been recognized as a hotbed of innovation in creative filmmaking practice, notwithstanding Rasmussen's legacy to the sector. We start this exploration with developments in computing, multimedia and internet sectors before we examine the emergence of real-time cinematic experiences and how they connect with machinima.

In 1992, the Australian company *Ozisoft* (formed in 1982) specialising in video game distribution was bought out by *Sega,* becoming *Sega Ozisoft. Ozisoft*'s founders were New Zealander Mark Dyne and his cousin South African Kevin Bermeister, who also founded *Packard Bell* and *Sega Enterprises Pty.* Bermeister, through his property consortium *Jacfun* (with partners including

Sega Japan, Mitsubishi Corp and *Mitsui Corp*), also established the *Sega World Sydney* amusement park (operated between 1997-2000) having negotiated the rights to Sydney's Darling Harbour. With its considerable industry experience and established game connections, in the mid-1990s *Sega Ozisoft* identified the potential of machinima as a real-time movie-making opportunity which in part led to the development of *Brilliant Digital Entertainment Inc.* (*BDE*).

Founded by Bermeister in 1996, who became its chairman and CEO, *BDE* developed internet interests including a contract with *Joltid* which then established *Altnet Inc.*, focussing on peer-to-peer networks and a service called *Global File Registry,* which aimed to connect content owners and internet service providers, using a pre-blockchain format database. By 2005, another of Bermeister's interests, a file-sharing service called *Kazaa,* was involved in one of the biggest US music industry legal cases at the time, culminating in a $150M settlement against the company (Ali, 2005). *Kazaa* argued that it was not responsible for the sharing activities of its users but the upshot was the platform was blacklisted by *Mckafee,* leading many IP owners to avoid the service because of its 'unethical practices' (e.g., Mansukhani, 2006). The debacle is one of the reasons why streaming platforms such as *YouTube* gained a foothold over P2P services. From 2006 onwards, Bermeister's investments included *Atrinsic Inc.* and *Skype,* in which he was a founding investor, illustrating how his interests evolved in communications technologies.

Notably, Bermeister registered a number of patents jointly with fellow South African Anthony Rose through a *BDE* subsidiary *Kinetech,* which took a majority share in *PersonalWeb Technologies. PersonalWeb*'s patented technologies identify content in distributed cloud-based networks, primarily music, through which the organization licenses content. The patents referred to are technologies which work by ranking distributed content according to its proximity to a searcher and by removing duplicate (pirated) copies of content to the most effective and efficient download. The organization has(d) an unusual approach to business in that it appears to focus on aggressively defending alleged patent infringements as its main income source. For example, it has attempted to claim substantial rights infringements against *Apple* and *Google* in 2011 and *Amazon* in 2020, albeit these have failed in court (US). Numerous other claims against the likes of *Nexsan, Microsoft, Hewlett Packard, Yahoo, Github, IBM,* appear to have been settled out of court (see *PersonalWeb.com*; Winterford, 2011; Moses, 2011; Forbes, 2020).

Rose, who was the chief technology officer at *Sega Ozisoft* and later at *Kazaa,* at the same time pulled together a development team that focussed on devising real-time 3D graphics for making what it described as 'interactive movies' for the *Sega* platform (Healey, 2012). Rose also developed a series of patented methods for effecting automated transactions as early as 1990 and subsequently developed technologies that optimized 3D animation for variable distributed computer networks (e.g., 2002 onwards). These technological innovations became a core part of what became known as the digital revolution in media industries, eventually leading to Rose being appointed as head of media technologies at the *BBC* in London (in 2007) where he is credited with the successful development of the *BBC iPlayer* on-demand service (the British equivalent of US *Hulu*) (Bowser, 2007; Chibber, 2009), and along with his colleagues, received a BAFTA award in 2008 (Connor, 2008).

Specifically, *BDE* was developed as a digital entertainment and production studio, creating content for multiple media formats, including the internet, PCs, TV and home video. Building on Rose's technological advancements, *BDE*'s specialism was in what it referred to as 'multi-path movies' which were 3D animated stories with multiple branches through which viewers could navigate to different endings. Its vision was to combine traditional film entertainment with game-like interactivity. Its first multi-path movie project was called *Cyberswine*, a co-development which was creatively led by *Sega Ozisoft* and released in 1997 (see Figure 7.2), based on an Australian comic series published by *Issue One*. *Cyberswine*'s movie-like qualities were most evident in the language used to promote the boxed content – for example, the programme for installing it on a PC was a 'projector' – it played 'movies' and was sold using 'movie tickets' at *Sega*'s 'box office' – although it was positioned in the market seemingly as a game. Player-viewers could choose their pathway through the film following hundreds of potential plot twists based on decisions they made related to mood preferences for characters.

Figure 7.2: Screencap *Cyberswine*.

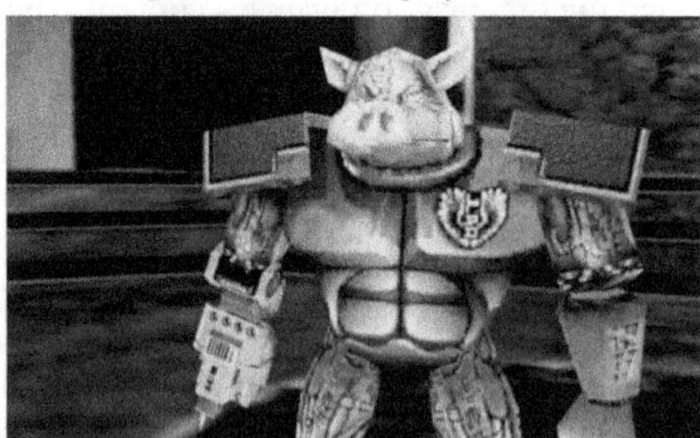

Source: *GamePlayShare*, 2014.

In an interview for *Hyper Magazine* (Clarke, 1996) prior to its launch, Rose, then representing *Sega Australia New Developments* (*SAND*), described how *Cyberswine* was different from games:

> We're not creating a game – we're creating a movie. You never go back and slaughter more monsters to go to the next level. You don't die and you can't win or lose. We're making what we think movies will be like in the future – a complex blend of the script writer's input coupled with your own desires. Our movies will run for about 100 minutes – the same as a feature film. Our movies are also not adventure games – the action never stops, you never need to decide whether to go left or right...
>
> Anthony Rose (in Clarke, 1996)

He goes on to describe the underlying suite of technological advancements which had been developed to enable scripts to automatically create screenplays by associating text with characters in a 3D environment. This included navigation, lip-sync and an object-oriented layout toolset, the latter of which would enable creators to publish their output to any platform such as *PlayStation*, PC/Mac, the internet or as a CD (DVDs were not launched until mid-1997 and of course *YouTube* was years away):

> What we want to do is enable existing creative people to be able to take their work through to the final product rather than just writing a short synopsis... We've developed a simple script language and we've allowed script writers to work in ways they are familiar with – standard screenplay format... Our *Script Navigator* will load word scripts, work out where things are being said, assign those lines to the names of the characters that are saying it, and take that right through to the final product. When you have some lip-sync dropped in, it can be attached to a line of dialogue, and then the 3D character will actually speak.
>
> Anthony Rose (in Clarke, 1996)

The *Navigator* tool facilitated branching stories by enabling real-time run-throughs using a mood database from which to select options. This effectively enabled filmmakers to very quickly make sense of the different threads in the multiple pathways they created. With scripts four times longer than standard films, Rose explained that their aim was to enable three to four branches per decision point. *Cyberswine* illustrated the approach with branches every 30 seconds culminating in around 500 scenes over the 100 minutes of film duration. Characters were rendered in real-time, depending on the choices made using *Softimage* and *3D Studio*. For extending the creative format to other content, the vision for distribution was that assets such as characters and backgrounds could be made available on CDs whilst the animation data, sound and story plots would be made available over the internet, leaving the player-viewer to create their own multi-path movies at home. Assets could comprise any animated content. *Cyberswine* was therefore a shop window project.

Cyberswine was launched at *E3* in Los Angeles in May 1996, and was one of several products launched that year that were described as interactive movies. Others included *SouthPeak Interactive*'s *Temujin* (released 1997), a supernatural mystery, and *Westwood Studio*'s adaptation of Ridley Scott's *Blade Runner*. Interactive movies were not a new genre since the first such film is considered to be the Czech movie *Kinoautomat* (released 1967). Early interactive movie experiences, however, tended to involve theatrical performances delivered in large-scale adapted environments. *Kinoautomat*, for example, was screened in a custom-built cinema where seats had been modified with buttons for audience members to select options. Somewhat different from an audience experience perspective yet still reminiscent of the motion picture industry processes, *Temujin* had been filmed in 35mm on sets using *SouthPeak*'s proprietary *Video Reality* technology which combined movie sequences with the ability to move characters thereby creating immersive experiences. Some described its combined feature film production values and immersive technology as the best example of the interactive movie genre to date (Sweetman, 1997). *SouthPeak*'s *Video Reality* game engine technology was subsequently used in two other projects, *Dark Side of the Moon* (released 1998) and *20,000 Leagues*, but the second was never released. *Video Reality* development was discontinued and the studio closed in 2000.

Adapting a movie's interactive experience for the emergent small home screen of the computer via the internet by using advanced asset control technologies was, from the film industry's perspective, a progressive step. From the game industry's perspective, it opened new doors for licensing assets from film brands for games and there are numerous examples of studios doing this eg., *Telltale* (*Wallace & Gromit, Back to the Future, Jurassic Park, The Walking Dead, Batman, Game of Thrones*). But the concept of interactive film in the game sector has generally remained poorly understood (see, e.g., Sohn, 2016) – it is neither film nor game, and furthermore, it is wholly reliant on the audience's perspective depending on the platform on which it is viewed. Other studios, however, created their own engines and story concepts eg., *Quantic Dream* (*Omikron: The Nomad Soul, Fahrenheit, Detroit: Become Human*). *Quantic*'s interactive experiences were described more as 'interactive dramas' as compared to adventure games (Murphy, 2013) of which an early example is the *Tex Murphy* series (which had so inspired Rasmussen, Chapter 6). Thus, positioning real-time 3D interactive cinematic experiences has been a key challenge. For example, *Quantic*'s game engine technology was used for motion capture in the 2004 film, *Immortal*, and is one of the earliest examples of a game engine being used to provide digital assets as cinematic backdrops for filming. Clearly, some projects have been more successful than others, largely depending on how well-known or well-promoted the assets are, as well as how accessible the streaming platform is for the audience. *Quantic*, however, subsequently became known as a studio for pushing the boundaries of games, rather than as an interactive movie maker (e.g., Burks, 2016).

BDE's vision was more expansive than this, and arguably their experience across technologies sectors had positioned it as more market savvy. Its aim was to power real-time storytelling using its proprietary game-film technologies as a process for the production of films and TV. By 1999, *BDE* had created numerous multi-path movie episodes and webisodes, secured licensing deals with a number of well-known characters including *DC Comics' Superman, Warner Bros' Ace Ventura, Pet Detective* and *Universal*'s *Xena: Princess Warrior,* produced music videos for the likes of *Kiss (Kiss Immortals* series) and *Def Jam,* created its own original content and launched a web-based service. It had also agreed to a distribution deal with *Time Warner*-owned *Entertaindom,* a new type of online interactive media streaming and community service that launched with a number of its multi-path movie products (Stone, 1999). Of course, in 1999, bandwidth for streamed interactive content was a key challenge for servers, which were quickly overcome. Furthermore, the requirement to download *Macromedia*'s *Flash Player* and *BDE*'s *Projector* to view and create content presented barriers to mainstream adoption.

Ultimately, *Entertaindom* failed, closing in February 2002, a victim of the dot com bubble burst (Hansen, 2002). In the meantime, however, *BDE* had secured funding investment of $4M in 2000 to develop content for the Asian market. Nonetheless, by 2001 its multi-path movies content productions ceased being part of *BDE*'s operations (Annual Report, 2001). Whilst it had secured between 4-5M downloads of its *Projector* product bundled with content, *BDE* quickly changed its distribution strategy to focus on increasing market share for its technology innovations. *Projector* became part of *Sharman Networks*' P2P proposition, realizing 10sM users in the process, by enabling organizations to distribute content through their own websites to a client base that included music labels, film production studios, software publishers and also game developers. It is *BDE*'s success with this strategy that led it to develop *Altnet,* its own P2P service in 2002.

It is somewhat ironic that Michela Ledwidge, the inaugural recipient of the *Peter Rasmussen Innovation Award in 2009* (Chapter 6) had cut her teeth as the first commissioned multi-path filmmaker, working for *BDE* in its Sydney studios. In 1997, she worked on a project, *Headbin,* to create story treatments but retained the copyright and continues to work on developing the concept as a remixable film project under her own studio title, *Mod.* She also ran *BDE*'s interactive film-writing competition (interview, 2020). And furthermore, years later Ledwidge was part of the BAFTA award-winning team working with Rose at the *BBC,* serving as the lead architect on the *iPlayer* project. Ledwidge is clear that *BDE*'s approach to real-time filmmaking was machinima. Of her experience, she commented:

> My first contact with machinima was unusual because I got commissioned in 1997 to write a feature-length title for a real-time engine company that thought they were going to take over Hollywood with what they called multi-path films... it's machinima in the sense of technology: technology-wise, it's real-time filmmaking but the bit that was the engine was designed specifically for this purpose and, long story short, this company did ship a bunch of titles but they never took over Hollywood as they tried to do! The whole idea of 'choose your own interactive movies', which was their shtick, didn't really work creatively as well.
>
> Michela Ledwidge (interview, 2020)

In effect, *Sega Ozisoft* and *BDE* had pioneered a real-time 3D filmmaking process through which they blurred the boundaries between game and film and also found a way to monetize their own IP in the development of toolsets. This enabled them to devise a business model with which to operate in. Their main challenge was persuading content owners to buy into their framework and to carve out a creative consumer base for the game-like experiences. Its similarities to the machinima methods employed by the creative community, which was beginning to evolve in a similar period in time, are evident but this also intimates how assets could be controlled by original IP owners. Whereas the machinima community used every part of a game as an asset including its engine code to develop increasingly creative outputs, the *Sega Ozisoft/BDE* model was wholly dependent on managing creative boundaries with asset owners. Furthermore, the machinima community rapidly developed audiences for creative outputs as finished artefacts which transcended platform services, as we have discussed in previous chapters.

With the expanding list of games available, the machinima community, centred on *Machinima.com*, collectively explored the visual and technological landscapes of games resulting in new avenues for promoting creative work through film. Game themed repositories of artefacts emerged across the internet and the underlying modding community grew alongside them. The community benefitted by having more tools and content to create with – in the case of *Diary of the Camper* (Chapter 2) and *The French Democracy* (Chapter 5) the underlying original assets were not changed whereas other examples we have described, were modified considerably more as part of the creative process which can, in turn, be explained as real-time and performative. Therefore, whilst it was machinima-based, *BDE*'s model would ultimately never have realized demand from viewing audiences beyond its real-time performative creative process – it simply was not that kind of product. The model it had used was more reminiscent of an unbundled predecessor to *Lionhead*'s *The Movies* game.

7.4 New Beginnings

BDE and *Quantic* are examples of key threads in understanding the emergence of *Epic*'s *Unreal Engine* (*UE*) and the evolutionary path to its current position as the pre-eminent toolset for making real-time 3D animated stories and cinematic experiences (see Chapter 2). The current nexus is the combination of game, film and streaming tools: it is a merger of game-based virtual cinematography and real-time visualization with film-based performance capture and streaming services. The first two components – game and film – were advanced significantly by the machinima pioneers as we have previously discussed, along with the puppeteering or performative aspects of animated characters as part of the third component, that is to say, the knowhow to manipulate digital assets in 3D virtual environments in real-time (eg., Nitsche et al, 2013). As Marc Petit, general manager of *Epic*'s *Unreal Engine*, stated:

> [Machinima] was the proving ground but we should define virtual production, there are different elements of virtual production. One of them is real-time visualization, and the obvious thing we see is to use a real-time rendering technology but this is a very narrow view of virtual production. The real view we get from machinima is using the game mechanics to simplify the processes, like driving a vehicle or the locomotion system for a character, which is now how we approach making games, where we frame and then play things back... that use of game mechanics, that for me is the heart of machinima – the use of game mechanics to create a virtual narrative.
>
> Marc Petit (interview, 2020)

Thus, the use of motion capture technologies to digitize assets and produce computer graphics images that could then be integrated with scenes and performance became the most recent mainstreamed development in the real-time 3D animation sector (e.g., Manovich, 2011). Whilst some of the technology was already incorporated into games, this was arguably beyond the focus of the original machinima community not least because access to the assets and resources required to develop the suites of technologies were out of scope. Indeed, our alternative beginning highlights how even big business investments in technological advancements failed to capture the attention of relevant markets at the right time. The complete toolset was, however, always under our noses.

UE was originally created by *Epic* to power its first-person shooter game, *Unreal* (released in 1998), and quickly became a popular machinima tool within the community. Indeed, both its *Unreal Tournament* game (which included a character tool called *Impersonator*) and *Unreal 3* (which included a cinematic creation package, *Matinee)* had been designed in consultation with the machinima community (Hancock and Ingram, 2007; Petit, 2020). Therefore it is not surprising that *UE* then also became a popular tool for game developers, who were primarily interested in its 3D graphics capabilities to enhance game cinematics, and for film and TV makers, who made use of its real-time capabilities to significantly speed up production workflow. *UE*'s use in the latter sector was primarily as a rendering tool for pre-visualizing storytellers' variations of scenes in order to determine and refine set-ups, camera positions, etc. The notable example of this was the director's set up for *A.I.* (2001) for which *Industrial Light & Magic* (*ILM*) developed its *Rogue City*, an expansive and futuristic world that had originally been envisioned by Stephen Spielberg and Stanley Kubrick (see ilm.com). As an output tool for this sector, however, its ability to produce high-quality visual effects in a finished artefact was insufficient, as Kim Libreri highlights in our Prologue interview. Indeed, it is quality of rendered output of early machinima films as artefacts that put off mainstream audiences beyond games in which they were created, many of whom had little experience with animation beyond *Disney* and *Studio Ghibli*.

It is with computing advancements and performance capture technologies that live action could be used to control virtual assets and real-time would become integrated into production processes. This is illustrated in films such as *Jurassic Park* (1993) where *ILM* had been the first to integrate *Softimage*'s 3D CG software into its workflow to create moving dinosaurs. Subsequently, similar technologies were used to animate *The Mummy* (1999), Andy Serkis' *Gollum/Smeagol* in *Lord of the Rings* (2001), Tom Hanks' character in *The Polar Express* (2004), *King Kong* (2005), *Beowulf* (2007), the *Na'vi* in *Avatar* (2009) and *Lion King* (2019) among many others. These examples illustrate how CG became increasingly sophisticated not just in its photorealistic outputs but in its approach to fusing imagery through the advancement of capture technologies. Most recently, for example, *Lion King* was described by *Disney*, its producer, as a 'live action' computer-generated animation, having used virtual reality as a performance capture methodology in its production workflow.

The role of *Softimage* is instrumental in understanding the latest developments. It was bought out by *Microsoft* in 1994 but ultimately became part of *Autodesk*'s software, *Maya* and *3D Studio* (in 2008), finally being discontinued in 2015 (Burns, 2014). *Maya* is the basis of *Weta Digital*'s toolset, Peter Jackson's studio (Alias Systems, 2003) and *3D Studio* is part of *Disney*'s studio (Turney, 2016). A free version of *Softimage*, called the *Softimage Mod Tool*, had also been used in *Epic*'s *UE*. It was not until *UE4* was released in 2014 that its potential became clear to mainstream producers with advanced illumination and a workflow that brought technical artists, designers and programmers closer together. Machinima producers had, however, been creating with *UE* since *Tournament* in 1998. *UE5*, launched in 2021, is positioned as a further significant advancement: it contains proprietary 'nanite' technology that automatically optimizes digitized assets which can be rendered in 8K textures. This enables very high levels of detail to be rendered in real-time, enhancing effects such as illumination, ray-traced shadows, reflections, translucency and virtually real movement. These are the very effects that Rosedale sought to build when he began programming *Second Life* back in 1999.

The computer-controlled real-time 3D animation of imagery has advanced from being a keyboard/console input to a motion capture suit. Computer control can now be markerless motion tracking and room-scale mounted systems (e.g., *The Mandalorian*) as well as virtual reality technologies including haptic devices. These technological advancements intimate that storytelling is becoming more of an embodied performative process. Of course, this has significantly changed the way studios work and actors perform, in many ways emphasizing the need for an actor to have more classic theatre training. Of the motion capture suit performance experience, for example, Sam Worthington, actor and the *Jake Sully* character in *Avatar*, commented on his role:

> The most exciting thing is, it is my performance – this thing walks and talks and acts like me, it's my interpretation… there's nowhere to hide so every take you have to be truthful. Even though I'm big, nine feet tall and blue, it's got my personality, it's got my soul. That's quite spectacular that a computer-generated image can do that – it really surprised me.
>
> Sam Worthington (in *Media Magik Entertainment*, 2009)

The streamlined production process is indeed reminiscent of Stanivlaski's minimalistic method for theatrical performance and cost savings result from the digital application of treatments, rather than physical: actors no longer need to spend hours in make-up, designers no longer need to make authentic costumes, exotic locations are not required, etc. Even greenscreen and bluescreen backdrops are not needed. Whilst there has been some resistance to this workflow, the global coronavirus pandemic in 2020 forced many studios to re-evaluate their production processes (e.g., Russo, 2020; Libreri, 2020). Furthermore, advancements in scaling the streaming technologies have helped to create new methodologies for performance capture.

Taking a lead from machinima, in recent years, some creative studios have explored the possibilities of motion capture suits, for example, *Vista Animations* (documented by *Draxtor*'s *Drax Files*, episode 41, 2016) uses the technology to create life-like movements as assets for avatars in *Second Life*; *Accursed Farms* studio used suit technology in its *Civil Protection* series to enhance the performance of game assets; and Ricard Gras, co-founder of *Timepath Studio* a VR/AI specialist, founder of *La Interactiva* a machinima production studio and one of the European members of *AMAS*, explored its potential in numerous large-scale real-time projects involving multiple simultaneous actors in thousands of cubic meters of physical space (Gras, 2020). Thus, technological advancement adds to the workflow by capturing life-like actions and interactions by enabling a real-time performance flow through movement. Furthermore, Gras is currently extending and enhancing his workflow with vol-cap (volumetric capture) and AI technologies.

The motion capture suits and systems through which to capture data are expensive, even at the low end of the spectrum. It was only when the *Playstation Eye* (2007), a computer vision-based sensor, and the *Xbox Kinect* motion sensor (2010) products launched that performance capture became a technology within reach of the no/low budget 'indie' producer. For example, *iPi Soft*, a Russian motion capture system launched in 2008, presented its *Kinect*-based markerless tracking solution at the 2012 *Machinima Expo* (see Figure 7.3) to an avid audience and has since supported machinima creators to explore the technology with numerous examples uploaded to its community website. *iPi Soft* is proprietary software that incorporates its own motion transfer system making it capable of working with any digitized input, integrating markerless tracking technology to capture movement and then exporting it to a compatible engine (e.g., *Unreal, Unity, Source*). Within the machinima community, the pioneer of its use is Ian Chisholm, who incorporated it into the workflow for his award-winning series *Clear Skies* (see Figure 7.4) while *iPi Soft* was in open beta (*Clear Skies 3*, released May 2011). Chisholm commented:

> It *[iPi Soft]* is a fantastically capable entry level mocap system... My workflow with *Clear Skies 3* was longer and harder with the introduction of mocap simply because I wasn't just picking from the stock gestures included in the *Half Life 2* characters any more. I had to figure out the best way to do things and get the captured performances into the *HL2* characters, and I was working around all the issues it generated with dodgy leg captures and so forth. However, you can cover a lot of problems with a good camera angle and a fast cut, and it was worth all these problems as the mocap opened up a whole new world of performance possibilities for the film - without it I probably wouldn't have made the film as I'd used every built-in gesture so many times and it was all getting very samey.
>
> Ian Chisholm (interview, 2020)

Whilst *iPi Soft*'s original target market was game development, its relative ease of use has, according to its CEO Michael Nikonov, also attracted the attention of the film industry, albeit the software has primarily become a pre-visualization tool (interview, 2020). Of its emergence for real-time motion capture, however, Nikonov believes more emphasis is now needed on physical performance and artistic skills to take it to the next level for storytelling:

> One of the things holding up our sales now is that there are not many people who understand the artistic side of mocap… using a mocap system is a very quick way to produce animation of course. Some people found it difficult to use but I think the main problems are not technical but rather there is a big problem with machinima creators not understanding acting – it's not a technical problem, it's an artistic problem. If you don't understand acting, then everything becomes difficult. People who understand acting, well they have less problems with the technology.
>
> Michael Nikonov (interview, 2020)

Figure 7.3: *iPi Soft* markerless tracking presented at the *Machinima Expo* 2012.

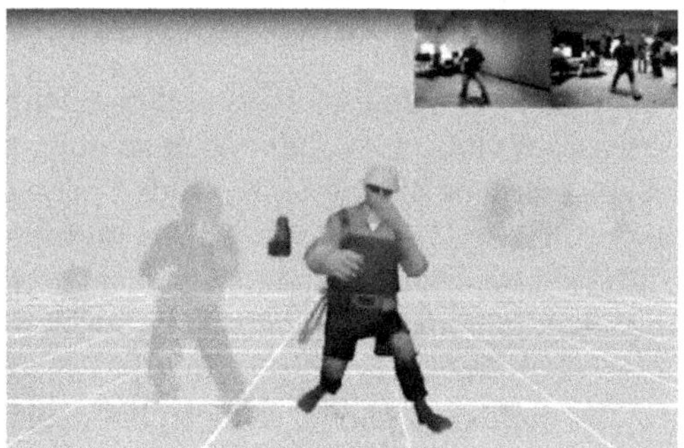

Source: *iPi Soft*, 2020.

Figure 7.4: Screencap *Clear Skies 3* (2011).

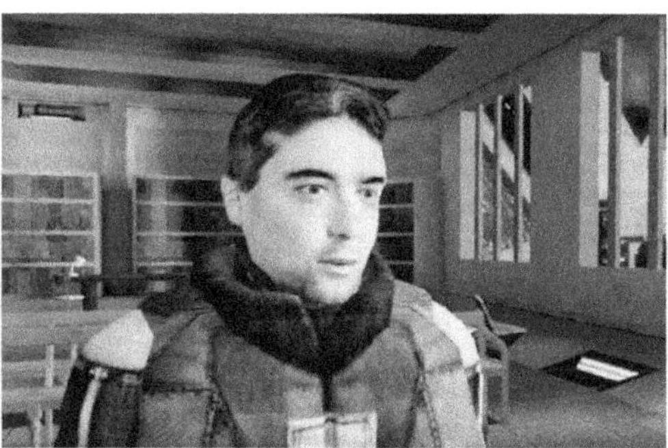

Feature-length machinima demonstrates smooth character movement from motion capture. Source: Chisholm, 2020.

The point is reflected in comments made by Chisholm:

> I know I'd never go back to making animation without the ability to performance capture because all built-in stock animations don't really look convincing or flow naturally… if you can stretch to [investing financially in performance capture equipment] and have a performance space, you'll never look back. If you want people to watch a story instead of an animation, I think it's a key part.
>
> Ian Chisholm (interview, 2020)

Virtual Reality (VR) performance capture is still in its infancy, with relatively few game mods having been developed. Indeed, most developers are evidently still playing with the concept of VR game experiences which began to accelerate as a game format in 2016, albeit the technology moves game further towards the multi-path navigable concept originated by *BDE*. For example, John Romero, founder of *id Software* and creator of *Doom*, suggested VR has significant potential for making game content, specifically as a tool for building environments and character models (correspondence with authors, 2020). Recent VR game releases include *LucasFilm* 2016 spinout *ILMxLAB Studio*'s *Vader Immortal*, an episodic *Star Wars* series (episode 1 released May 2019) and its latest *Tales from the Galaxy's Edge* (released 2020) another spin-off *Star Wars* 'action-adventure' VR experience, which were produced in collaboration with *Oculus Studios*; and, *Half Life Alyx* (released March 2020) and a subsequent game modification toolkit (released July 2020). Of course, where the VR experience differs to the multi-path model is the embeddedness of the choices captured in real-time movement within the virtual environment rather than overt selections being made through some sort of branching narrative process.

With the adaptation of these kinds of established stories and tropes, this approach has been described as a 'theme park film' (Robertson, 2019), a term coined by director Martin Scorsese and intended as a negative observation of what he saw as the *Marvel*-ization of cinema. Effectively, licensed content is represented in new formats. The approach perfectly reflects the DNA of the machinima pioneers' efforts to create new stories with existing assets using performative modes of creativity, and is also the way in which *BDE* shaped its production model. Furthermore, its use at *ILMxLAB* is no accident: John Gaeta, its founding executive creative director, specifically created a format that brought together technologists, storytellers and theme park designers to design and develop virtual worlds for storytelling (Bye, 2016).

Thus, what is highlighted with the technological advancements is an image-based and performance language for real-time experiences which is at present probably more of a hybrid of author-narrative and emergent-navigated immersive storytelling. Gaeta refers to this as 'virtual choreography', albeit his focus is primarily on production. It is, however, the performative image-language and embodied process of storytelling involving the audience that is closest to what Greenaway referred to in his keynote in 2010 – and this is machinima at its heart. As Petit comments:

> We oscillate between the isolation of the VR and the social component of [theatre] shows by having those big LED screens and at some point in the near future we are going to have AR, with transparent screens with *Harry Potter* magic and things showing up. When all windows can be a screen, you will see some fantastic content, with cameras in there, you can see real-time and it is going to be fabulous when you can mix the real and virtual and digital content blends very seamlessly into a stage, or in a venue or at a house so that you can have an interesting experience. This comes back to machinima, they were really the pioneers in these kinds of interactive techniques, and also by necessity because you had to convert video games to get what you wanted to get, but those skills and that thinking is very important and the people that understand how to do machinima have a leg up on the others in terms of content creation because they've wrestled and understood what you can and cannot do with virtual mechanics.
>
> Marc Petit (interview 2020)

Taking these processes further, *ILM* and *Weta Digital* have now room scaled virtual reality with walls of LED screens to create their collaborative virtual production toolsets (e.g., *The Mandalorian* and *Avatar 2*). The environment is reminiscent of the early immersive virtual reality *CAVE* (Cave automatic virtual environment) projection room-based system developed at the University of Illinois and launched in 1992 (Cruz-Neiru et al.). Whilst currently these methods are primarily used for virtual production and real-time rendering, many see this as the future of film and television production for creating immersive shooting environments, crafting in-camera VFX shots, etc. (Failes, 2020). Scaling such technologies, however, also creates a life-size means to explore both authored and emergent performative storytelling in real-time.

Expanding beyond the privileged few of a Hollywood film production set is the next obvious step. In many ways, this reimagines and converges a number of established interactive formats, for example, theatre, theme park, fan conventions, immersive cinema, digital art experiences and escape rooms. Such formats are not new: immersive theatre existed 8,000 years ago; modern theme parks began in the 1890s (*Coney Island*); fan conventions began in the 1930s (e.g., *Philcon, Worldcon*) and comic-cons, cosplay and larping (live-action role-playing), as various forms of interactive and themed fan event, have become increasingly popular ever since; immersive digital arts are increasingly popular galleried experiences (e.g., *Atelier des Lumière* in Paris); immersive cinema (e.g., *Secret Cinema*, founded 2007 in London) is a scaled theatrical experience that combines interactive performance with larping and theme park tropes, in purpose-built sets which focus on narrative-based film concepts (such as *Star Wars, Bladerunner* and *Casino Royale*). And escape rooms (began in 2007 in Japan by *SCRAP*) emulate early game-themed immersive experiences.

As the convergence of technology-enhanced immersion progresses, it is the creative possibilities that emerge from them, grounded in machinima practices, which will evolve new forms of entertainment. Figure 7.5 summarizes the multi-dimensional domains and cross-cutting themes of real-time 3D immersive experiences.

Figure 7.5: The future of storytelling: convergence of creative industries.

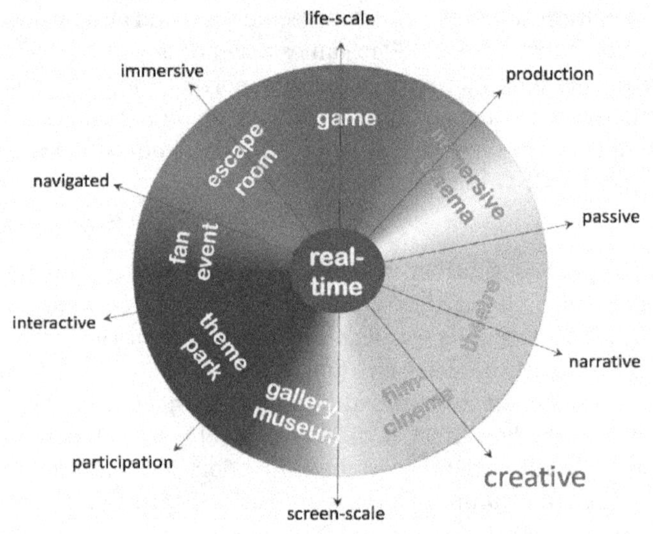

Source: authors.

As Petit comments:

> What's interesting with interactive 3D and real-time game engine technology is that, especially with *Unreal,* we can blend all of the various forms of media. You can do games and movies from the same assets now. We can support so many different platforms from virtual mapping. You can develop a piece of content and you can project it in Madison Square Garden on the biggest system on the planet with 26 projectors or consume it on an *iPhone,* it's the same content. Now the same interactivity has a different point of view, whether you are immersed in a concert hall or VR headset or whether you look at it on a phone, so it

> challenges a 125-year-old model of framing to tell your story, which is the system of cinematography. We have a lot of people who used to do ballets, operas and theatre plays and there is a lot of storytelling technologies when you do not control the point of view of the user, which was the thing with cinema, and now we are starting to see the old techniques converge on how you drive people's attention... what I'm saying is, it's the convergence. With the same assets, same content you can see all kinds of things happening.
>
> Marc Petit (interview, 2020)

Given the significant struggles faced by the pioneering creators within the machinima community, it is somewhat bitter-sweet to finally hear others across the breadth of creative industries recognize machinima's potential. For example, Diana Williams (a founding team member of *ILMxLAB* and current executive vice president of content at *MWM Universe*, an entertainment production company that works across the boundaries of new technologies, transmedia and immersive design to cross-pollinate new modes of storytelling) has advocated unbundling IP from so-called boilerplate contracts that have grown up with genres such as game and film (Stolz, 2020; Stolz et al., 2020). In doing so, she argues, the re-use of assets in entirely new ways becomes possible. She also points out how the current conglomerated storytelling frameworks are unhelpful in finding new possibilities to tell stories because, under the franchising model, the focus is on established industry pipelines.

As we have illustrated in Chapters 3 and 4, pioneering creators quickly became absorbed by big businesses – *Machinima Inc.* harvested innovative concepts and turned *Machinima.com* from an inspirational creative community into a production studio and a licensing platform; *Rooster Teeth* was more successful in retaining its community but it too is now part of *AT&T*. It sits alongside a number of other creative media content development studios and technology development platform enterprises that incorporate publishing, audio, mobile, game, film, streaming, etc. (including the remains of *Machinima Inc.*). What the pioneers teach us is that convergence in media industries settles on cashflow models rather than creativity and community. But it is the interdependencies between industries and communities that realize innovations which, in turn, engage and inspire audiences. For thoughts on this, Petit reflects on how innovations may evolve. He commented:

> I think of us *[Unreal]* as being the great equalizer because if you go to someone who understands, you know, if you look at Michele and Victoire [directors] at *Cirque du Soleil*, they tell the story of *Pandora* not through cameras but through a piece of great art that's 26x52 meters! So they've learned something, it's a very different craft than what Cameron

> did on the movie *Avatar*. The thing is now we can go to these two great teams and they will work off of each other and I can't wait to work together where we start mixing the narrative component with the navigational component – think about movies, or even the *Game of Thrones* today, we can create all of that universe as content. It is frustrating to see it only through the lens of a story. For me personally, I want to have a kind of online version for kids where they can go and just sit or discover and explore and spend more time in the environment with those characters. So when we build a TV series or a movie and the game with the same content, those assets will be available to you after the story has been told – and so you can even imagine releasing them to the machinima community and have people tell more stories, or different stories, or tell the stories differently – that is what is going to be very interesting, those collisions of all of that knowledge, and I'm very hopeful that we are going to be that platform where people can congregate and bring with them their knowledge to create something new... It is not the technology, the technology bridges the artforms. Remember, a pencil to an artist is nothing more than that.
>
> Marc Petit (interview, 2020)

It is clear, however, that there must be a new model that supports the indies to succeed through these kinds of collaborative endeavours. What is particularly interesting about the *Unreal* model today is the way it is funded. As Petit stated:

> We're all about empowering the community. We are actually seeing it through COVID because a lot of indies now they have the computers and cameras, Blender is free, UE is free, and they can create very sophisticated movies from home using all those what I call DIY technology. I would love to be able to say that *UE* has been an enabler if you are in the filmmaker community because we take a very complex programme and made it accessible. Both from the accessibility of our technology because it's very easy to use, you don't need to be a programmer to use it to produce a blueprint but also from the fact that its free to use, free of royalties, free of everything. In hindsight hopefully people can think of this pandemic as an accelerator of that enablement because it kind of forces people to work together, because we have the capabilities within the engine that enables small teams to work together. It was originally developed to support the workflows on a movie set where everybody had to see the same thing concurrently at the same time... the hardware costs are under control, software costs are under control as I mentioned, and the other thing we need is the enablement of online collaboration, because people like to work together, it's very

> fluid when people are on a project and I think we have that figured out now… The way we run the business is that the access and technology is free and we offer an optional support contract because some people would much rather have some support than none. That's what effectively allows us to offer the technology for free for indies.
>
> Mark Petit (interview, 2020)

With access to creative tools free at the point of use, early machinima pioneers whose workflow included the development of their own worlds and new kinds of immersive stories, Ledwidge, Morse and others for example, would be in their element. For those whose work extends game spaces with new stories, they too would find opportunities in transporting assets to the platform to support real-time creative project development. For others, who seek to retell or extend game stories, there remains a question mark over the levels of support more traditional games may afford because, fundamentally, there is no point in transferring the whole environment to a new real-time space. It has, for example, long been said that a game is merely a set of working tools to a creator and what *Unreal*'s model provides is an extensive framework that transcends the craft traditions associated with creative industries.

In summary, machinima still has much to offer albeit we have highlighted the need for innovation to develop new storytelling methods: our provocation is for the community to begin again. As Tina Crawford (aka Romily), organizer of numerous machinima panels at film festivals and host of the machinima panel at *DragonCon* between 2007-2015, reflected:

> If you see today's special effects used for big budget films like *Jumanji: The Next Level* you can see companies like *The Third Floor* doing previz using very machinima-like 3D animation reminiscent of what might be creative successors of *MovieStorm*. In our panel *[DragonCon]* we discussed how machinima would certainly be a money-saving technique and a launch pad for creativity for Hollywood. It's far safer and cheaper to blow up a 3D animation building and play with difficult shot angles in a digital medium than to deal with live stunt work, pyrotechnics, and sets only to have to redo them or be stuck with a suboptimal shot. Play the shot a hundred different ways with machinima and you're still spending less time and money to develop your ideas before you move your final draft to a live action shoot…
>
> I think we'll be seeing a continuation of the trends we're already seeing – more use in making big-budget (and small budget!) movies, continued use in games for cut scenes and trailers, as well as folks who want to dabble, learn, and maybe become pro, working with the publicly available options – game engines, 3D animation and AI programs, etc. –

> to do so. I suspect that the time won't be far off, especially now that the pandemic has changed how we interact with each other, that advances in tools will make machinima replacing live action a reality even in some big budget movies.
>
> Tina Crawford (interview, 2020)

Thus, renewed interest in machinima practices as a creative medium will continue to change the entire game-film-animation space forever – 'all the [virtual] world's a stage, and all the men and women merely players' (Shakespeare)!

Chapter 8

Conclusion

> Once people experience this new way of working, they will find that it is much more efficient and cost-effective... It is safe to say that virtual production is here to stay.
>
> Kim Libreri, Chief Technology Officer, *Epic Games*
> (in Dimitropoulos, 2020)

8.1 Introduction

In this chapter, we draw out the key themes highlighted from the evaluations we have presented in each of the chapters in this text. The themes have emerged in different ways in the works discussed. Whilst the chapters each represent an historical review and analysis of the impacts from within the communities directly influenced by the machinima works, in this chapter, we discuss these impacts from a more holistic perspective. We identify four themes and draw on each of the chapters to present the findings of our analysis: community, commercialization, convergence and creativity (figure 8.1). These are not easily separated from each other but are interwoven throughout our discussion.

Figure 8.1: Four Themes: Pioneers in Machinima.

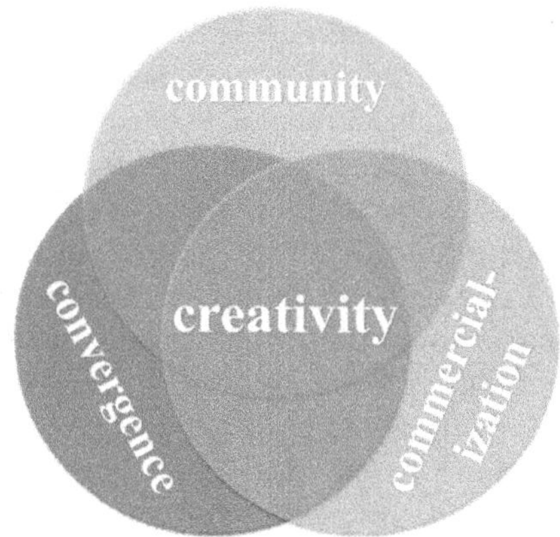

Source: authors.

8.2 Community

First and foremost, from its earliest days, machinima has been a story of community – be it about game players forming clans, production teams forming indie studios, followers and participants in the *Machinima.com* or *Rooster Teeth* platforms, or of the breadth of subsequent fan events taking place around the world. Community has been the bedrock of machinima as it has evolved.

In Chapter 2, we identified how the foundational film, *Diary of a Camper*, inspired others to create, which in turn led others to become key creative influencers as the community began to develop. We highlighted that whilst the foundational piece demonstrates virtual production, alongside it grew a mod community of asset and game developers who produced toolsets for machinima creators. These two groups of creatives were like a binary star system, revolving around each other and each feeding off the other to grow.

In Chapter 3, the success of *Machinima.com* and its professional sister site, *Machinima.org* managed by *AMAS*, was entirely predicated on the attitude of the founders who were focussed on knowledge exchange, collaboration, shared experience and increasing professionalization in virtual production, as well as being advocates of avant-garde storytelling. Machinima creators were passionate about the intersection of games and film and were inspired by both. The methodologies they developed were rooted in each but evolved into something new and different. The goal was to push creative boundaries and each other in every way.

In Chapter 4, we describe how *Rooster Teeth*'s success was originally built on a fan-based community, rather than creative one. *Red vs Blue*, their first machinima series, became the most successful machinima and web series ever produced, and it did so within days of its release in April 2003. Using their community as the basis for development, they extended their brand to offline events, new shows and different media formats. Their values of having fun with bleeding-edge technology, helped them position as a global brand. They were the first to use a subscription model on the internet for streamed content, which was entirely predicated on the strength of the relationship they had with their increasingly active community. They were the first to gamify the community's experience, use the community's interest in their work to fund raise their first live action film production, and to export an established media form, Japanese anime, from the US back to Japan. The team became celebrities and *Rooster Teeth* became an umbrella brand, enabling them to launch and establish new shows which then carved out their own respective niche communities. They have become the masters of creating an ecosystem of fandoms by being agile and responsive to their evolving community interests.

In Chapters 5 and 6, we examined the work of two independent creators who based their emergent practice within the machinima community, and from which they influenced new audiences with significant resulting impacts. In the case of Chan (Chapter 5), *The French Democracy* became an influential political tool. In the case of Rasmussen (Chapter 6), *Stolen Life* and its experimental virtual production processes were shaped within the community but his production was subsequently recognized as pioneering practice with a broader impact on creative industries. In many ways, the respective successes of Chan and Rasmussen are testimony to the power of community but the chapters also highlight challenges and limitations, not least the lack of funding for pioneer creators.

In Chapter 7, we highlighted an alternative evolutionary path of early stakeholders involved in developing creative practices. The organizations we examined recognized the potential of community but were unable to provide the platforms on which it could be supported to evolve over an extended period of time. Some scenarios are still developing, and we identified new opportunities for growth, rooted in the practices developed by the pioneering machinima community. Importantly, our analysis highlights that for long-term success of recent technological advancements, there needs to be a clear trajectory for a passionate and creative community to form and for different creative practices to be recognized within it.

8.3 Commercialization

Through the chapters, we identify that early commercialization of machinima was indirect through the adaptation of games by developers who had been influenced by the way in which machinima creators used their products. In chapters 2, 3 and 4, we highlighted how videographic technologies became increasingly part of the assets of games such as *Quake* and *Halo* as computing power developed on which the higher quality graphics could run.

As interest in machinima grew on the *Machinima.com* platform, we discussed in Chapter 3 how three significant challenges emerged. Firstly, with limited financial backing, *Strange Company* struggled to maintain a level of service that the community demanded. Its ability to manage the site's capacity became impaired, and coupled with Hancock's desire to focus on his creative work, there was little option but to find a new home for it. His choice at that point did not favour the community on which *Machinima.com* had been founded. Ultimately, the site became subsumed within a media empire which encompassed platform and content strategies – the community was left out in the cold. Whilst relationships with the original community floundered, the newly formed *Machinima Inc.* focused on aggressively acquiring new communities through its *Network Channel Partnership* strategy using *YouTube* as a platform on which to grow. It exploited both creators and games developers and publishers with the promise of indie-style content through which their work could be promoted and monetized.

Machinima Inc.'s strategy then influenced the larger community both directly and indirectly. Its perpetual contracts locked in indie creators (its partners), effectively assuring the longevity of both itself and *YouTube* whose business model was based on revenue sharing. As an indie, earning a share of that revenue was a function of being successful in generating audiences, which in turn required them to release more content. Production values of the creative work, such as that developed by early machinima pioneers, became a thing of the past.

Alongside this, the skillsets and creative values which had sustained the *Machinima.com* community were recognized and subsumed by the creative industries, leaving just a few of the original pioneers as hardcore independents. Machinima creators were employed primarily by games developers who integrated their creative real-time 3D animation and filmmaking expertise into their workflows. Games developers were themselves increasingly being squeezed as demand for new games grew. Their spot had been how to utilize gameplay content as advertising material, coupled with desirable creative technologies skillsets honed from years of real-time (machinima) storytelling practice.

The impact of the absorption of the community into the game industry and the shift in focus of *Machinima.com* changed the nature of machinima for the pioneering indies completely, something that caused it to fragment and coalesce around new platforms.

In Chapter 4, we highlighted how *Rooster Teeth* exploited its relationship with its community to develop a sustainable business model that included commercial stakeholders. The approach had originally been informed by the challenges the producers had faced in distributing an earlier creative project. The solution walked a fine line between relationship and business, but its success was because their communication strategy was clear to the community, 'support our work, or we die', or as their community put it, 'Sponsor or Freeload'. We identified how their business model evolved, focussing on increasing professionalization of content creation as the studio proposition developed. It is its closeness and understanding of its community, coupled with an agile approach to developing new content, that enabled *Rooster Teeth* to succeed. Its gamification strategy was useful in retaining community but it was the core values *Rooster Teeth* evolved that underpinned advocacy in the community. They used this to build new IP beyond the originating game IP which, in turn, facilitated revenue generation. With their own IP, *Rooster Teeth* became an umbrella brand which enabled them to launch numerous new creative works and forms of content, often by drawing in community members directly to form new shows. It combined this with a unique distribution platform strategy that was channel agnostic, enabling it to reach maximum audiences and communities with its breadth of content.

What Chapters 3 and 4 illustrate is how the grassroots creatives that carved out the new media sector struggled to survive as their potential was identified and exploited by more commercially savvy others. This left little space for the community through which development of new practices, new forms of content and new tool sets had evolved. Those that took their inspiration from the machinima communities and successfully monetized it, gave little back. The significance of value within the sector has ultimately seen a series of mergers and acquisitions of studios by global conglomerates that were both efficient in facilitating the development of content and which attracted direct-to-consumer income through the emergent platform-based economy. Reflecting Hancock's analysis of the *Machinima.com* platform he created, Gutstein (former CEO of *Machinima Inc.*) once said, *"In a world of infinite choice, the curator is king"* (in Jacobs, 2015) but actually, this misjudged the strength of community ethos we have illustrated and which is also borne out in Chapters 5 and 6. In these chapters, we highlighted that neither Chan nor Rasmussen was financially motivated in their creative endeavor, albeit this was not without consequences.

In Chapter 7, we identified how technology pioneers began by rethinking what creative practice may be possible in what they perceived as the convergence of the game-film space. Many of the organizations we identified were commercially motivated from the outset, however, this was proven to be a challenging strategy. In losing sight of community, or failing to identify a community in the first place, the products were only ever going to be short-lived experiments. This is a classic example of product-focussed strategy and reflects what many now think of the entertainment sector (e.g., Greenaway, Scorsese, Libreri, et al.). We discussed how new technologies currently evolving, such as *Unreal Engine* and performance capture devices, have given rise to new creative practices in virtual production which are clearly rooted in machinima. What is interesting, however, is the way in which traditional commercial models are being challenged in the process, clearly because of the recognition that there needs to be give as well as take for long-term success. Perhaps, with this approach to IP and creativity, future pioneering creatives will be rewarded with an equitable share of any commercial pot – or at least, they will be the wiser for having witnessed the first iterations of corporate takeovers in the machinima community, and make an informed decision.

8.4 Convergence

In Chapter 2, we discussed how the convergence between game and film for storytelling emerged. The backstory to *Diary of a Camper* illustrated how storytelling was a natural progression to geeky gameplay but the emergence of technologies to support it was key. With few tools to assist within the games of choice, pioneers evolved creative practices that enabled them to extend their gameplay into whole new areas – they forced play in new ways, they modified assets to achieve their own ends and they devised virtual production methods that interpreted filmmaking for their gameplay practice. Pioneers saw games as real-time 3D story environments: virtual spaces in which to position their imaginary characters and actors, where they made them play out new roles until they as directors and producers were happy with the creative outcome. This convergence of technology, performance and practice is the foundation of real-time virtual production today.

In Chapter 3, we highlighted how demand for real-time 3D content began to build quickly as the community grew. Demand was a consequence of the convergence of technological advancements in computational power and graphics capability, the evolution of platform capabilities which impacted accessibility of creative work, and the rapid development of game aesthetics with increasing photorealistic content making games look more like filmsets. In other words, better content, easier access, better quality. Audience demand for game-inspired content grew alongside the culture that facilitated creative practice to evolve. Whilst often described as a sub-culture within gaming, the rapid emergence of products and services that targeted the machinima community intimates more of an iceberg calving process resulting in a whole new industry. Its rapid growth and subsequent exploitation by *Machinima Inc.* before it had barely become established forced a change in direction, spawning other new industries such as e-sports and influencer cultures. Our review highlighted how a few committed pioneers continued to push the boundaries within the converged creative technological framework that remained but, fundamentally, the original trajectory for machinima never recovered its direction within the founding community.

In Chapter 4, convergence was evident in the way *Rooster Teeth* combined and devised different media formats to create new propositions – it adapted a TV series methodology for game-based content, devised and popularized new ways to reach audiences through online platforms (eg., webisodes) and then took the creative format of offline events for live performance. Up close and personal interaction with its community became a central tenet, converging online with offline in ways that had never been seen before. As *Rooster Teeth* learned more about the evolving interests of its community, so the producers pushed themselves to develop new series and types of content to keep the community involved and coming back for more. Their fecund creativity has been sustained for, so far, over seventeen years since the release of the first episode of *Red vs Blue*. *Rooster Teeth* has become a transmedia specialist with creative practice transcending machinima, with live action role play, let's play, podcasting, vlogging, film, game, improv performance, comics, publishing, events, etc. It will therefore be interesting to see how becoming an increasingly embedded part of the *AT&T* media empire will influence its agile approach in the future.

In Chapter 5, we explored how machinima as a creative tool became a political tool converging with publishing media tropes. We demonstrated how machinima using the voice of an individual could capture the attention of the world. Even some fifteen years after its release, *The French Democracy* still inspires others to continue to use games to reach audiences with political messages. Arvers, for example, has platformed machinima as a methodology and provided impetus for thousands of potential 'gonzo reporters' to use video games to tell their stories in any way they can. This was mediatization, but not as it had been seen before, where first-person narrative is performed and storified from repurposed assets.

In Chapter 6, Rasmussen's creative trajectory extended the earliest machinima methodologies and converged the practices and technologies related to game with his own professional film industry expertise. Whilst ostensibly the practices he developed were to help him address and overcome a serious health condition which ultimately contributed to his untimely passing, his thoughts and contribution to machinima as a convergent and emergent art form inspired the machinima community and has subsequently been recognized more broadly in professional transmedia industries. The chapter set out a microcosmic example of virtual production best practices for indie creators which is highly relevant to contemporary developments by such as *Epic* and emergent others today.

In Chapter 7, we highlighted largely unfamiliar stories of industry-led convergent media practices which drew on the machinima community. Convergence is evident in creative practice, performance and technological advancements that machinima pioneers would be familiar with but which are now being adopted by big-budget studios. Workflows highlighted are reminiscent of the early machinima days and the rationale for its development is exactly what the machinima community always said it would: reduced workflow times in order to speed up time-to-market, reduced budget spending (because of cost savings in production), pre-visualizing scenes and shots in order to frame the best possible option, and provided virtual camera angles and now, with considerably enhanced computing power, the ability to render high-quality content in real-time. Creators can scale up or down at the press of a key, a benefit derived directly from the convergence of game and film production methodologies. In this chapter, however, we also highlighted how other creative industries' perspectives are being drawn into the mix from theatre, museums, theme parks and other production and performance formats which are increasingly interwoven in creative practices. In turn, these are revolving around new technological advancements that enhance real-time 3D animated production, such as motion capture, haptic devices, AI, scaled parallax screen controls, etc.

8.5 Real-Time Creativity

At its heart, machinima was always about real-time creativity, but what does this actually mean?

In Chapters 2 and 3, we discussed how real-time creativity was a function of practice. Producers of content were essentially compelling improv performers, using the games' pre-rendered assets as creative constraints and the codified movements of artefacts within the games as subtexts to their stories. Machinima is described as an organic rather than a commercial outgrowth of the convergence of game and film. In Chapter 2, machinima was thus a creative practice that had the net impact of extending the game beyond its normal lifecycle – new stories, new plots, new audiences.

In Chapter 3, we discussed how the community became a hotbed of creativity, influenced by the sharing of best practice, new methods, tips and hints in using tools and assets. For many of the pioneers we talked to, the 'golden age' of machinima was before *Machinima.com* became *Inc.* In the words of one machinima creator we cited: "*I really believed that people were in the business of fostering creativity and entertainment that could not only launch careers, but unite and inspire people around the world*" (Hughes, 2011). The disappointment at the commercial route taken is tangible. It is not solely the loss of money that is mourned but it is the destruction of the creative community that ensued through which members had continually pushed each other to create more, do more, explore, share and debate.

Alongside *Inc.*, we discussed how *AMAS* (through *Machinima.org*) was successful in professionalizing machinima as a creative approach to filmmaking. This was evidenced in how the community became employable as creative professionals with their own unique skillsets. Dyson, the creator of *Star Wars' R2D2* and a machinima producer himself, eloquently summed this up as 'real-time imagination'.

In Chapter 4, we described the prolific creativity of *Rooster Teeth*, spurred on by its avid community of followers, fans and activists. Its creative ethos of 'only making the content its producers wanted to see themselves' became a mantra that pushed them further and harder in their search for new stories told in different ways. Whilst this approach brought in others who shared both vision and passion, we highlighted that it was the experience of being 'maverick' machinima creators, that gave the producers the confidence to continually try new things – creativity begot more creativity. The success of *Rooster Teeth* is, however, because it took its community along on the journey.

In Chapter 5, Chan's film is a jump-off point in the creative development of machinima. As a political piece, *The French Democracy*, forced many to take notice of a form that previously none had heard of. Games and game culture were not accepted in France, where Chan made his film. After the media storm around the work had quietened, its recognition became overt at the highest levels of society and politicians inhabited the virtual spaces of *Second Life* to explore its potential. It inspired other creators to consider how they too may use machinima to give a voice to stories often left untold.

In this chapter, we also touch on one of the arguments put forward for the reduction in creativity in the community. We have heard from a number of sources that complexity of emerging games meant it was harder to work with them as assets for machinima storytelling. This is, however, not the case. It was because the community splintered and pioneers that had built the community ethos to be one of sharing and support moved away from the commercial exploitation of their own and others' outputs. What is notable about this is that the whole process of community formation to the point where a force of creativity was possible was predominantly achieved through virtual means. Quite simply, it is without comparison in contemporary creative industries practice even today. For example, much effort now goes into developing a virtual and 'remote' creativity-led production pipeline but the machinima community had been working in this way since the mid-1990s. Real-time is therefore a term that describes every aspect of the creative processes employed.

In Chapter 6, we examined Rasmussen's portfolio of machinima work, centred on his masterpiece, *Stolen Life*, illustrating how his creative process had evolved over a period of time. Rasmussen was one of the first to point out how different machinima is from film and game as a creative practice. His experience as a traditionally trained yet established experimental filmmaker gave him the credibility within the community to make these observations resonate more broadly. He highlighted that it was the re-usability of assets *reminiscent of game* that made machinima such a powerful creative medium for filmmaking, which he then demonstrated through a body of work that included everything from digital doodles to an award-winning feature-length film. He coined the term 'digital clay' in the process, reflecting the malleability of machinima achieved through coding and performance-based evaluation of real-time storytelling.

As machinima creative practice evolved alongside the development of mods that helped to capture game content for storytelling, new kinds of stories began to emerge that were not really scripted in ways that the film industry was familiar with. Despite the interest in the machinima pioneers, which we have reported on through Chapters 2-6, it seems that industries had to find this out for themselves. Thus, in Chapter 7, our review considered how creativity was dealt with from industry perspectives.

We highlighted Greenaway's seminal comments on how real-time 3D animation processes employed in machinima-making provide an opportunity to move beyond narration as a creative practice to navigation and devising for storytelling. Greenaway argued that the Hollywood film aesthetic which has dominated storytelling produces no more than 'illustrated books', whereas the numerous examples we draw on from the world of machinima throughout this text illustrate that it is still really only the beginning of a digital image-based paradigm shift. Indeed, this is particularly exemplified in a statement from one of the community members who reflected that the influence of machinima on creative practice was "*a bit like asking how animation had impacted Disney*" (Winn, 2020). What this draws attention to is the creative process rather than the actual machinima film outcome. It is important that this is recognized because it draws attention to how the power of the form emanates from the process of performing machinima, albeit the output is the evidence of the process which can eventually be commercialized.

In Chapter 7, therefore, we discussed how the creative process has evolved within creative industries. What we found is how creative practices have been directly and profoundly influenced by machinima, most specifically from its earliest days of pioneering activities by the community. Indeed, many have in one form or another been a part of the community over the years – through game, through participation in filmmaking, in events and as friends of more active community members. We highlighted the example of *Epic* to shine a light on the nature of the exchange between the community and its *Unreal Engine*. *Epic*'s current business model is one which is highly supportive of indie creatives without necessarily exploiting them – it provides tools, workshops, assets, tips and hints and a platform for sharing good practice. Importantly, it allows creators to profit from their own work and retain IP (up to a level). As Libreri, the chief technology officer of *Epic* and former head of VFX at *ILM* under which Gaeta created the *Matrix* effects, stated:

> *Unreal Engine 5* promises to further free the artistic process by making it easier to take virtual worlds developed for feature film and television, and run them in the game engine in real-time.
>
> Kim Libreri (in Dimitropoulos, 2020)

Furthermore, Petit, the general manager of *Epic*, explained to us how the vision of the future of real-time creativity is not limited to a convergence of established media forms but open to seamless experiences across multiple platforms. He reflected on how this comes back to machinima, whose creators were the pioneers of these kinds of interactive techniques. *Epic*'s approach is therefore commendable, yet it remains to be seen how it will build a community environment in which creativity as seen among those early machinima pioneers can be achieved.

In conclusion, our text is both an evaluation and recognition of the pioneers of machinima as well as a provocation to those who have been inspired by the stories of its emergence and by the voices of those who participated in the early years of machinima as a creative technologies practice.

References

@Jericho (2019). Tweet, 19 January, https://twitter.com/JERICHO/status/1086487306297434112?ref_src=twsrc%5Etfw%7Ctwcamp%5Etweetembed%7Ctwterm%5E1086487306297434112&ref_url=https%3A%2F%2Fwww.dailydot.com%2Fparsec%2Fmachinima-youtube-deleted%2F, accessed 6 May 2020.

@RebelTaxi (2020). MTV Video Mods [machinima], https://www.youtube.com/watch?v=8PmTPhEIGQs.

20minutes.fr (2007). De 'French Democracy' a 'World of Electors', *20 Minutes*, 15 April, https://www.20minutes.fr/culture/151831-20070415-french-democracy-a-world-of-electors, accessed 18 May 2020.

Abbruzzese, J. (2015). Fullscreen is coming to the big screen, *Mashable UK*, 23 January, https://mashable.com/2015/01/23/fullscreen-youtube-movies, accessed 4 May 2020.

Adams, D. (2004). The Strangerhood: Stranger than fiction? *IGN.com*, 24 August, http://pc.ign.com/articles/557/557891.html, accessed 24 Aug 2005.

AFP (2005). Small animation on French riots makes big waves, *Yahoo! News*, 18 December, http://news.yahoo.com/s/afp/afpentertainmentfranc...5dIAFBxFb8C;_ylu=X3oDMTA5aHJvMDdwBHNlYwN5bmNhdA, accessed 20 December 2005.

Aguilar, C. (2019). Rooster Teeth CEO apologizes for poor work conditions at Austin animation studio, *Cartoon Brew*, 20 June, https://www.cartoonbrew.com/artist-rights/rooster-teeth-ceo-apologizes-for-poor-work-conditions-at-dallas-animation-studio-175948.html, accessed 6 May 2020.

Ali, R. (2005). Australian court rules against Kazaa, Gigaom, 5 Sept, https://gigaom.com/2005/09/05/australian-court-rules-against-kazaa/, accessed 15 July 2020.

Alias Systems (2003). Alias' Maya provides core 3D animation software for Lord of the Rings: The Return of the King, *Business Wire*, 23 Dec, https://www.businesswire.com/news/home/20031223005244/en/Alias-Maya-Core-3D-Animation-Software-Lord, accessed 16 July 2020.

Allen, G. (2004). Virtual warriors have feelings too, *The New York Times*, 14 November, http://www.nytimes.com/2004/11/14/arts/14alle.html, accessed 17 Nov 2004.

Altberg, E. (2014). Interview with Tracy Harwood, 21 July.

Arvers, I. (2020). Interview with authors, 22 May.

Azhar, A. (2003). Play it again, Sam, *The Guardian*, 20 November, https://www.theguardian.com/online/story/0,3605,1088445,00.html, accessed 21 Nov 2003.

Baculi, S. (2020). RWBY lead animator Ian Kedward leaves Rooster Teeth after 7 years: 'Some good. Then there was all the bad', *BoundingintoComics.com*, 15 January, https://boundingintocomics.com/2020/01/15/rwby-lead-animator-ian-kedward-leaves-rooster-teeth-after-7-years-some-good-then-there-was-all-the-bad/, 7 May 2020.

Bailenson, J. (2017). Virtual reality can help politicians make responsible decisions about the environment, *National Geographic*, 25 Oct, https://blog.nationalgeographic.org/2017/10/25/virtual-reality-can-help-politicians-make-responsible-decisions-about-the-environment/, accessed 21 June 2020.

Bailey, A. (2006). Correspondence with Ben Grussi, 26 January.

Baumgarten, J. (2018). Ezra Cooperstein named president of Rooster Teeth, *Multichannel.com*, 26 January, https://www.multichannel.com/news/ezra-cooperstein-named-president-rooster-teeth-417734, accessed 6 May 2020.

BBC News (2009). Whitehall defends 'fantasy world', 19 Mar, http://news.bbc.co.uk /1/hi/uk_politics/7952213.stm, accessed 21 June 2020.

Biever, C. (2003). The Animation Game, *New Scientist*, 25 October.

Binary Picture Show (2006). Beast [machinima], https://www.youtube.com/watch ?v=DjmLhR6jnjo&t=208s.

Bittanti, M. (2011). Don't mess with *The Warriors*: the politics of machinima, in H. Lowood and M. Nitsche (eds.), *The Machinima Reader*, pp. 159-174, Cambridge, MA: MIT Press.

Black, C. (2007). Interview: Stolen Life, *Nanoflix Productions*, 4 July, https://www.youtube.com/watch?v=5WzDEycU5xU, accessed 15 June 2020.

Blake, M. (2019). A turbulent week for WarnerMedia, *LA Business Journal*, 13 September, https://labusinessjournal.com/news/2019/sep/13/turbulent-week-warnermedia/, accessed 6 May 2020.

Boellstorff, T. (2008). *Coming of age in Second Life: An anthropologist explores the virtually human*, Woodstock: Princeton University Press.

Boomer, J. (2014). Interview with T. Harwood, 30 May.

Boomer, J. (2020). Interview with authors, 11 May.

Booton, J. (2014). Tech mergers hotter than in the dot-com era, *Marketwatch.com*, 14 November, https://www.marketwatch.com/story/tech-mergers-hotter-than-in-the-dot-com-era-2014-11-13, accessed 4 May 2020.

Bowser, J. (2007). BBC appoints head of digital media technology, *Campaign*, 17 Sept, https://www.campaignlive.co.uk/article/bbc-appoints-head-digital-media-technology/738431, accessed 14 July 2020.

Brilliant Digital Entertainment Annual Report 2001, https://sec.report/Document/0001011438-02-000252/, accessed 15 July 2020.

Brouwer, B. (2016). Rooster Teeth's Burnie Burns and Gavin Free reminisce about the brand, online video's past, *Forbes*, 8 July, https://www.forbes.com/sites/bree brouwer/2016/07/08/rooster-teeth-online-video-history-burnie-burns-gavin-free/#30e1806119b5, accessed 22 Apr 2020.

Brown, H. (2005). Forum post: Machinima and Yahoo, *Machinima.com*, 12 October.

Brown, H. (2008). Correspondence with Ben Grussi.

Brown, S. (2003). *Artery: Machinima*, https://archive.org/details/Artery-Machinima, accessed 30 March 2020.

Brown, W. and Holtmeier, M. (2013). Machinima: Cinema in a minor or multitudinous key? In Ng, J., *Understanding machinima: essays on filmmaking in virtual worlds*, pp. 3-22, London: Bloomsbury Press.

Bungie.net (2004). Red vs Blue: The Interview Strikes Back, 25 November, http://www.bungie.net/News/TopStory.aspx?story=rvbinterview, accessed 25 Nov 2004.

Burke, C. (2020). Interview with authors, 14 June and 15 July.

Burke, C. (2020). This Spartan Life (Halo) [machinima], https://www.youtube.com/channel/UCNMAnXsLhWNG5lsVLziT1Ig

Burkeman, O. (2007). Exploding pigs and volleys of gunfire as Le Pen opens HQ in virtual world, The Guardian, 20 Jan, https://www.theguardian.com/technology/2007/jan/20/news.france, accessed 21 June 2020.

Burks, R. (2016). How Quantic Dream continues to change the way we perceive gaming, *Tech Times*, 23 Jun, https://www.techtimes.com/articles/166695/20160623/how-quantic-dream-continues-to-change-the-way-we-perceive-gaming.htm, accessed 15 July 2020.

Burns, B. (2012). Burnie Burns talks to TSTV, interview, 7 March, https://www.youtube.com/watch?v=1ai1UzX0UDc, accessed 23 Apr 2020

Burns, B. (2017). Burnie Vlog, 27 February, Roosterteeth.com, accessed 11 May 2020.

Burns, B. (2017). Vlog: RTX2017 Austin Clips, https://www.youtube.com/watch?v=ozP7nBxbwe0&list=PLI03SDc_TzzIHSH02uRQ6pLqNDlbQPPLe&index=3, accessed 2 May 2020.

Burns, B. (2020a). https://twitter.com/burnie/status/1268628119075926018, Twitter, 4 Jun (8:38pm).

Burns, B. (2020b). gg new map, *Burnie.com*, 10 June, accessed 10 June 2020.

Burns, M. (2014). The long and lonely death of Softimage, *Digital Arts*, 17 Mar, https://www.digitalartsonline.co.uk/features/motion-graphics/long-lonely-death-of-softimage/, accessed 16 July 2020.

Busch, A. (2014). Indiegogo record for film campaign: 'Lazer Team' wins with $2.4M, *Deadline.com*, https://deadline.com/2014/07/indiegogo-record-for-film-campaign-lazer-team-wins-with-2-4m-800085/, accessed 4 May 2020.

Business Wire (2015). Fullscreen acquires McBeard, *Businesswire.com*, 4 May 2015, https://www.businesswire.com/news/home/20150504005659/en, accessed 4 May 2020.

Bye, K. (2016). #294: John Gaeta on ILMxLAB and immersive storytelling, *Voices of VR Podcast*, 8 Feb, https://voicesofvr.com/294-john-gaeta-on-ilmxlab-immersive-storytelling/, accessed 18 July 2020.

Byerley, M. (2019). Podcast: Philip Rosedale interviewed by Linden Vet about building virtual world, New World Notes, 22 Apr, https://nwn.blogs.com/nwn/2019/04/philip-rosedale-linden-lab-high-fidelity-social-vr.html, accessed 13 July 2020.

Castillo, M. (2010). Top 10 video games: Mass Effect 2, *Time.com*, http://content.time.com/time/specials/packages/article/0,28804,2035319_2034548_2034561,00.html, accessed 14 April 2020.

Chan, A. (2005). The French Democracy [machinima], https://archive.org/details/thefrenchdemocracy.

Cheredar, T. (2014). Fullscreen acquires Rooster Teeth, video studio behind Red vs. Blue, *Venture Beat*, https://venturebeat.com/2014/11/10/fullscreen-acquires-rooster-teeth-video-studio-behind-red-vs-blue/, accessed 4 May 2020.

Chibber, K. (2009). The man who saved the BBC, *Wired*, 15 Apr, https://www.wired.co.uk/article/the-man-who-saved-the-bbc, accessed 14 July 2020.

Chisholm, I. (2020). Clear Skies 3 [machinima], https://ianchisholmva.wordpress.com/clear-skies/.

Chisholm, I. (2020). Interview with authors, 16 December.

Chmielewski, D. (2013). Ridley Scott and Machinima sci-fi collaboration fizzles, *Los Angeles Times*, 22 November, https://www.latimes.com/entertainment/envelope/cotown/la-et-ct-ridley-scott-machinima-shorts-20131122-story.html, accessed 13 April 2020

Chmielewski, D. (2018). Otter Media lays off 10% of staff in restructuring of digital properties, *Deadline.com*, https://deadline.com/2018/12/otter-media-layoffs-10-percent-staff-restructuring-of-digital-operations-1202513797/, accessed 6 May 2020.

Chrisafis, A. (2012). Seven years after the riots, the suburbs of Paris still simmer with resentment, *The Guardian*, 3 November, https://www.theguardian.com/world/2012/nov/03/estate-racial-hatred-poisoning-france?CMP=twt_gu, accessed 15 May 2020.

Chrisafis, A. (2015a). The trial that could lay bare France's racial divide, *The Guardian*, 15 March, https://www.theguardian.com/world/2015/mar/15/trial-france-racial-divide, accessed 17 May 2020.

Chrisafis, A. (2015b). 'Nothing's changed': 10 years after French riots, banlieues remain in crisis, *The Guardian*, 22 October, https://www.theguardian.com/world/2015/oct/22/nothings-changed-10-years-after-french-riots-banlieues-remain-in-crisis, 15 May 2020.

Clan Phantasm/Starfury Productions (1998). Devil's Covenant [machinima], https://web.archive.org/web/20010606204040/http://machinima.com/phantasm/.

Clarke, A. (1996). This pig ain't no Babe, *Hyper Magazine*, Oct, https://retrocdn.net/images/5/51/Hyper_AU_036.pdf, accessed 14 July 2020.

Clarke, A. and Mitchell, G. (2007). *Videogames and Art*, Bristol, UK: Intellect Books.

Clarke, S. (2018). 'Game of Thrones' star Maisie Williams joins Rooster Teeth animated series gen:LOCK, *Variety.com*, 15 September, https://variety.com/2018/digital/news/game-of-thrones-maisie-williams-joins-rooster-teeth-genlock-1202943191/, accessed 6 May 2020.

Clarke, S. (2018). Red vs Blue producer Rooster Teeth opens up in London, *Variety.com*, 23 April, https://variety.com/2018/digital/news/red-vs-blue-rooster-teeth-london-1202780342/, accessed 7 May 2020.

Claudia Black Unofficial (2013). Claudia Black about Stolen Life and Machinima 2009, *YouTube*, 3 Mar, https://www.youtube.com/watch?v=_a1Or988DMU, 7 June 2020.

Cockburn, P. (2018). Obituary: Hugh Russell Paul Hancock, "Machinima" founder and virtual reality pioneer, *The Herald*, 2 March, https://www.heraldscotland.com/opinion/16060383.obituary-hugh-russell-paul-hancock-machinima-founder-and-virtual-reality-pioneer/, accessed 1 April 2020.

Connolly, R. (2020). Interview with authors, 18 June.

Connor, A. (2008). Pic of the day: iPlayer BAFTA, BBC, 12 May, https://www.bbc.co.uk/blogs/bbcinternet/2008/05/pic_of_the_day_iplayer_bafta.html, accessed 14 July 2020.

Crabtree, S. (2006). Machinima becoming used for social criticism, *Backstage.com*, 7 April, https://www.backstage.com/magazine/article/machinima-becoming-used-social-criticism-49454/, accessed 9 April 2006.

Craddock, D. (2016). Machinima magic: the death and rebirth of Ranger Gone Bad, Shacknews.com, available online at https://www.shacknews.com/article/96624/machinima-magic-the-death-and-rebirth-of-ranger-gone-bad, accessed 4 Mar 2020.

Crawford, T. (2020). Interview with authors, 15 July.

Crikey (2011). Hillary Clinton flirts with Second Life, 11 July, https://www.crikey.com.au/2007/07/11/hillary-clinton-flirts-with-second-life/, 9 Nov 2020.

Crossick, G. and Kaszynska, P. (2014). Understanding the value of arts and culture, *Arts and Humanities Research Council*, https://ahrc.ukri.org/documents/publications/cultural-value-project-final-report/, accessed 25 July 2020.

Cruz-Neira, C., Sandin, D.J., DeFanti, T.A, Kenyon, R.V. and Hart, J.C. (1992). The CAVE: Audio Visual Experience Automatic Virtual Environment, Communications of the Association of Computing Machinery, 35(6): pp. 64-72.

CTV News (2005). Riots herald 'machinima' film breakthrough, *CTV.ca*, 15 December, www.ctv.ca/servlet/ArticleNews/story/CTVNews/20051215/machinima_20051215/20051215?hub=Entertainmen, accessed 19 December 2005.

Delaney, K. (2004). When art imitates videogames, you have 'Red vs Blue' *The Wall Street Journal*, 9 April, http://interactive.wsj.com/dividends/retrieve.cgi?id=/text/wsjie/data/SB108145721789778243.djm&d2hconverter=display-d2h&template=dividends, accessed 24 Apr 2020.

DeLappe, J. (2013). Playing politics: machinima as live performance and document, in J. Ng, *Understanding machinima*, pp. 147-166, New York: Bloomsbury Press.

Dellario, F. (2020). Interview with authors, 3 March.

Demoscene – the Art of Coding (2019), http://demoscene-the-art-of-coding.net/the-demoscene/, accessed 18 April 2020

Dibbell, J. (2005). Site specific: Pixar plays, *The Village Voice*, New York, 50(45), p. 25.

Dimitropoulos, S. (2020). Why Hollywood needs computer games tech more than ever, BBC News, 10 Jul, https://www.bbc.co.uk/news/business-51799504, accessed 12 July 2020.

Drunk Gamers (2001). N64 | The Lost Reviews Pt 1: Conker's Bad Fur Day, 29 June, https://web.archive.org/web/20020214180655/http://www.drunkgamers.com/lost1.shtml, accessed 22 Apr 2020.

Ducrey, V. (2007). Sarkozy takes presidential campaign into the online game 'Second Life', AP Television, 20 Feb, http://www.aparchive.com/metadata/youtube/15db7d52b6a07a63197089fbd1b45df6, accessed 21 June 2020.

Dyson, T. (2012). Interview with Tracy Harwood, 22 February.

Ebert, R. (2001). Final Fantasy: The Spirits Within, RogerEbert.com, 11 July, http://www.rogerebert.com/reviews/final-fantasy-the-spirits-within-2001, accessed 2 April 2020

Eng, P. (2020). The history of Rooster Teeth, https://www.patrickeng.com/history-of-rooster-teeth-infographic#table, accessed 29 Apr 2020.

Errera, C. (2004). Louis Wu: The Spread of RVB, *Halo.Bungie.org*, 6 March.

Errera, C. (2020). Interview with the authors, 24 April.

Eschwege, A. (2007). Second Life: phenomene ou epiphenomena? Emarketing.fr, 1 Oct, https://www.e-marketing.fr/Marketing-Magazine/Article/Second-Life-phenomene-ou-epiphenomene--20690-1.htm, accessed 29 June 2020.

Failes, I. (2020). Westworld's journey into the LED screen revolution, Befores and Afters, 25 Jun, https://beforesandafters.com/2020/06/25/westworlds-journey-into-the-led-screen-revolution/, accessed 16 July 2020.

Falcione, J. (2020). Interview with authors, 13 May.

Feldman, C. (2004). The Sims 2 undergoes machinima makeover, *Gamespot*, 30 September.

Fingus, R. (2015). Google announces ad-free YouTube Red subscriptions with Music service & offline caching, *AppleInsider.com*, 21 October, https://appleinsider.com/articles/15/10/21/google-announces-ad-free-youtube-red-subscriptions-with-music-service-offline-caching, accessed 4 May 2020.

Fixmer, A. (2014). Fullscreen buys Rooster Teeth, its first acquisition under Chernin ownership, *Mashable UK*, 10 November, https://mashable.com/2014/11/10/fullscreen-buys-rooster-teeth, accessed 4 May 2020.

Forbes (2006). Red vs Blue: the cash is always greener, *Forbes.com*, 14 December, https://www.forbes.com/2006/12/10/red-vs-blue-tech-cx_de_games06_1212cash.html, accessed 2 May 2020.

Forbes, E. (2020). Patent case of the week: In re: PersonalWeb Technologies LLC, Appeal No. 2019-1918 (Fed. Cir. June 17, 2020), *Schwabe.com*, 22 June, https://www.schwabe.com/newsroom-publications-in-re-personalweb-technologies-llc-appeal-no-2019-1918-fed-cir-june-17-2020, accessed 14 July 2020.

Foyler, C. (2007). French government knights Peter Molyneux, *Shack News*, 6 April, https://www.shacknews.com/article/46446/french-government-knights-peter-molyneux, accessed 23 May 2020.

Frankie (2006). Red vs who? *Bungie.net*, https://www.bungie.net/News/TopStory.aspx?link=redvswho, accessed 9 April 2006.

Fritz, B. (2006). Smoke and mirrors: new content is viewer's choice, *Variety*, 403(9), p 48.

Gaeta, J. (2004). Foreword, in Marino, P., *3D Game-based Filmmaking: The Art of Machinima*, Scottsdale, ZA: Paraglyph Press.

Gajsek, D. (2020). Unity vs Unreal Engine for XR development: which one is better? *Circuit Stream*, 16 Mar, https://circuitstream.com/blog/unity-vs-unreal/, accessed 21 June 2020.

GamePlayShare (2014). Gameplay screencap: Cyberswine, *YouTube*, 16 Sept, https://www.youtube.com/watch?v=kWDbLMCazTU, accessed 14 July 2020.

Gestalt (2000). Interview with Hugh Hancock of Strange Company, *Eurogamer.net*, https://www.eurogamer.net/articles/i_strangecompany, accessed 30 March 2020.

GG (2001). Reshoot-'em-ups, *Entertainment Weekly*, 7 July, p.148.

Girlich, U. (1996), The Unofficial DEM Format Description (Version 1.02), http://www.gamers.org/dEngine/Quake/Qdem/dem-1.0.2-3.html#ss3.2, accessed 18 April 2020.

Gish, H. (2008). Trauma engines: representing school shootings through Halo, *UCLA's Journal of Cinema and Media Studies: Mediascape*, Spring, http://www.tft.ucla.edu/mediascape/Spring08_TraumaEngines.html, accessed 18 May 2020.

Gladstone, D. (2006). The little picture: should machinimists quit their day jobs? *Computer Gaming World*, 2 June, http://www.1up.com/do/feature?pager.offset=0&cId=3151146, accessed 7 Jun 2006.

Gladstone, D. (2006). The little picture: should machinimists quit their day jobs? *Computer Gaming World Magazine*, 2 June, http://www.1up.com/do/feature?pager.offset=0&cId=3151146, accessed 7 Jun 2006.

Goss, J. (2004). Red vs Blue = Green, *Austin American Statesman*, 6 July, pp. 1, D6.

Goss, J. (2020). Interview with authors, 26 February.

Gras, R. (2008). Interview with Tracy Harwood, 13 May.

Gras, R. (2020). Interview with authors, 20 July.

Greenaway, P. (2010). Keynote, 48 Hour Filmmaking Project Machinima, 23 Sept, https://vimeo.com/15253336, accessed 13 July 2020.

Grove, R. (2008). On the death of Peter Rasmussen, *Machiniplex*, 19 March, http://machiniplex3.blogspot.com/2008/03/on-death-of-peter-rasmussen_19.html, accessed 8 June 2020.

Grove, R. (2017). Interview with Tracy Harwood, 12 July.

Grussi, B. (2008) Unpublished manuscript, Machinima (1996-2008).

Grussi, B. (2020). Personal communication with Tracy Harwood.

Ha, A. (2018). AT&T is now the sole owner of Otter Media, *Techcrunch.com*, 7 August, https://techcrunch.com/2018/08/07/att-otter-media/, accessed 6 May 2020.

Hamer-Morton, J. (2020). Interview with authors, 30 April.

Hancock, H. (2000). Veridian, Corporatism and Machinima, 1 January, *Machinima.com,* http://www.machinima.com/displayarticle2.php?article=393, accessed 1 April 2020.

Hancock, H. (2000). Welcome to Machinima.com! 3 January, *Machinima.com,* https://web.archive.org/web/20000817214136/http://www.machinima.com/articles/Machinima-com%20intro/page1.shtml, accessed 8 Mar 2020.

Hancock, H. (2003). Commercial machinima and the law, 13 October, *Machinima.com,* http://www.machinima.com/displayarticle2.php?article=375, accessed 2 April 2020.

Hancock, H. (2006). Hugh Hancock leaves Machinima.com, 30 January, http://www.machinima.com/article.php?article=444, accessed 8 April 2020.

Hancock, H. (2014). Interview with Tracy Harwood, 20 May.

Hancock, H. and Ingram, J. (2007). *Machinima for Dummies*, Hoboken NJ: Wiley Publishers.

Hancock, H. and Ingram, J. (2007). *Machinima for Dummies*, Hoboken, NJ, Wiley Publications.

Hansen, E. (2002). Entertaindom, Cnet.com, 10 Mar, https://www.cnet.com/news/aol-time-warner-plans-to-close-entertaindom/, accessed 15 July 2020.

Hardin, M.-O. (2019). Branded a no-go zone: a trip inside the 93, France's most notorious banlieue, *The Guardian*, 4 April, https://www.theguardian.com/artanddesign/2019/apr/04/photographer-banlieue-monsieur-bonheur-department-93-paris-france-fox-news-no-go-zone, accessed 15 May. 2020.

Harsin, J. (2014). 'The French Democracy': mapping promise and limitation of glocal digital protest, *Communication, Culture and Critique*, Vol. 7, pp. 174-191.

Harwood, T. (2011). Towards a manifesto for Machinima, *Journal of Visual Culture*, Vol. 13 No. 1, pp. 6-12.

Harwood, T. (2011). Towards a manifesto for machinima, *Journal of Visual Culture*, 10(1), pp. 6-12.

Harwood, T. (2014). *Machinima: Investigating the Cultural Values*, Machinima.dmu.ac.uk, accessed 25 July 2020.

Harwood, T. and Garry, T. (2013). 'It's mine!' – Participation and ownership within virtual co-creation environments, in S. Tagg, A. Stevenson and T. Viscovi (eds.), *New Developments in Online Marketing*, pp. 127-138, Routledge.

Healey, T. (2012). Little grey cells #2… any implied 'how you should do it' – you should throw away, *Mob76 Outlook*, 23 May, https://www.mob76outlook.com/any-implied-how-you-should-do-it-you-should-throw-away/#more-1223, accessed 14 July 2020.

Henderson, B. (2020). Interview with authors, 4 March.

Henley, J. (2005). Sarkozy pledges police crackdown after riots in Paris, *The Guardian*, https://www.theguardian.com/world/2005/nov/01/france.jonhenley, accessed 17 May 2020.

Hill, J. (2006). Dream machinima, *The Sydney Morning Herald*, 8 June, https://www.smh.com.au/technology/dream-machinima-20060608-gdnpah.html, accessed 21 Apr 2020.

Hogg, C. (2007). Japanese MP opens cyber office, BBC News, 11 Jun, http://news.bbc.co.uk/1/hi/world/asia-pacific/6739857.stm, accessed 21 June 2020.

Horiuchi, V. (2005). Rise of the machines, The Salt Lake Tribune, 28 January, http://www.sltrib.com/healthscience/ci_2535215, accessed 27 Jan 2005.

Howlett, C. (2020). Correspondence with authors, 7 June.

Howlett, C. (2020). PhD Thesis: Mapping the techno-stice: dissensual territories. In-between technology and contemporary art, *Queensland University of Technology*, https://eprints.qut.edu.au/174605/1/Christopher_Howlett_Thesis.pdf, accessed 19 May 2020.

Hughes, B. (2011). Before you sign that Machinima contract, *ObviouslyBenHughes.com*, 8 December, http://www.obviouslybenhughes.com/post/13933948148/before-you-sign-that-machinima-contract, accessed 12 December 2011

Hurst, S. (2016a). Indiegogo success Lazer Team scores over $1M in theatrical pre-sales, *CrowdfundInsider.com*, 28 January, https://www.crowdfundinsider.com/2016/01/80925-indiegogo-success-lazer-team-scores-over-1m-in-theatrical-release-pre-sales/, accessed 4 May 2020.

Hurst, S. (2016b). Rooster Teeth's new game 'Million Dollars, But…' smashes $10,000 goal just minutes after Kickstarter launch, *CrowdfundInsider.com*, 12 May, https://www.crowdfundinsider.com/2016/05/85514-rooster-teeths-new-game-million-dollars-but-smashes-100000-goal-just-minutes-after-kickstarter-launch/, accessed 4 May 2020.

Hurst, S. (2016c). Rooster Teeth's 'Million Dollars, But…The Game' finishes Kickstarter round and captures $1.3M, *CrowdfundInsider.com*, 10 June, https://www.crowdfundinsider.com/2016/06/86722-rooster-teeths-million-dollars-but-the-game-finishes-kickstarter-round-captures-over-1-3m/, accessed 4 May 2020.

IceAxe Productions (2007). Clockwork [machinima], https://vimeo.com/4914117.

IGN FilmForce (2006). Interview: Tommy Pallotta, *IGN Magazine*, 30 May, https://uk.ign.com/articles/2006/05/30/interview-tommy-pallotta, accessed 2 April 2020.

ILL Clan (1998). Apartment Huntin' [machinima], http://www.machinima.com/files/Films/Conventional_Media/AH-Final.shtml.

ILMVFX (2020). The virtual production of The Mandalorian, Season One, *YouTube.com*, 20 February https://www.youtube.com/watch?v=gUnxzVOs3rk, accessed 13 April 2020

Ingraham, N. (2013). With Hollywood partnerships, Machinima wants to be the HBO of gaming video, *The Verge*, 18 July, https://www.theverge.com/2013/7/18/4536414/machinima-wants-to-be-the-hbo-of-gaming, accessed 10 April 2020.

Inside Film (2008). NWS FTO scholarship in Rasmussen's honour, 18 Jun, https://www.if.com.au/nsw-fto-scholarship-in-rasmussens-honour/, accessed 6 June 2020.

Inside Film (2010). Peter Morse wins Peter Rasmussen Award, 15 Jun, https://www.if.com.au/peter-morse-wins-peter-rasmussen-award/, accessed 6 June 2020.

Ivey, R. (2012). Interview with Chris Jones and Aaron Conners of Big Finish Games, *Just Adventure*, 23 May, https://www.justadventure.com/2012/05/23/interview-with-chris-jones-and-aaron-conners-of-big-finish-games/, accessed 6 June 2020.

Jacobs, H. (2015). CEO of huge YouTube network explains why he's betting on Vimeo, *Business Insider*, 4 June, https://www.businessinsider.com/machinima-ceo-chad-gutstein-explains-vimeo-and-vessel-deals-2015-6?r=US&IR=T, accessed 11 April 2020.

Jandoc, W. (2004). Red vs. Blue mines game for comedy gold, Honolulu Star, 5 December, http://starbulletin.com/2004/12/05/features/story4.html, accessed 6 Dec 2004.

Jarvey, N. (2016). Fullscreen CMO Jason Klarman exits, Alan Beard promoted, Hollywood Reporter, 6 September, https://www.hollywoodreporter.com/news/fullscreen-cmo-jason-klarman-exits-919062, accessed 5 May 2020.

Jarvey, N. (2018). David Tennant joins Rooster Teeth's gen:LOCK, *Hollywood Reporter*, 27 July, https://www.hollywoodreporter.com/news/david-tennant-joins-rooster-teeths-genlock-1130449, accessed 6 May 2020.

Jarvey, N. (2018). Warner Bros. unveils Machinima rebrand after year of integration, *Hollywood Reporter*, 14 February, https://www.hollywoodreporter.com/news/warner-bros-unveils-machinima-rebrand-year-integration-1084733, accessed 12 April 2020.

Jenkins, H. (2006). *Convergence culture: where old and new media collide*, New York: New York University Press.

Johnson, E. (2014a). Nerdist knocks YouTube's stickiness, commenters at Comic-Con, *Vox.com*, 27 July, https://www.vox.com/2014/7/27/11629208/nerdist-knocks-youtubes-stickiness-commenters-at-comic-con, accessed 4 May 2020.

Johnson, E. (2014b). Rooster Teeth says independence has served it well, Vox.com, 1 May, https://www.vox.com/2014/5/1/11626336/a-year-after-machinima-split-rooster-teeth-says-gamer-dudes-are-still, accessed 4 May 2020.

Johnson, E. (2014c). From Oculus to Twitch to Minecraft, why gamers are in hot demand, *Vox.com*, 10 September, https://www.vox.com/2014/9/10/11630730/

from-oculus-to-twitch-to-minecraft-why-gamers-are-in-hot-demand, accessed 4 May 2020.

Johnson, P. (2010). *Second Life, media, and the other society*, New York: Peter Lang.

Jones, C. (2007). Interview: Stolen Life, *Nanoflix Productions*, 4 July, https://www.youtube.com/watch?v=4PkNFuxPFz4, accessed 15 June 2020.

Jones, R. (2011). Does machinima really democratize? *Journal of Visual Culture*, 10(1): 59-65.

Kafka, P. (2013). Machinima wants a mega-round. Who wants to invest in a YouTube giant? *AllThingsD.com*, 20 June, http://allthingsd.com/20130620/machinima-wants-a-mega-round-who-wants-to-invest-in-a-youtube-giant/, accessed 10 April 2020.

Kafka, P. (2017). Transcript: Rooster Teeth's co-founder Michael 'Burnie' Burns on Recode Media, *Vox.com*, 20 January, https://www.vox.com/2017/1/19/14325758/full-transcript-michael-burnie-burns-rooster-teeth-viral-video-youtube, accessed 29 Apr 2020.

Kahan, D. (2019). The exploitation of American creators: Rooster Teeth's abusive crunch culture, *Popdust.com*, 17 June, https://www.popdust.com/rooster-teeth-crunch-2638895587.html, accessed 6 May 2020.

Kang, K.A. (1999). A KAK sponsored contest, https://web.archive.org/web/20001213033500/http://q3arena.com/news/archive.php3?archive_id=550, accessed 30 March 2020.

Kang, K.A. (2004). Anna [machinima], https://archive.org/details/anna_fountainhead.

Kathunter (2005). The Sims 2 gets even stranger, *GamePro Magazine*, April, p. 22.

Kelland, M. (2008). Interview with Tracy Harwood, 2 November.

Kelland, M. (2011). From game mod to low-budget film: the evolution of machinima, in Lowood, H. and M. Nitsche, *The Machinima Reader*, pp. 23-36, Cambridge, MA: MIT Press.

Kelly, K. (2019). Technium: Virtual live-action in a virtually real film, *kk.org*, 30 April, https://kk.org/thetechnium/virtual-live-action-in-a-virtually-real-film/, accessed 14 April 2020.

Knoop, J. (2019). All of Machinima's YouTube videos are gone, stunning creators and fans, *Dailydot.com*, 21 January, https://www.dailydot.com/parsec/machinima-youtube-deleted/, accessed 6 May 2020.

Kolan, P. (2007). Stolen Life interview: Peter Rasmussen, *IGN*, 6 Jun, https://www.ign.com/articles/2007/06/06/stolen-life-interview-peter-rasmussen, accessed 7 June 2020.

Konow, D. (2005). The cult of Red vs Blue, *Tom's Hardware Guide: Games & Entertainment*, 24 September, http://www.tomshardware.com/game/200509241, accessed 25 Sept 2005.

Krahulik, M. and Holkins, J. (2005). Comic strip: Red vs Blue vs Decorum, *Penny-Arcade.com*, 31 August, https://www.penny-arcade.com/comic/2005/08/31, accessed 28 Apr 2020.

Kramer, S.D. (2011). YouTube launches massive programming push, *Gigaom.com*, 28 October, https://gigaom.com/2011/10/28/419-youtube-launches-massive-programming-push/, accessed 9 April 2020

Krapp, P. (2011). Of games and gestures: machinima and the suspension of animation, in H. Lowood and M. Nitsche (eds.), *The Machinima Reader*, pp. 315-338, Cambridge, MA: MIT Press.

L.H. (2004). Innovators bit parts: That Xbox in your living room? A few tweaks and it's a movie studio, *New York Magazine*, 5 January.

Landa, C. (2013). 'Odds Are' you'll like the Rooster Teeth, Barenaked Ladies collaboration, *Tubefilter*, 11 October, https://www.tubefilter.com/2013/10/11/rooster-teeth-barenaked-ladies-odds-are-music-video/, accessed 25 Apr 2020.

Lardinois, F. (2016). YouTube will premiere its first original series and movies next week, including a new PewDiePie show, *Techcrunch.com*, 3 February, https://techcrunch.com/2016/02/03/scary-pewdiepie/, accessed 4 May 2020.

Lardy, X. (2014). Interview with Tracy Harwood, 21 May.

Lardy, X. (2020). Interview with authors, 20 May.

Lawler, R. (2013). Machinima names Stephen Semprevivo President and GM amidst management turnover, *Techcrunch.com*, https://techcrunch.com/2013/11/26/machinima-semprevivo-president-gm/, accessed 10 April 2020.

Lechner, M. (2005). La cite animee d'Alex Chan, Liberation.fr, 12 December, https://www.liberation.fr/grand-angle/2005/12/12/la-cite-animee-d-alex-chan_541546, accessed 18 May 2020.

Ledwidge, M. (2020). Interview with authors, 22 June.

Leggat, G. (2004a). Burnie Burns on RedvsBlue, *Filmmaker Magazine*, Fall, pp. 2, 8.

Leggat, G. (2004b). Movies for the game crowd, *Daily News* (New York), 1 February.

Libreri, K. (2020). Interview with authors, 30 November.

Logue, T. (2020). Interview with authors, 2 April.

Louderback, J. (2004). Cyber stuff: Play. Cut. Create, *USAWeekend.com*, 21 Nov, http://www.usaweekend.com/04_issues/041121/041121web.html, accessed 21 Nov 2004.

Lowood, H. (2005). Real-time performance: machinima and game studies, *The International Digital Media and Arts Association Journal*, 3(1):10-17.

Lowood, H. (2006). High-performance play: the making of machinima, *Journal of Media Practice*, 7(1), pp. 25-42.

Lowood, H. (2006). Storyline, dance/music, or PvP?: Game movies and community players in World of Warcraft, *Games and Culture*, 1(4): 362-283.

Lowood, H. (2008). Found technology: players as innovators in the making of machinima, in McPherson, T. (ed.), *Digital Youth, Innovation, and the Unexpected*, pp. 165-196, The John D. and Catherine T. MacArthur Foundation Series on Digital Media and Learning, Cambridge, MA: The MIT Press.

Lowood, H. (2011). Perfect capture: three takes on replay, machinima and the history of virtual worlds, *Journal of Visual Culture*, 10(1): 113-124.

Lowood, H. (2011). Video capture: machinima, documentation, and the history of virtual worlds, in Lowood, H. and Nitsche, M., pp. 3-22, *The Machinima Reader*, Boston: MIT Press.

Lowood, H. and Nitsche, M. Eds. (2011). *The machinima reader*, Cambridge, MA: MIT Press.

Lowood, H. et al. (2011) *Special Issue: Machinima*, Journal of Visual Culture, 10(1).

Lucien-Bay, L. (2020). Interview with authors, 5 March.

Lum, S. (2000). The Cineplex: Closed…, 26 November, https://www.quakewiki.net/archives/cineplex/, accessed 1 April 2020.

Lynch, K. (2015). Oscars 2015: The Guinness World Records alternative Academy Awards, *Guinness World Records*, 20 February, https://www.guinnessworldrecords.com/news/2015/2/academy-awards-2015-the-guinness-world-records-alternative-oscars-373083, accessed 23 Apr 2020.

Mac, R. (2014). Amazon pounces on Twitch after Google balks due to antitrust concerns, Forbes Magazine, 25 August, https://www.forbes.com/sites/ryanmac/2014/08/25/amazon-pounces-on-twitch-after-google-balks-due-to-antitrust-concerns/, accessed 1 April 2020.

Machinima Inc. (2012). Consolidated Financial Statement, Ernst & Young LLP, *Gov.UK*, accessed 8 April 2020.

Machinima Judge's Panel (2010). Second Life, 48 Hour Film Project: Machinima [machinima], https://vimeo.com/15253336.

MacLain, L. (2020). Interview with authors, 5 May.

Main, S. (2017). Rooster Teeth hopes its new podcast network will attract creators facing YouTube's 'ad apocalypse', *Adweek*, 14 June, http://www.adweek.com/digital/rooster-teeths-hopes-its-new-podcast-network-will-attract-creators-facing-youtubes-ad-apocalypse/amp/, accessed 6 May 2020.

Makedonski, B. (2019). All of machinima's videos were removed without any prior warning, *Destructoid.com*, 19 January, https://www.destructoid.com/all-of-machinima-s-videos-were-removed-without-any-prior-warning-539519.phtml, accessed 6 May 2020.

Makuch, E. (2016). YouTube network 'deceived customers' with paid for Xbox One videos and [update: Federal Trade Commission settles a 'deceptive marketing' campaign with Machinima, Microsoft responds], *Gamespot.com*, 19 March, https://www.gamespot.com/articles/youtube-network-deceived-customers-with-paid-for-x/1100-6430268/, accessed 13 April 2020

Manovich, L. (2011). Image future, in Lowood, H. and Nitsche, M., *The Machinima Reader*, Cambridge, MA: The MIT Press.

Mansukhani, J. (2006). Mcafee discoves proof of concept virus, First Post, 3 Aug, https://www.firstpost.com/tech/mcafee-discovers-proof-of-concept-virus-3547635.html/amp, accessed 15 July 2020.

Marino, P. (2004). *3D Game-based filmmaking: The Art of Machinima*, Phoenix, AZ, Paraglyph Press.

Marino, P. (2020). Interview with authors, 7 April.

Marsden, R. (2013). Channels spawned by YouTube are making a fortune but are the people making the videos missing out? *The Independent*, 13 January, https://www.independent.co.uk/life-style/gadgets-and-tech/features/channels-spawned-by-youtube-are-making-a-fortune-but-are-the-people-making-the-videos-missing-out-8464004.html, accessed 13 April 2020.

Martin, J, II (2008). Interview with Tracy Harwood, 2 November.

Matlack, C. (2005). Young Spielbergs by the thousands, *Business Week*, 19 December, p 46.

Mayberry, B. (2020). Interview with authors, 14 April.

McAlone, N. (2017a). Why the cofounder of a 250-perso video company is 'overjoyed' by youTube's new cable TV competitor, *Business Insider*, 5 March, https://www.businessinsider.com.au/burnie-burns-of-rooster-teeth-overjoyed-with-youtube-tv-2017-3, accessed 6 May 2020.

McAlone, N. (2017b). How to turn a viral video hit into 250-person business, from someone who did it, *Business Insider*, 29 January, https://www.businessinsider.com/burnie-burns-of-rooster-teeth-explains-how-to-sustain-youtube-viral-video-hit-2017-1?r=US&IR=T, accessed 6 May 2020.

McDonald, G. (2020). Private correspondence with authors.

McDowell, M. (2020). Interview with authors, 13 July.

McMillan, G. (2019). DC teams with Rooster Teeth for RWBY, gen:LOCK comics, *Hollywood Reporter*, 5 July, https://www.hollywoodreporter.com/heat-vision/rwby-genlock-comics-coming-dc-rooster-teeth-1222595, accessed 6 May 2020.

Media Magik Entertainment (2009). Avatar exclusive: behind the scenes (the art of performance capture), *YouTube*, 16 Dec, https://www.youtube.com/watch?v=P2_vB7zx_SQ&feature=youtu.be, accessed 16 July 2020.

Messinger, P.R. and Ge, X. (2011). Advertising in virtual worlds: facilitating a hierarchy of engagement, in Eastin, M.S., T. Daugherty and N.M. Burns, *Handbook of Research on Digital Media and Advertising: User Generated Content Consumption*, pp. 73-108, Hershey, PA: Information Science Reference.

Minor, J. (2015). Valve's movie brats: inside the Source Filmmaker community, PC Mag, 5 Oct, https://uk.pcmag.com/pc-games-2/71665/valves-movie-brats-inside-the-source-filmmaker-community, accessed 19 July 2020.

Mirapaul, M. (2002). Arts online: computer games as the tools for digital filmmakers, *The New York Times*, 22 July.

Moon, I. (2020). Interview with authors, 2 April.

Morse, P. (2020). Interview with authors, 20 July.

Moses, A. (2011). Kevin v the world: reformed pirate sues tech giants for millions, *Sydney Morning Herald*, 12 Dec, https://www.smh.com.au/technology/kevin-v-the-world-reformed-pirate-sues-tech-giants-for-millions-20111212-1oqi9.html, accessed 14 July 2020.

Murphy, R. (2013). David Bowie cameos and fully rendered penises – the bizarre history of Quantic Dream, *Games Radar*, 7 Oct, https://www.gamesradar.com/david-bowie-cameos-and-fully-rendered-penises-bizarre-history-quantic-dream/, accessed 15 July 2020.

Musgrove, M. (2005). Game turns players into indie moviemakers, *Washington Post*, 1 December, http://www.washingtonpost.com/wp-dyn/content/article/2005/11/30/AR2005113002117_pf.html, accessed 2 December 2005.

Ng, J. (2013). *Understanding machinima: essays on filmmaking in virtual worlds*, London: Bloomsbury.

Nguyen, T. (2006). An Unfair War [machinima], https://archive.org/details/AnUnfairWar.

Nikonov, M. (2020). Interview with authors, 17 July.

Nitsche, M. (2005). Film live: And Excursion into Machinima, in Bushoff B. (ed.), *Developing Interactive Narrative Content: sagas_sagasnet_reader*, pp. 210-243, Munich: High Text.

Nitsche, M. (2011). Machinima as media, in Lowood, H. and Nitsche, M., pp. 113-126, *The Machinima Reader*, Boston: MIT Press.

Nitsche, M., Mazalek, A. and Clifton, P. (2013). Moving digital puppets, in Ng, J., *Understanding machinima: essays on filmmaking in virtual worlds*, New York: Bloomsbury.

Nyuyen, T. (2020). Interview with authors, 21 May.

Onanuga, T. (2019). The collapse of Machinima is a stark warning to YouTube creators, *Wired Magazine*, 27 January, https://www.youtube.com/watch?v=KWCxMnboT4E, accessed 1 April 2020.

Ong, J. (2013). Ridley Scott teams up with top YouTube channel Machinima to produce 12 original sci-fi short films, *TheNextWeb.com*, 12 March, https://thenextweb.com/media/2013/03/12/ridley-scott-teams-up-with-machinima-to-produce-12-original-science-fiction-short-films/, accessed 10 April 2020.

Pallotta, T. (2003). In the Waiting Line by Zero 7 [machinima], https://vimeo.com/16960879.

Pasha, S. (2005). One word for you Hollywood: Machinima, 12 August, *CNN Money*, https://money.cnn.com/2005/08/12/technology/machinima_hollywood/, accessed 8 March 2020.

Patel, S. (2016). How Rooster Teeth gets 135,000 people to pay for gaming and comedy content, *Digiday.com*, 28 June, https://digiday.com/media/rooster-teeth-gets-135000-people-pay-gaming-comedy-content/, accessed 5 May 2020.

Patel, S. (2017). How YouTube networks are pivoting to studios, media brand models, *Digiday.com*, 17 April, https://digiday.com/future-of-tv/inside-the-reinvention-youtube-networks-look-to-shed-the-mcn-stigma/, accessed 6 May 2020.

Patel, S. (2017). Warner Bros. digital studio Stage 13 is making shows for emerging platforms, *Digiday.com*, 4 August, https://digiday.com/future-of-tv/warner-bros-digital-studio-stage-13-making-shows-emerging-platforms/, accessed 12 April 2020.

Patel, S. (2018). Rooster Teeth creates $2.5 million development fund for animation creators, *Digiday.com*, 3 August, https://digiday.com/future-of-tv/rooster-teeth-creates-2-5-million-development-fund-animation-creators, accessed 6 May 2020.

PCGamer (2005). Eyewitness: The Strangerhood – developer talkback, 10 January, http://www.pcgamer.com/eyeonline/eyeonline_2005-01-10.html, accessed 14 Jan 2005.

Perez, S. (2018). Vizio launches its own streaming service powered by Pluto TV, *Techcrunch.com*, 1 August, https://techcrunch.com/2018/08/01/vizio-launches-its-own-streaming-service-powered-by-pluto-tv/, accessed 12 April 2020.

Perrier, F. (2007). World of Electors from Alex Chan, *Frank Perrier*, 16 April, https://www.franckperrier.com/world-of-electors-from-alex-chan/, accessed 18 May 2020.

Petit, M. (2020). Interview with authors, 20 July.

Piras, C. (2020). Interview with authors, 13 June.

Pollack, N. (2013). You are watching machinima, the future of TV, *Wired Magazine*, 12 February, https://www.wired.com/2013/02/ff-you-are-watching-machinima/, accessed 10 April 2020.

Popper, B. (2012). Google investing in Machinima and the future of TV, *The Verge*, 7 May, https://www.theverge.com/2012/5/7/3004414/google-invests-in-machinima, accessed 10 April 2020.

QML (2002). Extract from forum, https://web.archive.org/web/20021204205006/http://machinima.com/qml/, accessed 2 April 2020.

Ramsey, G. (2019). Geoff's feed, Roosterteeth.com, 25 September, https://roosterteeth.com/g/post/1d2ad096-ef65-488f-9664-3c87ffc28f5e, accessed 6 May 2020.

Rasmussen, P. (2000). Joy [machinima], https://web.archive.org/web/20200216181639/http://nanoflix.net/.

Rasmussen, P. (2000). Red Igloo (author file), https://www.youtube.com/watch?v=s5DblUGDRec&feature=youtu.be, accessed 15 June 2020.

Rasmussen, P. (2000). Red Igloo [machinima], https://web.archive.org/web/20200216181639/http://nanoflix.net/.

Rasmussen, P. (2000). Rendevous [machinima], https://web.archive.org/web/20200216181639/http://nanoflix.net/.

Rasmussen, P. (2000). Rendevous, *Nanoflix Productions*, https://vimeo.com/89817936, accessed 6 June 2020.

Rasmussen, P. (2001). Joy (author file), https://www.youtube.com/watch?v=sQrDYFLpzrI&feature=youtu.be, accessed 15 June 2020.

Rasmussen, P. (2003). Interview, *AMAS: Machinima Film Festival DVD*, https://www.youtube.com/watch?v=pdfJN24ZZN8&feature=youtu.be, accessed 13 June 2020.

Rasmussen, P. (2003). Killer Robot {machinima], https://web.archive.org/web/20200216181639/http://nanoflix.net/.

Rasmussen, P. (2004). Killer Robot, *Nanoflix Productions*, https://vimeo.com/89817937, accessed 6 June 2020.

Rasmussen, P. (2007a). Blog: Stolen Life rough cut, *Nanoflix*, 6 Mar, https://nanoflix.wordpress.com/category/stolen-life/page/6/, accessed 9 June 2020.

Rasmussen, P. (2007b). Blog: Rough cut finished, *Nanoflix*, 14 Apr, https://nanoflix.wordpress.com/category/stolen-life/, accessed 21 May 2020.

Rasmussen, P. (2007c). Blog: Why machinima is different, *Nanoflix*, 29 Apr, https://nanoflix.wordpress.com/2007/04/29/why-machinima-is-different/, accessed 7 June 2020.

Rasmussen, P. (2007d). Blog: Machinima distribution, *Nanoflix*, 7 Aug, https://nanoflix.wordpress.com/category/stolen-life/, accessed 21 May 2020.

Rasmussen, P. and Turnure, J. (2007). Stolen Life [machinima], https://web.archive.org/web/20200216181639/http://nanoflix.net/.

Rasmussen, P. and Turnure, J. (2007). Stolen Life, *Nanoflix Productions*, https://vimeo.com/104179019, accessed 6 June 2020.

Reid, C. (2008). Fair game: the application of fair use doctrine to machinima, *Fordham Intellectual Property, Media and Entertainment Law Journal*, 19, pp. 831-876.

Reilly, P.J. (2014). Bitcoins not tax fairy dust – Second Life still a tax haven? *Forbes*, 26 Mar, https://www.forbes.com/sites/peterjreilly/2014/03/26/bitcoins-not-tax-fairy-dust-second-life-still-a-tax-haven/#2e35de606615, accessed 13 July 2020.

Rice, P. (2006). *Male Restroom Etiquette*, Guinness World Records Gamer's Edition, 2009.

Rice, P. (2007). Podcast: The Overcast #17, 9 May, http://theovercast.com/feed/, accessed 7 June 2020.

Rice, P. (2020). Interview with authors, 1 April.

Rice, P. (2020). Interview with authors, 16 June.

Rigney, R. (2012). How Rooster Teeth won the internet with Red vs Blue, Wired, 25 May, https://www.wired.com/2012/05/rooster-teeth-red-vs-blue/, accessed 24 Apr 2020.

Rigney, R. (2012). Trailer: Elijah Wood debuts in Red vs. Blue May 28, *Wired Magazine*, 24 April, https://www.wired.com/2012/04/red-vs-blue-season-10-elijah-wood-premiere/, accessed 4 May 2020.

Robertson, A. (2019). Vader Immortal is what a 'theme park film' actually looks like, and it's great, *The Verge*, 23 Nov, https://www.theverge.com/2019/11/23/20972243/vader-immortal-ilmxlab-vr-quest-rift-star-wars-game-review, accessed 17 July 2020.

Robertson, B. (2003). Films of the future, Computer Graphics World, 26(4), http://www.cgw.com/Publications/CGW/2003/Volume-26-Issue-4-April-2003-/Films-of-the-Future.aspx, accessed 3 April 2020.

Robertson, E. (2005). Captain Butch Flowers, *BNLBlog.com*, 1 Mar.

Roettgers, J. (2012). Machinima is YouTube's content king, *Gigaom.com*, 5 March, https://gigaom.com/2012/03/05/machinima-youtube-comscore-january/, accessed 9 April 2020

RogueShadowAngel (2011). Egyptian politics invade Second Life, YouTube, 5 Feb, https://www.youtube.com/watch?v=BA-vBg9Ld70, accessed 21 June 2020.

Romero, J. (2020). Correspondence with authors.

Rooster Teeth (2003). RVB Video Projects, 11 June, http://drunkgamers.com/bloodgulch.shtml, accessed 22 Apr 2020.

Russo, D. (2020). Why Hollywood movie-making may become more virtual in a post-coronavirus world, *CNBC*, 23 May, https://www.cnbc.com/2020/05/23/how-hollywood-movie-making-becomes-virtual-after-coronavirus.html, accessed 16 July 2020.

Salen. K. (2011). Arrested development: why machinima can't (or shouldn't) grow up, In Lowood, H. and Nitsche, M. (eds.), *The Machinima Reader*, pp. 37-50, Cambridge, MA, MIT Press.

Sam (2019). Hanabee Entertainment announce plans for 2020, end Rooster Teeth partnership, *The Okatu's Study*, 10 December, https://www.otakustudy.com/anime/2019/12/hanabee-entertainment-announce-plans-for-2020-ending-rooster-teeth-partnership/, accessed 7 May 2020.

Schweitzer, D. (ed) (1972). The Derleth Mythos, *Discovering H.P. Lovecraft*, Wildside Press.

Seth, S. (2019). The world's top ten media companies, Investopedia, 29 August, https://www.investopedia.com/stock-analysis/021815/worlds-top-ten-media-companies-dis-cmcsa-fox.aspx, accessed 11 May 2020.

Shanley, P. (2019). Rooster Teeth lays off 13 percent of staff, *Hollywood Reporter*, 12 September, https://www.hollywoodreporter.com/news/rooster-teeth-lays-13-percent-staff-1239225, accessed 6 May 2020.

Shea, C. (2007). Aussie Machinima Film Festival: Robots <i>can</i>cry, *IGN*, 9 Feb, https://www.ign.com/articles/2007/02/09/aussie-machinima-film-festival, 7 June 2020.

Shearer, H. (2020). Son-in-Law, *YouTube*, 23 Jul, https://www.youtube.com/watch?v=ZtptN8bfl3M&feature=youtu.be, accessed 25 July 2020.

Shiff, T. (2004). MTV2 Video Mods – Interview with the producer, *Nzone.com*, September, http://www.nzone.com/object/nzone_videomods_graphics.html, accessed 3 April 2020

Shiff, T. (2020). Interview with authors, 9 April.

Shivakumar, F. (2016). Rooster Teeth's Burnie Burns on pioneering online-only video, *Techcrunch.com*, 6 July, https://techcrunch.com/2016/07/06/rooster-teeth-burnie-burns-qa/, accessed 5 May 2020.

Silverman, J. (2006). Hack this film, *Wired Magazine*, 14 Jan, https://www.wired.com/2006/01/hack-this-film/, accessed 23 June 2020.

Sinclair, B. (2004). Rise of the machinima: what happens when the new frontier in guerrilla filmmaking meets the wild west of underground game development? *Polygon Magazine*, pp. 28-38.

Sloan, S. (2007). Podcast: Slice of SciFi #117: Karl Miller and Kiki Stockhammer, Scifi Rock Band Warp 11, 14 July, https://www.sliceofscifi.com/2007/07/14/slice-of-scifi-117/, accessed 7 June 2020.

Sluganski, R (2007). The making of Stolen Life, *Just Adventure*, 23 April, https://web.archive.org/web/20070423122427/http://www.justadventure.com/articles/StolenLife/MakingOf.shtm, accessed 6 June 2020.

Smith, C. (2005). What is machinima? *Day 7: Daily Insider, Sundance Film Festival*, 27 January, pp. 1, 4.

Sohn, J.-Y. (2016). What are Telltale games? How are they like interactive TV shows? *Screenprism*, 10 Aug, http://screenprism.com/insights/article/how-are-telltale-games-like-interactive-television-shows, accessed 15 July 2020.

Sorrel, C. (2010). Video: Driving a real car like a video-game car, *Wired Magazine*, 7 April, https://www.wired.com/2010/04/video-driving-a-real-car-like-a-video-game-car/, accessed 4 May 2020.

Sotamaa, O. (2007). Let me take you to The Movies, *Convergence*, Vol. 13 No. 4, pp. 383-401.

Spanger, T. (2019c). WarnerMedia's Rooster Teeth names co-heads of animation to replace Gray Haddock, Variety.com, 13 December, https://variety.com/2019/digital/uncategorized/rooster-teeth-animation-joe-clary-sean-hinz-replace-gray-haddock-1203435591/, accessed 7 May 2020.

Spangler, T. (2016a). Fullscreen's Rooster Teeth seeks wider appeal for 'First' rebranded subscription VOD service, *Variety.com*, 28 June, https://variety.com/2016/digital/news/rooster-teeth-first-subscription-vod-service-double-gold-1201804574/, accessed 5 May 2020.

Spangler, T. (2016a). Machinima, with YouTube blocked in China, pacts with Sohu to enter World's biggest market, *Variety*, 21 July, https://variety.com/2016/digital/news/machinima-china-sohu-1201819325/, accessed 11 April 2020.

Spangler, T. (2016b). 'Knight Rider' reboot from Justin Lin set at Machinima, *Variety*, 25 October, https://variety.com/2016/digital/news/knight-rider-justin-lin-machinima-1201899839/, accessed 11 April 2020.

Spangler, T. (2016b). Rooster Teeth hits HDTVs: subscription VOD service launches on AppleTV, XboxOne, *Variety.com*, 7 November, https://variety.com/2016/digital/news/rooster-teeth-apple-tv-xbox-one-1201911356/, accessed 5 May 2020.

Spangler, T. (2016c). Fullscreen's Rooster Teeth hires trio of content execs for subscription VOD push, *Variety.com*, 25 July, https://variety.com/2016/digital/news/fullscreen-rooster-teeth-svod-executive-hires-1201821781/, accessed 5 May 2020.

Spangler, T. (2018). AT&T buys out Chernin Group's stake in Otter Media, *Variety.com*, 7 August, https://variety.com/2018/digital/news/att-buys-out-chernin-groups-stake-in-otter-media-1202898339/, accessed 6 May 2020.

Spangler, T. (2019a). After Machinima shutdown, Rooster Teeth revives 'Inside Gaming' and rescues other Machinima shows, *Variety.com*, https://variety.com/2019/digital/news/machinima-rooster-teeth-inside-gaming-1203136988/, accessed 6 May 2020.

Spangler, T. (2019b). Gen:LOCK Season 2 starring Michael B. Jordan will get HBO Max premiere, *Variety.com*, 24 October, https://variety.com/2019/digital/news/genlock-season-2-hbo-max-rooster-teeth-1203382069/, accessed 7 May 2020.

Steigrad, A (2020). Hollywood quietly turns to video-game tech to restart movie shoots, *New York Post*, 26 April, https://nypost.com/2020/04/26/studios-take-cues-from-video-game-tech-after-delayed-productions/, accessed 2 May 2020.

Stephens, T. (2008). A bright life in film, darkened by loss, *The Sydney Morning Herald*, 15 May, https://www.smh.com.au/national/a-bright-life-in-film-darkened-by-loss-20080515-gdsdnl.html, accessed 15 June 2020.

Sterling, G. (2000). Viridian Note 00181: Infotech and Creativity, http://www.viridiandesign.org/notes/176-200/00181_infotech_and_creativity.html, accessed 1 April 2020.

Steurer, E. (2005). Meet the makers of The Strangerhood, Wired, January, http://www.wired.com/wired/archive/13.01/play.html?pg=1, accessed 29 December, 2004.

Stolz, A. (2020). Eight lessons for the future of film from 'Rebels of Storytelling', 8 July, https://www.linkedin.com/pulse/eight-lessons-future-film-from-rebels-storytelling-alex-stolz/, accessed 19 July 2020.

Stolz, A., Atkinson, A. and Kennedy, H.W. (2020) *The Future of Film Report*, London: King's College London.

Stone, M. (1999). Entertaindom: bold concept, but… ZD Net, 30 Nov, https://www.zdnet.com/article/entertaindom-bold-concept-but/, accessed 15 July 2020.

Strange Company (1999). Eschaton: Nightfall [machinima], https://web.archive.org/web/20010406065723/http://www.strangecompany.org/main.htm.

Stross, C. (2002). New art forms #2 machinima, https://www.antipope.org/charlie/blog-archive/July_2002.html, accessed 8 Mar 2020.

Stuart, T. (2013). Rage against the Machinima, *Houston Press*, 9 January, https://www.houstonpress.com/arts/rage-against-the-machinima-6596834, accessed 13 April 2020.

Sweetman, B. (1997). Video Innovations: EC, net effect, *Playback*, 30 Jun, https://playbackonline.ca/1997/06/30/16242-19970630/, accessed 15 July 2020.

Takahashi, D. (2010). Using games to make movies, Machinima.com raises $9M, *Venture Beat,* 14 June, https://venturebeat.com/2010/06/14/using-games-to-make-movies-machinima-com-raises-9m/, accessed 9 April 2020.

Takahashi, D. (2011). Machinima hits 1 billion monthly video views, *Venture Beat,* 6 December, https://venturebeat.com/2011/12/06/machinima-hits-1-billion-monthly-video-views/, accessed 9 April 2020.

Takahashi, D. (2012). Machinima scores partnership to promote highly anticipated Hawken game (exclusive), *Venture Beat,* 1 June, https://venturebeat.com/2012/06/01/machinima-scores-partnership-to-promote-highly-anticipated-hawken-game-exclusive/, accessed 9 April 2020.

Takahashi, D. (2014a). Warner Bros. rumoured to consider investment in YouTube video site Machinima, *Venture Beat,* 26 February, https://venturebeat.com/2014/02/26/warner-bros-rumored-to-consider-investment-in-youtube-video-site-machinima/, accessed 10 April 2020.

Takahashi, D. (2014b). Machinima names new CEO in wake of funding for fanboy and fangirl video-entertainment network, *Venture Beat,* 31 March, https://venturebeat.com/2014/03/31/machinima-names-new-ceo-in-wake-of-funding-for-fanboy-video-entertainment-network/, accessed 10 April 2020.

Takahashi, D. (2015). Warner Bros. invests $24M more into game video site Machinima, *Venture Beat,* 19 February, https://venturebeat.com/2015/02/19/warner-bros-invests-24m-more-into-game-video-site-machinima/, accessed 11 April 2020.

Takahashi, D. (2017). Rooster Teeth will support indie developers with new game publishing chief, *Venture Beat,* 2 June, https://venturebeat.com/2017/06/02/rooster-teeth-will-support-indie-developers-with-new-game-publishing-chief/amp/, accessed 6 May 2020.

Takahashi, D. (2017). Warner Bro. names game veteran Russell Arons as Machinima boss, *Venture Beat,* 17 March, https://venturebeat.com/2017/03/17/warner-bros-names-game-veteran-russell-arons-as-machinima-boss/, accessed 12 April 2020.

Terbeek, M. (2015). How to break through online video clutter, *Techcrunch.com,* 28 April, https://techcrunch.com/2015/04/28/how-to-break-through-online-video-clutter/, accessed 11 April 2020.

Terdiman, D. (2007). Counting the real Second Life population, Cnet.com, 4 Jan, https://www.cnet.com/news/counting-the-real-second-life-population/, accessed 13 July 2020.

Thain, K. (2020). Interview with authors, 26 April.

Thompson, C. (2005). A machinima commentary on the riots in France, *Collisiondetection.com,* 23 November, http://www.collisiondetection.net/mt/archives/2005/11/_heres_an_extre.html, accessed 16 May 2020.

Thompson, C. (2005). The Xbox Auteurs, *New York Times,* 7 August, http://www.nytimes.com/2005/08/07/magazine/07MACHINI.html, accessed 7 Aug 2005.

Thompson, C. (2020). Interview with authors, 25 May.

Thuyen, N. (2020). Interview with authors, 21 May.

Totilo, S. (2005). First film about French riots comes courtesy of a video game, *MTV.com*, 5 December, http://www.mtv.com/news/articles/1517481/20051205/index.jhtml, accessed 8 December 2005.

Totilo, S. (2005). Machinima pros make a living playing 'Halo' – with their feet, *MTV.com*, 28 September, http://www.mtv.com/news/articles/1510551/20050928/index.jhtml, accessed 29 Sept 2005.

Tritin Films (2000). Quad God [machinima], http://www.machinima.com/files/Films/Conventional_Media/QuadGod_Cable_Full.shtml.

Trundle, V. (2014). Videogames and innovation, in Beavis, C., J. O'Mara, L. McNeice (eds.), *Digital Games: Literacy in Action*, pp. 121-126, South Australia: Wakefield Press.

Tshimanga, C. (2009). Let the music play: the African diaspora, popular culture, and national identity in contemporary France, in C. Tshimanga, C. Didier Gondola and P. Bloom, *Frenchness and the African Diaspora*, pp. 248-276, Bloomington and Indianapolis: Indiana University Press.

Turney, D. (2016). Wave of animation: Disney's Moana ups the CGI ante, *Autodesk*, 23 Nov, https://www.autodesk.com/redshift/moana-animation/, accessed 16 July 2020.

Turnure, J. (2007). Directorial statement: Stolen Life, *Vimeo*, https://vimeo.com/104179019, accessed 7 June 2020.

Turnure, J. (2020). Interview with authors, 14 June.

Twist, J. (2014). Interview with Tracy Harwood, 5 May.

United Nation's Universal Declaration of Human Rights, http://libraryresources.unog.ch/udhr, accessed 14 May 2020

United Rangers Films (1996). Diary of a Camper [machinima], https://archive.org/details/DiaryOfACamper.

United Rangers Films (1997). Ranger Gone Bad II: Assault on Gloom Keep, https://archive.org/details/ranger-gone-bad-ii-assault-on-gloom-keep.

Unreal (2019). Behind the scenes with UE4's next-gen virtual production tools | project spotlight | Unreal Engine, *YouTube.com*, 12 November, https://www.youtube.com/watch?v=Hjb-AqMD-a4, accessed 13 April 2020.

Unscrewed with Martin Sargent (2004), *TV.com*, 19 February and 9 November, http://www.tv.com/shows/unscrewed-with-martin-sargent/episodes/, accessed 25 Apr 2020.

Valentine, D. (2020). Interview with authors, 15 May.

Van Rhoon, M. (2007). Blog: Stolen Life review, Unofficial Tex Murphy website, 17 April, http://www.unofficialtexmurphy.com/messageboard/viewtopic.php?t=1077&start=0&postdays=0&postorder=asc&highlight=&sid=3cebc4a908ca6e34ae8399fcd258518f, 7 June 2020.

Varney, A. (2007). The French Democracy: a machinima smash raises questions about art – and copyright, *The Escapist*, 13 March, https://v1.escapistmagazine.com/articles/view/video-games/issues/issue_88/496-The-French-Democracy.2, accessed 18 May 2020.

Walk, H. (2016). YouTube's Vanessa Pappas: "The distance that mainstream media manufactured between a celebrity and fan has all but eroded online", *HunterWalk.com*, 12 February, https://hunterwalk.com/2016/02/12/youtubesvanessa-pappas-the-distance-that-mainstream-media-manufactured-between-a-celebrity-and-fan-has-all-but-eroded-online/, accessed 4 May 2020.

Waters, D. (2003). Animators turn to video games, *BBC Entertainment*, 7 August, http://news.bbc.co.uk/1/hi/entertainment/3107599.stm, accessed 24 Apr 2020.

Watkins, R. (2020). Interview with authors, 26 April.

Weber, H. (2014). Gaming video site Machinima confirms $18M round after major layoffs, *Venture Beat*, 10 March, https://venturebeat.com/2014/03/10/gaming-video-site-machinima-confirms-18m-round-after-major-layoffs/, accessed 10 April 2020.

Webley, M. (2008). The Movies Online History, *Lionhead.com*, 6 December, http://www.lionhead.com/themovies/TMO.aspx, accessed 17 May 2020.

Webster, C. (2020). Interview with authors, 27 June.

Weiss, G. (2018). Otter Media lays off 140 staffers amid reorganization of Rooster Teeth, Fullscreen, Machinima, more, *Tubefilter.com*, 5 December, https://www.tubefilter.com/2018/12/05/otter-media-layoffs-reorganization-rooster-teeth-fullscreen-machinima/, accessed 12 April 2020.

Whittaker, R. (2019). Massive shakeup in top management at Rooster Teeth, Austin Chronicle, 24 September, https://www.austinchronicle.com/daily/screens/2019-09-24/massive-shakeup-in-top-management-at-rooster-teeth/, accessed 6 May 2020.

Whittaker, R. (2020). Burnie Burns leaves Rooster Teeth, *Austin Chronicle*, 11 Jun, https://www.austinchronicle.com/daily/screens/2020-06-11/burnie-burns-leaves-rooster-teeth/, accessed 11 June 2020.

Whittaker, R. (2020a). Rooster Teeth rescheduling RTX gathering, *Austin Chronicle*, 6 April, https://www.austinchronicle.com/daily/screens/2020-04-06/rooster-teeth-rescheduling-rtx-gathering/, 7 May 2020.

Whittaker, R. (2020b). Rooster Teeth unleashes Red Vs Blue: Zero release date, *Austin Chronicle*, 15 September, https://www.austinchronicle.com/daily/screens/2020-09-15/rooster-teeth-unleashes-red-vs-blue-zero-release-date/m/screens/2020-09-11/rtx-at-home-rethinks-the-fan-community-space/m/screens/2020-09-11/rtx-at-home-rethinks-the-fan-community-space/, 9 Nov 2020.

Williamson, S. (2006). Burnie Burns of Red Vs Blue fame talk machinima, *Hexus.net*, 22 August, https://hexus.net/gaming/features/industry/6540-burnie-burns-red-vs-blue-fame-talks-machinima/, accessed 24 Apr 2020.

WillTroll (2019). RTX is coming up; use your questions at panels to address Crunch time, *Reddit*, 16 June, https://www.reddit.com/r/roosterteeth/comments/c1ejgt/rtx_is_coming_up_use_your_questions_at_panels_to/, accessed 6 May 2020.

Winn, A. (2020). Interview with authors, 7 June.

Winterford, B. (2011). Aussie eyes Apple, Google over 'cloud' music patents, *IT News*, 6 Jul, https://www.itnews.com.au/news/aussie-eyes-apple-google-over-cloud-music-patents-262659, accessed 14 July 2020.

Wired (2004). Music videos tap video games, *Wired Magazine*, 30 September, https://www.wired.com/2004/09/music-videos-tap-video-games/, accessed 2 April 2020.

Wisniewski, A. (2001). Shoot 'em up: machinima animators use Quake and other first-person shooters to make real movies, *Time Out New York*, 7 May, p.178.

Xbox Nation (2004). Red vs Blue: Deus ex Machinima, *1up.com*, Nov, p. 74.

Yade, R. (2007). Breaking the lines: Sarkozy's presidential campaign, *Brookings Institution*, 7 October, https://franceintheus.org/IMG/pdf/Brookings_yade.pdf, accessed 23 May 2020.

Yarrow, J. (2014). Microsoft is buying the company behind Minecraft for $2.5 billion, Business Insider, 15 September, https://www.businessinsider.com/microsoft-buys-minecraft-2014-9?r=US&IR=T, accessed 5 May 2020.

Zarathustra Studios/Krad Productions (2007). [COMPANY]Rulez! [machinima], https://www.youtube.com/watch?v=djCSaA8B7Dw.

Index

People

A

B

C

M

N

O

P

Q

R

Films (and Music)

F

G

H

I

J

K

L

M

N

O

P

Q

R

S

T

Companies / producers / brands

Q

R

S

Games

S

T

U

V

W

Z

Keywords

A

Software

T

W

www.ingramcontent.com/pod-product-compliance
Lightning Source LLC
LaVergne TN
LVHW050614100826
845148LV00011B/1589

* 9 7 8 1 6 4 8 8 9 2 0 6 6 *